# THE IRISH-AMERICANS

# THE IRISH-AMERICANS

*See last pages of this volume
for a complete list of titles*

# IRISH-AMERICANS
# AND ANGLO-AMERICAN RELATIONS,
# 1880-1888

Joseph Patrick O'Grady

ARNO PRESS

A New York Times Company

New York — 1976

Editorial Supervision: ANDREA HICKS

———◆———

First publication in book form, 1976,
  by Arno Press, Inc.
Copyright © 1976 by Joseph Patrick O'Grady

THE IRISH-AMERICANS
ISBN for complete set: 0-405-09317-9
See last pages of this volume for titles.

Manufactured in the United States of America

———◆———

Library of Congress Cataloging in Publication Data

O'Grady, Joseph P
   Irish-Americans and Anglo-American relations,
1880-1888.

   (The Irish-Americans)
   Reprint of the author's thesis, University of
Pennsylvania, 1965.
   1.   United States--Foreign relations--Great Bri-
tain.   2.   Great Britain--Foreign relations--United
States.   3.   Irish Americans--Politics and govern-
ment.   4.   Irish question.   I.   Title.   II.   Series.
E183.8.G7044   1976      327.73'041      76-6360
ISBN 0-405-09353-5

IRISH-AMERICANS

AND

ANGLO-AMERICAN RELATIONS, 1880-1888

Joseph Patrick O'Grady

A DISSERTATION

in

History

Presented to the Faculty of the Graduate School of Arts and Sciences
of the University of Pennsylvania in Partial Fulfillment of the
Requirements for the Degree of Doctor of Philosophy

1965

# Index

Featherstone, James - see O'Kennedy.

Feely, Dennis - 89.

Fenian Ram - 175, 276.

Fenians - 7, 8, 9, 10, 14, 73, 74, 168, 170, 171, 175.

Fennell, Thomas - 51.

Finerty, John F. - 11, 51, 58, 64, 84, 191, 227, 228, 256, 257.

Fish, Carl - 30.

Fish, Hamilton - 9, 30, 121, 208.

Ford, Patrick - 11, 18, 49, 51, 58, 64, 65, 73, 79, 80, 81, 82, 83, 86, 87, 92, 93, 96, 97, 153, 159, 171, 200, 202, 224, 256, 257.

Forster, William E. - 76, 80, 83, 86, 148, 149, 157, 160.

Fortune Bay Incident - 31, 109, 112, 114, 115, 116, 126, 127, 272.

Free Trade - 41, 46, 48, 50, 65, 66, 106.

Frelinghuysen, Frederick - 108, 120, 121, 122, 123, 125, 126, 149, 151, 152, 153, 154, 159, 160, 162, 163, 164, 165, 178, 179, 182, 184, 189, 191, 192, 193, 194, 273, 274, 275, 276.

Frye, William P. - 130, 131, 218, 231, 232, 233, 259.

fur-seals - 133, 238.


Gallagher, Thomas - 185.

Garfield, James G. - 40, 41, 52.

George, Henry - 165, 166, 284.

Gladstone, William - 3, 30, 57, 74, 77, 78, 80, 81, 82, 83, 86, 87, 92, 93, 96, 97, 146, 163, 200, 215, 216, 219, 237, 274.

Godkin - 180, 187, 200, 224.

Grace, William C. - 13, 27, 57, 68, 153.

Grant, U. S. - 9, 13, 21, 27, 209, 212.

# Bibliography

## Bibliographical Aids

The starting point of this study is S. F. Bemis and G. G. Griffin, _Guide to the Diplomatic History of the United States_ (Washington, 1935). References to more recent diplomatic studies are found in Thomas A. Bailey, _A Diplomatic History of the American People_ (New York, 1958). The _Harvard Guide to American History_ (Cambridge, 1954), edited by Oscar Handlin and others, is useful for the political scene, though additional titles can be found with the aid of the _Index to the Writings on American History 1902-1940_ (Washington, 1956), edited by D. M. Matteson, Ester Z. Bailey and Rose Engleman. The basic bibliography for the Anglo-Irish question is James Carty, _Bibliography of Irish History, 1870-1911_ (Dublin), 1940). Recent studies are noted in the bibliography of Conor Cruise O'Brien, _Parnell and His Party, 1880-1890_ (Dublin, 1958). For references to the Irish in America, see Carl Wittke, _The Irish in America_ (Baton Rouge, 1956) and Charles C. Tansill, _America and the Fight for Irish Freedom, 1886-1922_ (New York, 1956).

## Published Sources

### (A) Government Documents

Government documents form the bulk of the primary sources, especially the diplomatic correspondence found in _Papers Relating to the Foreign Policy of the United States_ and _British and Foreign State Papers_. A few volumes in the series _Senate Executive Documents_ and _House Executive Documents_ supply some additional information, while the _Congressional Record_ is used to discover the mood of Congress on the various issues. The

information on the Phelps-Rosebery Extradition Treaty appears in the Proceedings of the United States' Senate in Executive Session.

(B) Contemporary Accounts, Letters and Memoirs

Second only to the government documents with respect to the amount
of material provided are contemporary accounts, letters and memoirs.
The most valuable source in this category is Paul Knaplund and C. M.
Clews, "Private Letters from the British Embassy in Washington to the
Foreign Secretary, Lord Granville, 1880-1885," American Historical Association's Annual Report, 1941 (Washington, 1942), simply because the
British often failed to include in the official diplomatic correspondence
the Anglo-American differences created by the Irish-Americans. By publishing the private letters Knaplund and Clews provide a basic source
for the understanding of this minority group. The letters of John Devoy,
edited by William O'Brien and Desmond Ryan as Devoy's Post Bag (Dublin,
1953) serve as the second major source in this category because they
provide the basic knowledge of the Irish-American activities during
this decade. Four memoirs in particular supplement these letters;
T. J. P. Tynam, The Irish National Invincibles (New York, 1894); Michael
Davitt, The Fall of Feudalism in Ireland (New York, 1904); Sir Robert
Anderson, Sidelights on the Home Rule Movement (New York, 1906); and
Henri LeCaron, Twenty-five Years in the Secret Service (London, 1892).
Tynam was the famous leader of the "Invincibles"; Davitt, the Father
of the Land League; Anderson, the director of British efforts to gain
access to the Irish nationalist movements; and LeCaron, the famous spy
who, for twenty-five years, served in both the British Secret Service

and the Clan-Na-Gael. The relationship of the Irish-American to the American community is found in two studies, William Grace, The Irish in America (Chicago, 1886) and P. H. Bagnel, The American Irish (London, 1882). The writings of prominent Americans, such as Carl Schurz, James G. Blaine, Grover Cleveland, James R. Lowell, John Sherman, Benjamin Harrison and others, shed light on their relations with the Irish vote as well as the American political scene. The shrewd Englishman, Sir Cecil Spring-Rice, at the time attached to the British Embassy in Washington, is the source of some interesting observations found in his letters, edited by Stephen Gwynn, The Letters and Friendships of Sir Cecil Spring-Rice (Boston, 1929). The Russian diplomat, Baron Rosen, manifests a similar ability in his Forty Years of Diplomacy (New York, 1922). A number of official political campaign text books and other publications are included as sources of information on how both parties catered to the Irish vote. Finally, important reactions of the financial classes are found in the Proceedings of the Convention of the American Bankers Association, 1885 (New York, 1885), and Proceedings of the Convention of the American Bankers, 1887 (New York, 1887).

(C) Public Opinion Sources

A number of newspapers and weekly news magazines note the public's reaction to these various events. Irish-American reactions are found in the Boston Pilot (Democratic), the New York Irish-American (Democratic), the New York Irish World (Republican), and the Chicago Citizen (Republican). Occasionally, Catholic newspapers are used in this manner since Catholic and Irish-American opinion on these questions are synonymous. The New York _Times_ and the New York _Tribune_ give the views of representative Democratic and Republican dailies respectively. Both papers are especially helpful for information which their staffs were able to obtain from behind the closed doors of the Senate. The magazine, _Public Opinion_, first published in 1886, is an invaluable source of newspaper opinion for the latter part of the study. Three weekly magazines also furnished indications of public reactions: _The Nation_, a representative American magazine; the _American_, which reflected the pro-Irish leanings of its editor, Robert Ellis Thompson; and the _Saturday Review_, a representative British magazine.

(D) Secondary Studies — Books

As in any study of this type secondary sources provide a wealth of information. The books by Charles C. Tansill serve as the most important group in this category, especially _The Foreign Policy of Thomas F. Bayard_ (New York, 1941). The extensive quotes from the Bayard papers are significant contributions to the understanding of the Irish influence upon the Phelps-Rosebery Treaty and the Bayard-Chamberlain Treaty. Information on the Irish in America can be found in Carl Wittke, _The Irish in America_ (Baton Rouge, 1956) and Florence E. Gibson, _The Attitudes of the New York Irish on National and Local Affairs, 1848-1892_ (New York, 1951) and in two biographies, M. P. Curran, _The Life of Patrick A. Collins_ (Norwood, 1906) and James J. Roche, _The Life of John Boyle O'Reilly_ (New York, 1891). Facts on the Anglo-Irish struggle at home can be gathered by examining the biographies of leading men on both sides such as William E. Gladstone,

Charles Stewart Parnell, Sir William Harcourt and others. In addition, a number of monographic studies are literally filled with information on the Anglo-Irish struggle including Norman D. Palmer, The Land League Crisis (New Haven, 1940); John E. Pomfret, The Struggle for Land in Ireland, 1800-1923 (Princeton, 1930); and Conor C. O'Brien, Parnell and His Party, 1880-1890 (Dublin, 1958). This last work greatly clarifies the connection between Parnell and the movements in the United States. Biographies of the important American statesmen contend interesting items on the American side of the story and, to some extent, the connection between the American politician and the Irish vote. Foremost among these are the studies of James G. Blaine, Grover Cleveland and Benjamin Harrison. Monographic works also furnish much needed information for the political picture, especially Herbert Clancy, The Presidential Election of 1880 (Chicago, 1958); H. C. Thomas, The Return of the Democratic Party to Power in 1884 (New York, 1919); and William Burnham, Presidential Ballots, 1836-1892 (Baltimore, 1892). The diplomatic questions can be found in a large number of special studies.

(E) Articles

Information gathered from numerous articles greatly add to a study of this nature. Such articles as John Edgar Chamberlain, "The Foreign Element in our Population," Century, N.S. VI (September, 1884), 761, and Robert J. Creighton, "Influence of Foreign Issues on American Politics," International Review, XIII (August, 1882), 182, reflect American fears that foreign issues of no real concern to the United States would cause some kind of disaster if politicians continued to use such issues to gain votes. In the midst of the Irish "dynamite campaign," these fears increased as shown in two articles: Edward Self, "The Abuse of Citizenship," North American Review, CXXXVI (June, 1883), 541, and Henry W. Rodgers, "Harboring Conspiracy," North American Review, CXXXVIII (June, 1884), 521. Articles can also help in the understanding of the various diplomatic questions, especially with regard to the sumarine built for the Fenians by the Irish immigrant, John P. Holland. Two articles by Thomas N. Brown, "Nationalism and the Irish Peasant," Review of Politics, XV (October, 1953), 403, and "The Origin and Character of Irish-American Nationalism," Review of Politics, XVIII (July, 1956), 327, are indispensable on the character of the Irish.

Following is a list of the works consulted for this study:

I  Unpublished

Bernardo, C. J. "The Presidential Election of 1888." Unpublished Ph.D. dissertation, Georgetown University, 1949.

Burnette, Allen Lawrence. "The Senate Foreign Relations Committee and the Diplomacy of Garfield, Arthur, and Cleveland." Unpublished Ph.D. dissertation, University of Virginia, 1952.

Cuddy, Henry. "The Influence of the Fenian Movement on Anglo-American Relations, 1860-1872." Unpublished Ph.D. dissertation, Saint John's University, 1953.

Eckman, James. "The British Traveler in America, 1875-1920." Unpublished Ph.D. dissertation, Georgetown University, 1946.

Fifield, Walter W. "A History of the Extradition Treaties of the United States." Unpublished Ph.D. dissertation, University of Southern California, 1936.

House, Albert V. "The Political Career of Samuel Jackson Randall." Unpublished Ph.D. dissertation, University of Wisconsin, 1934.

Jameson, Edward A. "Irish-Americans, the Irish question, and American Diplomacy, 1895-1921." Unpublished Ph.D. dissertation, Harvard University, 1944.

Newman, Robert G. "Extradition and the Political Offender." Unpublished Ph.D. dissertation, University of Minnesota, 1946.

Selig, Adler. "The Senatorial Career of George Franklin Edmunds, 1866-1891." Unpublished Ph.D. dissertation, University of Illinois, 1934.

White, Edward A. "The Republican Party in National Affairs, 1888-1891." Unpublished Ph.D. dissertation, University of Wisconsin, 1941.

## II  Published Sources

### (A) Government Documents

British State and Foreign State Papers. Vols. 72-78. London, 1881-1888.

Malloy, William M. Treaties, Conventions, International Acts, Protocols and Agreements Between the United States of America and other Powers, 1776-1909. Vol. I. Washington, 1910.

Richardson, James D., ed. A Compilation of the Messages and Papers of the Presidents, 1789-1898. 10 Vols. Washington, 1899.

United States Congress. Congressional Record, 47th Congress—50th Congress. Washington, 1881-1889.

_____. House Executive Document 1, 50th Congress, 2nd Session. Washington, 1889. .

_____. House Executive Document 607, 81st Congress, 2nd Session: Biographical Directory of the American Congress, 1774-1949. Washington, 1952.

_____. Senate Executive Document 5, 47th Congress, Special Session. Washington, 1882.

United States Department of State. Papers Relating to the Foreign Relations of the United States, 1880-1888. Washington, 1881-1889.

United States Senate. Proceedings of the United States Senate in Executive Session. Vols. 23-27. Washington, 1901.

(B) Contemporary Accounts, Letters and Memoirs

Anderson, Sir.Robert. Sidelights on the Home Rule Movement. New York, 1906.

Bagnell, Philip H. The American Irish. Boston, 1882.

Bancroft, Frederic, ed. Speeches, Correspondence and Political Papers of Carl Schurz. 6 Vols. New York, 1913.

Blaine, James G. Political Discussions. Norwick, 1887.

_____. Twenty Years of Congress. 2 Vols. Norwick, 1886.

Bolles, Albert S. Practical Banking. 7th ed. New York, 1890.

Campaign Text Book of the Democratic Party, 1886. Washington, 1886.

Campaign Text Book of the Democratic Party of the United States for the Presidential Election of 1888. New York, 1888.

Chamberlain, Joseph. A Political Memoir, 1880-1892. London, 1953.

Clisher, Charles W., ed. Proceedings of the Eighth Republican National Convention, 1884. Chicago, 1884.

Cooper, Thomas V. Biographies of James G. Blaine and John A. Logan. San Francisco, 1884.

Davitt, Michael. Fall of Feudalism in Ireland. London, 1904.

Dawson, George Francis. The Republican Campaign Text-Book for 1888. New York, 1888.

Devoy, John. Recollections of an Irish Rebel. London, 1929.

DeWolfe, Harvey, M. A., ed. New Letters of James Russell Lowell. New York, 1932.

Dickinson, Edward. Official Proceedings of the National Democratic Convention, 1888. Saint Louis, 1888.

Foster, John W. Diplomatic Memoirs. 2 Vols. Boston, 1909.

Grace, William R. The Irish in America. Chicago, 1886.

Gwynn, Stephen, ed. The Letters and Friendships of Sir Cecil Spring-Rice: A Record. 2 Vols. Boston, 1929.

Hamilton, Gail. _Biography of James G. Blaine_. Norwich, 1895.

Healy, T. M. _Letters and Leaders of My Day_. 2 Vols. London, 1928.

Hoar, George F. _Autobiography of Seventy Years_. New York, 1905.

Hunt, Henry M. _The Crime of the Century_. Chicago, 1889.

Killen, James Bryce. _The Irish Question_. New York, 1886.

Knaplund, Paul, and Clewes, C. M., eds. "Private Letters from the British Embassy in Washington to the Foreign Secretary, Lord Granville, 1880-1885." _American Historical Association Annual Report, 1941_. Washington, 1942.

LeCaron, Major Henri. _Twenty-five Years in the Secret Service_. London, 1892.

Lodge, Henry Cabot. _Selections from the Correspondence of Theodore Roosevelt and Henry Cabot Lodge, 1884-1918_. New York, 1925.

Lowell, James R. "On a Certain Condescension in Foreigners." _Fireside Travels_. Boston, 1904. pp. 291-332.

McLaughlin, J. Fairfax. _The Life and Times of John Kelley_. New York, 1885.

Morton, Charles E., ed. _Letters of James Russell Lowell_. 2 Vols. New York, 1894.

Nevins, Allan, ed. _Letters of Grover Cleveland_. Boston, 1933.

O'Brien, William. _Evening Memories_. Dublin, 1920.

_____. _Recollections_. London, 1905.

O'Brien, William, and Ryan, D., eds. _Devoy's Post Bag_. 2 Vols. Dublin, 1953.

_Political Reformation of 1884, a Democratic Campaign Book_. New York, 1884.

_Proceedings of the Convention of the American Bankers Association, 1887_. New York, 1887.

_Proceedings of the Convention of the American Bankers Association, 1885_. New York, 1885.

Rosen, Baron. _Forty Years of Diplomacy_. 2 Vols. New York, 1922.

Ryan, Mark F. Fenian Memories. Dublin, 1946.

Sherman, John. Recollections of Forty Years in the House, Senate and Cabinet. 2 Vols. Chicago, 1895.

Smalley, George W. Anglo-American Memories. New York, 1911.

_____. Anglo-American Memories. Second Series. London, 1912.

Thorndike, Rochel Sherman, ed. The Sherman Letters. New York, 1894.

Tynam, P. J. P. The Irish National Invincibles. New York, 1894.

Volwiler, A. T., ed. The Correspondence Between Benjamin Harrison and James G. Blaine, 1882-1893. Philadelphia, 1940.

### (C) Sources of Public Opinion

#### (a) Newspapers

The American Catholic News, 1885-1888.

The Catholic Review, 1880-1888.

Boston Pilot, 1880-1888.

New York Freeman's Journal and Catholic Register, 1880-1888.

The New York Tablet, 1880-1888.

New York Tribune, 1880-1890.

New York Times, 1880-1890.

Chicago Citizen, 1882-1888.

#### (b) Magazines

American, 1880-1889.

Annual Register, 1880-1888.

Nation, 1880-1888.

Public Opinion, 1886-1889.

Saturday Review, 1880-1888.

(D) Books

Bailey, Thomas A. Diplomatic History of the American People. 6th ed. New York, 1958.

Barnard, Harry. Rutherford B. Hayes and His America. New York, 1954.

Barrows, Chester L. William M. Evarts, Lawyer, Diplomat, Statesman. Chapel Hill, 1941.

Bemis, Samuel Flagg, ed. American Secretaries of State and Their Diplomacy. New York, 1928.

——————————————. A Diplomatic History of the United States. 4th ed. New York, 1955.

Blake, Nelson M. William Mahone of Virginia: Soldier and Political Insurgent. Richmond, 1935.

Bland, Sister Joan. The Hibernian Crusade. Washington, 1951.

Brebner, John B. North Atlantic Triangle. New Haven, 1945.

Brooks, Robert C. Political Parties and Electoral Problems. 3rd ed. New York, 1933.

Burnham, W. Dean. Presidential Ballots, 1836-1892. Baltimore, 1955.

Caldwell, Robert B. James A. Garfield, Party Chieftain. New York, 1931.

Callahan, James Morton. American Foreign Policy in Canadian Relations. New York, 1937.

Cecil, Algernon. British Foreign Secretaries, 1807-1916. London, 1927.

Cecil, Lady Gwendolen. Life of Robert Marquis of Salisbury. 4 Vols. London, 1921.

Chadwick, French E. The Relations of the United States and Spain. New York, 1909.

Chidsey, Donald Barr. The Gentleman from New York: A Life of Roscoe Conkling. New Haven, 1935.

Churchill, W. S. Lord Randolf Churchill. 2 vols. London, 1936.

Clancy, Herbert J. The Presidential Election of 1880. Chicago, 1958.

Connaughton, Sister Mary Stanislaus. The Editorial Opinion of the Catholic Telegraph of Cincinnati on Contemporary Affairs and Politics, 1871-1921. Washington, D.C.; The Catholic University of America Press, 1943.

Cortissay, Royal. The Life of Whitelaw Reid. New York, 1921.

Curran, M. P. The Life of Patrick A. Collins. Norwood, 1906.

Curtis, Edmund. A History of Ireland. 6th ed. London, 1950.

Dangerfield, Rayden J. In Defense of the Senate: A Study in Treaty Making. Norman, 1933.

D'Arcy, William. The Fenian Movement in the United States, 1858-1886. Washington, 1947.

DeSantis, Vincent P. Republicans Face the Southern Question: The New Departure Years, 1877-1897. Baltimore, 1959.

Donahoe, Sister Joan Marie. The Irish Catholic Benevolent Union. Washington, 1953.

Dugdale, Blanche E. C. Arthur James Balfour. 2 vols. London, 1936.

Edwards, R. Dudly, and Williams, T. Desmond, eds. The Great Famine. New Haven, 1957.

Ensor, R. C. K. England, 1870-1914. Oxford, 1936.

Fish, Carl R. American Diplomacy. New York, 1916.

Fitzmaurice, Lord Edmond. The Second Earl Granville. London, 1906.

Fleming, Denna F. The Treaty Power of the American Senate. New York, 1930.

Ford, H. J. The Cleveland Era. New Haven, 1921.

Gardiner, A. G. Sir William Harcourt. 2 vols. London, 1923.

Garvin, J. L. The Life of Joseph Chamberlain. 2 vols. London, 1932.

Gibson, Florence. The Attitudes of the New York Irish to National and Local Affairs. New York, 1952.

Gwynn, S. T., and Tuckwell, G. Life of Sir Charles Dilke. 2 vols. London, 1927.

Hamilton, Gail. *Biography of James G. Blaine*. Norwich, 1895.

Hammond, J. L. *Gladstone and the Irish Nation*. New York, 1938.

Handlin, Oscar. *Boston's Immigrants, 1790-1865*. Cambridge, 1941.

Holt, W. Stull. *Treaties Defeated by the Senate*. Baltimore, 1933.

Howe, George F. *Chester A. Arthur—A Quarter Century of Machine Politics*. New York, 1934.

Josephson, Matthew. *The Politicos, 1865-1919*. New York, 1938.

Kent, F. R. *History of the Democratic Party*. New York, 1928.

Knaplund, Paul. *Gladstone's Foreign Policy*. London, 1935.

Lindsey, David. *"Sunset" Cox, Irrepressible Democrat*. Detroit, 1959.

Logan, Rayford W. *The Diplomatic Relations of the United States with Haiti, 1776-1891*. Chapel Hill, 1941.

Lyons, F. S. L. *The Fall of Parnell, 1890-91*. London, 1960.

McCall, Samuel W. *The Life of Thomas B. Reed*. Boston, 1917.

McDonald, Sister M. Justille. *The History of the Irish in Wisconsin in the 19th Century*. Washington, 1954.

McElroy, Robert. *Levi Parsons Morton: Banker, Diplomat and Statesman*. New York, 1930.

McInnis, Edgar W. *The Unguarded Frontier*. New York, 1942.

Masterman, Sylvia. *The Origins of International Rivalry in Samoa, 1845-1884*. Stanford, 1934.

Millington, Herbert. *American Diplomacy and the War of the Pacific*. New York, 1948.

Montague, Ludwell L. *Haiti and the United States, 1714-1938*. Durham, 1940.

Moore, Joseph West. *The American Congress*. New York, 1895.

——————————. *The Republicans: A History of Their Party*. New York, 1956.

Morley, John. *The Life of William Ewart Gladstone*. London, 1903.

Mowat, R. B.  The Diplomatic Relations of Great Britain and the United States.  London, 1925.

_____.  The Life of Lord Pauncefote.  Boston, 1929.

Muzzey, David S.  James G. Blaine, A Political Idol of Other Days.  New York, 1934.

Nevins, Allan.  Grover Cleveland: A Study in Courage.  New York, 1932.

_____.  Hamilton Fish: The Inner History of the Grant Administration.  New York, 1936.

_____.  Henry White: Thirty Years of American Diplomacy.  New York, 1930.

O'Brien, Conor Cruise.  Parnell and His Party, 1880-1890.  Oxford, 1957.

O'Brien, R. B.  The Life of Charles Stewart Parnell.  2 vols.  New York, 1898.

Palmer, Norman D.  The Irish Land League Crisis.  New Haven, 1940.

Patter, George.  To the Golden Door: The Story of the Irish in Ireland and America.  Boston, 1960.

Pearson, Charles C.  The Readjuster Movement in Virginia.  New Haven, 1917.

Perkins, Dexter.  The Monroe Doctrine, 1867-1907.  Baltimore, 1937.

Pomfret, John E.  The Struggle for Land in Ireland, 1800-1923.  Princeton, 1930.

Putnam, Carleton.  Theodore Roosevelt: The Formative Years, 1858-1886.  New York, 1958.

Reuter, Bertha A.  Anglo-American Diplomatic Relations during the Spanish-American War.  New York, 1924.

Roche, James J.  The Life of John Boyle O'Reilly.  New York, 1891.

Roseboom, Eugene H.  History of Presidential Elections.  New York, 1957.

Ryden, George Herbert.  The Foreign Policy of the United States in Relation to Samoa.  New Haven, 1933.

Scudder, Horace E.  James Russell Lowell.  Boston, 1901.

Shannon, James P.  Catholic Colonization of the Western Frontier.  New Haven, 1957.

Shippee, Lester B.  Canadian-American Relations, 1849-1874.  New Haven, 1943.

Sievers, Harry J.  Benjamin Harrison: Hoosier Statesman.  2 vols. New York, 1959.

Stevens, Sylvester K.  American Expansion in Hawaii, 1842-1898.  Harrisburg, 1945.

Syrett, Harold C.  The City of Brooklyn, 1865-1898.  New York, 1944.

Tansill, Charles C.  America and the Fight for Irish Freedom, 1866-1922.  New York, 1956.

_____.  Canadian-American Relations, 1875-1911.  New Haven, 1943.

_____.  The Congressional Career of Thomas Francis Bayard.  Washington, 1946.

_____.  Diplomatic Relations Between the United States and Hawaii, 1885-1889.  New York, 1940.

_____.  The Foreign Policy of Thomas F. Bayard.  New York, 1940.

Thomas, H. C.  The Return of the Democratic Party to Power in 1884.  New York, 1919.

Travis, Ira Dudley.  The History of the Clayton-Bulwer Treaty.  Minneapolis, 1900.

Tyler, Alice Felt.  The Foreign Policy of James G. Blaine.  Minneapolis, 1927.

Williams, Mary W.  Anglo-American Isthmanian Diplomacy,, 1815-1915.  Washington, 1916.

Willson, Beckles.  American's Ambassadors to England, 1775-1928.  London, 1928.

Wittke, Carl Frederick.  The Irish in America.  Baton Rouge, 1956.

(E) Articles

Adams, George H. "Our State Department and Extradition," <u>American Law Review</u>, XX (July-August, 1886), 540-552.

Anonymous. "Power of the Irish in American Cities," <u>Living Age</u>, CLXXI (November, 1886), 382-384.

Bailey, James H. "Anthony M. Keiley," <u>Virginia Magazine of History and Biography</u>, LXVII (January, 1959), 65-81.

Blaine, Walker. "Why Harrison Was Elected," <u>North American Review</u>, CXLVII (December, 1888), 686-695.

Bossard, James H. "Robert Ellis Thompson, Pioneer Professor in Social Science," <u>American Journal of Sociology</u>, XXXV (September, 1929), 239-249.

Brooks, Robert P. "John P. Holland (1841-1914) and His Submarines," <u>Proceedings of the New Jersey Historical Society</u>, XIII (April, 1928), 182-189.

Brown, Thomas N. "Nationalism and the Irish Peasant, 1800-1848," <u>Review of Politics</u>, XV (October, 1953), 403-445.

_____. "The Origins and Character of Irish-American National-ism," <u>Review of Politics</u>, XVIII (July, 1956), 327-358.

Bryce, James. "England and Ireland," <u>Century</u>, IV (June, 1883), 249-264.

Buley, R. C. "The Campaign of 1888 in Indiana," <u>Indiana Magazine of History</u>, X (June, 1914), 30-53.

Calton, Kenneth E. "Parnell's Mission to Iowa," <u>Annals of Iowa</u>, XXII (April, 1940), 312-327.

Carroll, William. "Irish Comment on an English Text," <u>North American Review</u>, CXLVII (September, 1888), 289-292.

Chamberlain, Joseph Edgar. "The Foreign Element in our Population," <u>Century</u>, VI (September, 1884), 761-783.

Clarke, Joseph I. C. "Irish Comment on an English Text," <u>North American Review</u>, CXLVII (September, 1888), 285-289.

Creighton, Robert J. "Influence of Foreign Issues on American Politics," <u>International Review</u>, XIII (August, 1882), 182-190.

deHart, E. L. "The Extradition of Political Offenders," Law Quarterly Review, II (April, 1886), 177-187.

DeSantis, Vincent P. "Republican Efforts to 'Crack' the Democratic South," Review of Politics, XIV (April, 1952), 244-264.

Devoy, John. "Irish Comments on an English Text," North American Review, CXLVII (September, 1888), 281-285.

Dillon, William. "Assassination and Dynamite," Fortnightly Review, XLI (April, 1884), 510-521.

"Editorial," Bankers' Magazine and Statistical Register, XXXIX (April, 1885), 789.

"Egan, Patrick," Dictionary of American Biography, VI (1936), 51.

Ford, Patrick. "The Irish Vote in the Pending Presidential Election," North American Review, CXLVII (August, 1888), 185-190.

Garfield, Dorothy. "The Influence of Wisconsin on Federal Politics, 1880-1907," Wisconsin Magazine of History, XVI (September, 1932),3-25.

Green, James J. "American Catholics and the Irish Land League, 1879-1882," Catholic Historical Review, XXXIX (January, 1949), 19-26.

Hardy, Osgood. "Was Patrick Egan a Blundering Minister," Hispanic American Historical Review, VIII (February, 1928), 65-81.

"Holland, John P.," Dictionary of American Biography, IX (1936), 45-46.

Jay, John. "The Presidential Election," International Review, IX (September, 1880), 320-342.

Kerwin, Michael. "Irish Comment on an English Text," North American Review, CXLVII (September, 1888), 292-296.

Lodge, Henry Cabot. "The Fisheries Question," North American Review, CXLVI (February, 1888), 121-130.

Marsh, A. H. "The Canadian Fisheries Question," American Law Review, XXI (May-June, 1887), 369-398.

O'Reilly, John Boyle. "At Last," North American Review, CXLII (January, 1886), 104-110.

_____. "Ireland's Opportunity, Will it be lost," American Catholic Quarterly Review, VII (January, 1882), 114-120.

Phelps, E. J. "The Behring Sea Controversy," Harper's Monthly Magazine, LXXXII (April, 1891), 766.

Quinn, P. T. "On the Dynamite Policy," Century, IV (June, 1883), 309.

Rice, Allen T., ed. "Extradition of Dynamite Criminals," North American Review, CXLI (July, 1885), 47-59.

Richmond, Arthur. "Letters to Prominent Persons—Number One to the Secretary of State," North American Review, CXLII (January, 1886), 90-103.

Rucker, Colby. "The Fenian Ram," Proceedings of the United States Naval Institute, LXI (January, 1935), 1136-1139.

Schwatka, Frederick. "The Fur Sea Fishery Dispute," North American Review, CXLVI (March, 1888), 390-399.

Sedquick, A. G. "Extradition," North American Review, CXXXVI (May, 1883), 497-505.

Seelye, Julius H. "Dynamite as a Factor in Civilization," North American Review, CXXXVII (July, 1883), 1-7.

Self, Edward. "The Abuse of Citizenship," North American Review, CXXXVI (June, 1883), 541-556.

Shea, John Gilmary. "No Actual Need of a Catholic Party in the United States," American Catholic Quarterly Review, XII (October, 1887), 705-713.

_____. "The Anti-Catholic Issue in the Late Election—The Relation of Catholics to the Political Parties," American Catholic Quarterly Review, VI (January, 1881), 36-50.

Sullivan, Alexander. "The American Republic and the Irish National League of America," American Catholic Quarterly Review, IX (January, 1884), 35-44.

Thompson, Robert Ellis. "Irish Comment on an English Text," North American Review, CXLVII (September, 1888), 297-301.

"Thompson, Robert Ellis." Dictionary of American Biography, IX (1936), 469-470.

_____. The National Cyclopaedia of American Biography, X, 18.

Walker, F. A. "American Irish and American German," <u>Scribner's Monthly</u>, VI (June, 1873), 172-179.

Woodbury, Charles L. "The Canadian Fisheries Dispute—An Open Letter to Senator Morgan," <u>American Law Review</u>, XXI (May-June, 1887), 431-445.

Woolsey, Theodore S. "The Fishery Question," <u>North American Review</u>, CXLII (March, 1886), 216-226.

# Preface

In recent years a number of scholars have studied the role played by the immigrant in American history and a few have been particularly interested in his role in the formation of American foreign policy. This dissertation is another example of that more specific interest and as such will attempt to analyze the Irish-American influence upon Anglo-American relations from 1880-1888.

Although not the first study of this specific topic, it is the first to analyze these years. In 1936 Nelson M. Blake submitted "The United States and the Irish Revolution, 1914-1922" for the Ph.D. at Clark University. Eight years later Edward A. Jamison completed his study, "Irish-Americans, The Irish Question and American diplomacy, 1895-1921," for the same degree at Harvard University. Then in 1953 Henry Cuddy submitted his doctoral dissertation, "The Influences of the Fenian Movement on Anglo-American Relations, 1860-1872," to Saint John's University. These three studies analyze the years from 1860 to 1922, except for the period from 1872 to 1895, but Charles C. Tansill implied in the title of his book, Americans and the Fight for Irish Freedom, 1866-1922 (1957), that he had filled this gap in our knowledge. However, a close examination of Professor Tansill's study reveals that, not only did he fail to analyze these years in any real detail, he even failed to explain America's part in the fight for Irish freedom. In reality he devoted his book to the defense of Judge Danial Cohalan against his many detractors on both sides of the Atlantic and left the years from 1872 to 1895 relatively untouched.

Justification for this study does not rest solely upon this point of originality.  It rests to a much greater extent upon developments in Anglo-Irish relations, American political life, and Anglo-American diplomatic relations.  The years of the 1880's witnessed the most important events in the Anglo-Irish struggle between the Great Famine and World War I.  At the same time a close balance of power characterized American politics, while a gradual deterioration of Anglo-American diplomacy led to the eventual outburst over the Venezuelan question in 1895.  In other words, as events in Ireland aroused the latent hatred in Irish-Americans for all things British, Anglophobia seemed to return to the surface of American life, while the political situation tended to increase the value of the Irish American vote.  Consequently, on the surface conditions were ideal for the Irish-American attempt to influence Anglo-American diplomacy.  Whether they succeeded or not remains to be seen, but their chances for success were greater at this time than at any other.

The dissertation is divided into two sections.  The introduction and first three chapters analyze first, the power of the Irish-American in American politics; secondly, his ability to influence the Anglo-Irish struggle and, finally, the state of Anglo-American relations.  The last four chapters analyze Irish-American influence upon Anglo-American relations.

# Introduction

Modern English efforts to control Ireland began in the sixteenth
century when Queen Elizabeth I colonized Irish estates with English
aristocrats. Cromwell continued this policy with ruthless effective-
ness in the 1650's. The further substitution of English for Irish
aristocrats that followed the defeat of James II in 1691 virtually completed the process. Not all the members of this aristocracy, the Anglo-
Irish Ascendancy came from these new transplants, for a few were old
families with long traditional holdings in Ireland, and although many
of the newcomers spent their time in London, a few became more Irish
than the Irish. Along with the lawyers and university men, the Ascendancy
dominated Irish life without threat of revolution in the century that
followed William's arrival.

As the nineteenth century drew near, the Ascendancy faced the beginning of a long series of attacks upon their position. The first, organized by Henry Grattan in the Irish Parliament at Dublin, demanded the
abolition of British rights to review and control laws passed by the
Irish legislators. Grattan's failure gave the more radical United Irishmen the opportunity to organize the Revolution of 1798. Meeting force
with force, the British crushed the revolt and as a more permanent solution to the problem, passed the Act of Union which abolished the Dublin
Parliament and gave Ireland representation in both the House of Lords
and the House of Commons. Nationalism was the wave of the future,
however, and in the first half of the nineteenth century Daniel
O'Connell aroused the Irish peasants with his determined assault upon
this unnatural union. By the early 1840's the Ascendancy feared that

1

O'Connell's adroit coupling of effective parliamentary representation to the growing unrest among the masses would eventually cause the repeal of the Act, which to them would signal the beginning of the end of their control of Irish lands.

At this critical juncture in Anglo-Irish relations three events occurred that saved the Ascendancy for at least another forty years. In 1843 because of O'Connell's unwillingness to use force to destroy the Act of Union, his Repeal Association movement collapsed and with it that form of Irish nationalism which looked to moderate constitutional and parliamentary methods as the means for gaining Irish freedom. Three years later the first of many successive crop failures signaled the opening round of what later became known as the Great Famine. By 1850 thousands upon thousands of Irish peasants had fled the certain death by starvation which stalked Ireland. Finally, in 1848 the Young Irelanders staged an abortive attempt to overthrow the British landlords and the failure scattered the young revolutionaries to the four corners of the world. The Ascendancy could only cheer as they saw the end of effective Irish representation in Parliament, the dispersal of the revolutionary elements, and the reduction of the peasant population to more realistic proportions. Ireland was still theirs.

It remained so without serious opposition until the 1880's, one of the most significant decades in the long history of the Anglo-Irish struggle. The Irish question so dominated the English mind at the time that Sir Charles Dilke complained:

> It is too much the case with England that we are
> occupied with the consideration of the Irish ques-
> tion . . . we allow the foreign affairs of the
> country to be translated in the dark.[1]

However, this Irish question of the 1880's was not the same question

that confronted English politicians in the 1840's. As Sir William

Harcourt, the Home Secretary in William Gladstone's second government,

so accurately perceived:

> In former Irish rebellions the Irish were in Ireland.
> We could reach their forces, cut off their resources in
> men and money and then to subjugate was comparatively
> easy. Now there is an Irish nation in the United States,
> equally hostile, with plenty of money, absolutely beyond
> our reach and yet within ten days sail of our shores.[2]

This seemed so true to his contemporaries that the London _Times_ re-

duced the whole question to "mainly an Irish-American one,"[3] and modern

historians who have studied the problem all agree that the Irish-American

played an extremely significant, if not decisive, role in this phase of

the Anglo-Irish struggle.

Yet agreement here raises another question. If the Irish-

American possessed the ability to seriously interfere with a domestic

English question, did he possess the ability to project this same ques-

tion into Anglo-American relations? The answer can be found only in the

interplay of those relations with the Irish-American's capacity to influ-

ence simultaneously the American political scene and the Anglo-Irish

struggle. In the final analysis the answer will rest upon Irish-American

---

[1] S. T. Gwynn and G. Tuckwell, _Sir Charles Dilke_, 2 vols. (1917),
II, 262.

[2] Conor C. O'Brien, _Parnell and His Party_ (1957), 161.

[3] Thomas N. Brown, "The Origins and Character of Irish-American
Nationalism," _The Review of Politics_, XVIII (1956), 327.

power, but, since this ultimately found its vitality in what one historian called Irish-American nationalism,[4] which originated in the aftermath
of the events of the 1840's, the story of the Irish-American ability to
influence Anglo-American relations must begin with these events.

The basic ingredients of the new nationalism were produced by the
very events which earned the cheers of the Anglo-Irish Ascendancy.
The Great Famine drove almost 900,000 peasants to America in the five
years from 1846 to 1850[5] and they continued to arrive until by 1890
over 3,000,000 Irishmen had completed the journey. While the Famine
opened America's gates to the rising flow of immigrants, O'Connell's
failure forced the younger politicians to seek the solution to their
dreams in a more violent form of nationalism which produced the revolution in 1848. With its subsequent failure these revolutionaries gradually made their way to America where they found a large population of ex-
iled fellow countrymen in need of leadership. In other words the events
of the late 1840's gave to Irish-American nationalism its masses and
its leaders. In addition both the leaders and the led arrived with bitter memories of the Irish land system, the Ascendancy, and British rule—
memories that served as the foundation stones of their cause, the destruction of the land system, the elimination of the Ascendancy, and the end to
British rule, in short, Irish freedom, or in the terms of a later generation, self-determination.

---

[4] Thomas N. Brown, "Irish-American Nationalism, 1848-1891." Unpublished Doctoral Dissertation. Harvard University (1956).

[5] Carl Wittke, We Who Built America (1939), 130.

These were only the raw materials, however; they did not supply
the spark that created Irish-American nationalism. This came from
America. As the immigrants arrived prejudice and bigotry of all types
greeted them at every turn.[6] Coupled to the poverty and loneliness of
their lot, this reception forced them to seek safety in numbers and
"Irish towns" appeared in America's great cities. Their desire to live
in sharply defined geographic areas, often characterized by filth,
disease, crime, and drunkenness, alone with their preference to vote as
a block for the same party, caused native Americans to see in the Irish
a threat, not only to the well-being of the nation, but to its very existence.[7] This constant opposition created in the ex-peasant "a sense
of inferiority, a sensitiveness to criticism and a yearning for re-
spectability."[8] Yet he soon discovered that in America he did not have
to be poor; he did not have to be shunned from the main stream of society.
He could gain the respect he desired, but his ancestry handicapped him.[9]
If he could only convince the average American it was not his fault he
was poor, dirty, and crime infested, they would accept him and his
countrymen. The British government and the Ascendancy, who together
maintained that obnoxious land system, should shoulder the blame for

---

[6] Thomas N. Brown, "Nationalism and the Irish Peasant 1800-1848,"
Review of Politics, XV (1953), 403.

[7] Oliver MacDonagh, "Irish Emigration to the United States of America and the British Colonies During the Famine," in R. Dudley Edwards and
T. Desmond Williams, eds., The Great Famine (1957), 382, 383.

[8] Brown, "Origins and Character," 329.

[9] Ibid., 333.

the plight of the Irish in America. This could be proven, if only Ireland could gain her freedom—so argued the ignorant immigrant—and America would then accept them.[10] In other words the immigrant's desire to prove his right to be called an American produced his peculiar breed of nationalism. The oddity was that this approach created a marginal nation, neither Irish nor American, but Irish-American,

> whose principal literature was hostile to England, whose heroes and martyrs were either political prisoners or executed felons, and whose every aspiration and hope was at variance with the established order of things in the land which they had left.[11]

With this passionate nationalism as a dropback the remnants of the Young Ireland movement faced a relatively easy task of organizing the ex-peasants.[12] The homesick immigrants, packed into their "Irish towns," made it even easier as they formed numerous social, recreational, and beneficial societies, both local and national, all of which provided countless opportunities for discussion of news from "home" and for sharing experiences in America, out of which came a stronger, more dedicated Irish-American nationalism. As these organizations filled a social need, while indirectly intensifying the political, other Irish leaders

---

[10] New York Irish World, November 13, 1880. Michael Davitt made this point very clear in an address in New York when he told the Irish in America that they would have to remove the "stain of degradation from your birth and the Irish race here in America will get the respect you deserve."

[11] Phillip H. Bagnell, The American Irish (1886), 110.

[12] Alden Jameson, " Irish-Americans, The Irish Question and American Diplomacy, 1895-1921." Unpublished Doctoral Dissertation. Harvard University, 2 vols. (1944), I, 3.

worked to establish purely political organizations.[13]  After a number
of failures James Stephens founded the Irish Revolutionary Brotherhood
in Dublin and authorized John O'Mahoney to establish a branch in the
United States.  The Fenians, as the members were called in America, saw
their mission as one of organizing the Irish in America to contribute
both money and moral support to the struggle against England and of preparing a secret military force which would be ever ready to take advantage of England's difficulties.[14]  The establishment of this organization in 1858 marked the real emergence of the American Irish as a
force for consideration whenever the Irish question arose.  From that
date until the end of the struggle in 1923 they provided men, money,
and moral support for the cause.

The first attempt to take advantage of the organized and sentimental
Irish-American followed the end of the American Civil War.  By 1865
the I.R.B. leaders in both Ireland and the United States decided to
make final plans for the overthrow of English rule in Ireland.  The
American leaders felt that they could collect the necessary funds, since
collectively the ex-peasants had more than enough wealth to finance such
an undertaking.  They also wanted to take advantage of the military experience gained by thousands of Irish-Americans during the recent war.
Finally, Anglo-American relations had reached a low ebb as a result of

---

[13] Ibid., 8.

[14] William D'Arcy, The Fenian Movement in the United States, 1858-
1886 (1947), 17.

British actions in the course of the war—a fact that increased Irish hopes of a clash between England and the United States. For these reasons the Irish in America openly organized two military expeditions into Canada in 1866.[15] Theoretically these were to coincide with a revolution in Ireland, but the British received word of the coming attack, nipped it at the bud, and the Ascendancy remained firmly in control.

Meanwhile, the administration in Washington refused to interfere with the public preparations of the Fenians for two reasons. In the first place 1866 was a Congressional election year and Johnson, interested in winning the Irish vote for which the Democrats and Radical Republicans were also fighting, refused to jeopardize his chances.[16] Secondly, his Secretary of State, William Seward, hinted to the British that the administration would deliberately permit the Fenian fiasco to continue, if the British did not agree to the settlement of mutual disputes in a manner favorable to the United States.[17] In other words the aims of Irish-American nationalists coincided with those of American politicians and diplomats. In such an atmosphere Johnson permitted the Irish to do as they pleased as long as they did not go too far.[18] Once they actually attacked Canada, he issued a Proclamation of Neutrality, ordered General George G. Meade to confiscate the arms of the defeated Irish veterans, and even went as far as to arrest many of the leaders for

---

[15] John A. Cuddy, "The Influences of the Fenian Movement on Anglo-American Relations, 1860-1872." Unpublished Doctoral Dissertation, Saint John's University (1953), 19.

[16] D'Arcy, The Fenian Movement, 64.

[17] Ibid., 65.

[18] Major Henri Le Caron, Twenty Five Years in the Secret Service (1892), 31.

violation of the neutrality laws.  But within a short time the arms were quietly returned to their owners and those arrested released without a trial.[19]  The Irish tried again in June 1870, but times had changed.  The election of U.S. Grant in 1868 stabilized the political situation and by July 1869 Hamilton Fish opened serious conversations with Sir John Rose, the Canadian Minister of Finance, with the view of ending Anglo-American disputes.[20]  These eventually led to the signing of the highly success- ful Treaty of Washington which provided the machinery for the solution of every outstanding Anglo-American dispute.  Thus two of the props that supported the Fenian movement collapsed.  This fact, coupled to the utter failure of the movement itself, led to the gradual demise of the Brother- hood in America and with its demise the Irish question temporarily re- ceded from America's shores.[21]

With the decline of the Fenians Irish-American nationalism entered the decade of the 1870's in desperate need for reorganization to pre- pare for the inevitable renewal of the struggle with England.  When it came it resulted in a basic split in Irish-American nationalism. From 1848 to 1870 the radical, violent revolutionary element dominated the Irish in America.  After 1870 these "physical force" adherents shared control of Irish political aspirations with a more moderate faction which emphasized the constitutional, parliamentary approach as the

---

[19] Ibid., 58; D'Arcy, The Fenian Movement, 186.

[20] Thomas A. Bailey, Diplomatic History of the American People, 6th ed. (1958), 416.

[21] Cuddy, "The Influences of the Fenian Movement on Anglo- American Relations, 1860-1872." Unpublished Doctoral Dissertation. St. John's University (1953), 108.

solution to the Irish Question.[22]  During the decade John Boyle O'Reilly
and Patrick Collins, both of Boston, emerged as the leaders of this new
force.  Both had actively participated in the Fenian fiasco of 1866-67,
O'Reilly as an organizer in the British Army and Collins as an organizer
in the United States.  The failure of the revolt caused them to lose
confidence in the physical force approach.  O'Reilly withdrew from the
I.R.B. in 1870 and welcomed the Home Rule party when it emerged four
years later in Ireland.[23]  Collins meanwhile settled in Boston where he
entered upon a career in American politics.  By the end of the decade
both men had received wide recognition of their roles as leaders of this
more conservative movement.

The emergence of this force did not mean the elimination of the
more radical elements.  The decline of the Fenians was offset somewhat
by the formation of a separate organization for hard-core revolutionaries within the I.R.B.  Founded in 1867, this new group, the Clan-Na-
Gael, slowly developed as the dominant "physical force" power in Irish-
American nationalism.  By 1876 it numbered over 11,000 members and controlled sufficient wealth to think in terms of armed attacks upon English cities.[24]

While this split occurred in political organization and thought
new social organizations appeared, the more important being the Irish

---

[22] Jamison, "Irish-Americans, The Irish Question," 8.

[23] James J. Roche, The Life of John Boyle O'Reilly (1891), 143.

[24] Le Caron, Twenty Five Years, 107, 109.

Catholic Benevolent Union and the Catholic Total Abstinence Union.
Since these attracted the attention of Irishmen during a decade of
political inactivity, the followers of both factions in Irish politics
appeared at their annual national conventions. Unfortunately, by the
late 1870's and especially in the 1880's these purely social organizations lost their vitality when political issues returned to dominate
Irish minds.[25] Yet they did maintain and intensify Irish-American
nationalism by providing the immigrant with the opportunity to exchange views at a time when their experiences in America served as
virtually its only unifying force.

By 1880 they were losing even this limited role to the new
Irish press. In 1870 Patrick Ford founded the New York Irish World
which eventually became the most influential Irish paper in America
and possibly even in Ireland.[26] By 1880 four additional Irish papers
were published in New York, while every important center of Irish population supported at least one. In 1876 O'Reilly became the proprietor as
well as editor of the Boston Pilot which became the leading organ of
conservative Irish-American nationalism as Ford's became the organ of
the radicals.[27] In 1882 John F. Finerty established the Chicago Citizen as the second important radical sheet,[28] while papers appeared in

[25] Joan Bland, The Hibernian Crusade (1951), 109, 138; Joan M.
Donahue, The Irish Catholic Benevolent & Union (1953), 3.

[26] Brown, "Origins and Character," 349.

[27] William O'Brien and Dennis Ryan, eds., Devoy's Post Bag, 2 vols.
(1953), I, 15.

[28] United States Congress, House Executive Document 607, 81st
Congress, 2nd Session: Biographical Directory of the American Congress, 1774-1949 (1952), 1157.

Saint Louis, the <u>Western Watchman</u>, Saint Paul, the <u>Northwestern Chron-</u><u>icle</u> and Philadelphia, <u>Irish Catholic Benevolent Union Journal</u>.  Like other immigrant presses these thrived in periods of intense political activity and in the 1880's they became the "principle instrument of instruction in Irish-American nationalism."[29]

As the Irish in America recognized and prepared for the renewal of the struggle with England, they also began to reach responsible pos- itions in American society, especially in politics.  For instance, in 1873 Hugh McLaughlin gained control of the Democratic party machine in Brooklyn and ruled it until 1903 with few mishaps.[30]  By 1875 "Honest" John Kelley had consolidated his grip upon Tammany Hall while his lieutenant, Tom Grady, campaigned for the Democratic ticket at numerous national conventions of Irish societies.  Kelley held his position until his death in 1885, only to be succeeded by Richard Croker, another Irish- American.[31]  In 1876 an influential member of the I.C.B.U., Michael Jennings, won a seat on the City Council of Philadelphia and six years later William F. Harrity, an early graduate of La Salle College, became Chairman of the Democratic City Committee.  Harrity later served as the National Democratic Chairman from 1892 to 1896.  At least eight men, all prominent in the I.C.B.U., held judgeship during the 1870's and in 1880 Dennis Dwyer, the founder of the Union, won a seat on the New York State

---

29 Brown, "Origins and Character," 345.

30 Harold C. Syrett, <u>The City of Brooklyn, 1867-1898</u> (1944), 71.

31 Florence Gibson, <u>The Attitudes of the New York Irish to National</u> <u>and Local Affairs</u> (1951), 393.

Supreme Court. Americans born in Ireland served as Mayors in Richmond, Memphis, Baltimore, Wilmington, Scranton, and in 1880 New York, when William C. Grace won a bitter, bigoted campaign. The growing political influence was not limited to local politics, for in 1871 William R. Roberts, the leader of the Fenian attacks upon Canada in 1866, entered Congress as a Democratic representative from New York.[32] In the elections of 1876 James B. Reilly won a congressional seat in Pennsylvania while in 1879 three additional Irish-Americans entered Congress as Democrats. However, the Democrats did not have an absolute monopoly among Irish-American politicians. As early as 1868 Alexander Sullivan, who later became a dominant figure in the Clan-Na-Gael, actively campaigned for U.S. Grant. In return for his services he became Collector of Internal Revenue at Santa Fe.[33] In 1876 William J. Sewell of Camden served as a delegate to the National Republican Convention and later served in the Senate from the State of New Jersey. William Woodburn of Nevada was a Republican Congressman from 1875 to 1877, while two other Republican Irishmen entered the House in 1879. Senator Simon B. Conover, a Republican from Florida, served as an active member of the Clan-Na-Gael. During the 1880's fifteen Irish-Americans served in the House, four Republicans and eleven Democrats, while three served in the Senate, Sewell, James G. Fair, a Democrat from Nevada who was in partnership with J.C. Flood, an active member of the Clan-Na-Gael, and Charles W. Jones, a

---

[32] Biographical Directory of Congress, 1745.

[33] Le Caron, Twenty-Five Years, 63.

Democrat from Florida.[34] Two of the eleven Democratic Representatives actively participated in Fenian fiascos of the late 1860's.[35]

The career of Patrick Collins reflects the raising influence of Irish-Americans upon American politics better than the statistics above. Even as he was actively engaged in Fenian organizing work, he won a seat to the Massachusetts General Court in 1867. Three years later he moved to the State Senate and in 1873 became Democratic City Chairman in Boston. This led to his appointment as the State's Judge-Advocate General and as a Democratic National Committeeman. In the state elections of 1876 the party reaped the benefits from these offerings. In that year Charles Francis Adams carried the Democratic banner in his fight for the Governorship of Massachusetts, but Irish-Americans were displeased with him for his record as Minister to England during and after the Civil War. They accused him of refusing to defend Irish-born American citizens, arrested by the British on charges of inciting the Irish population to revolt. Collins himself made such accusations in 1867, but in 1876 he publicly reversed his position to defend Adams' record. Collins' biographer claims that his intervention saved at least 13,000 votes for the Democrats. Whether this was true or not never seemed to bother the Democratic leaders as Collins continued to rise in Democratic circles. He attended the National Convention in 1880, received the nomination to a newly-created, overwhelmingly safe

---

[34] Biographical Directory of Congress, 1143; O'Brien, Post Bag, II, 563.

[35] Le Caron, Twenty-Five Years, 74.

Congressional district in Boston, and played a prominent role in
the elections of 1884, 1888, and 1892.  He capped his national career
with an appointment as Consul General in London at the hand of Grover
Cleveland.  However, his influence declined rapidly after 1896, so that
by 1900 he no longer carried national weight, although he remained
strong locally; in fact, he became Mayor of Boston in 1902.[36]  His national influence, interestingly enough, coincided with the era of close
political power balance, that is, from 1876 to 1896.

Why he lost his influence goes beyond the scope of this study, but
his career does indicate that by 1880 the Irish-American had risen to
a position of power, whether Americans realized it or not.  As one
editor stated:

> We have the Irishman, excitable, over-imaginative,
> improvident, as it is generally thought, but given free
> play in business and public affairs, it can not be denied
> that his political achievements among us, whatever else
> may be said of them, have shown great adroitness and
> method; and the celt in this country also makes money,
> builds up fortunes.[37]

This "rising influence of the Irish in America"[38] prompted one recent
student of the Irish Question to claim that it changed the whole
character of the Anglo-Irish struggle from a national movement in the
1840's to an international one in the 1880's.  This political influence, coupled to the fact that the Irish in America collectively controlled sufficient wealth to support major campaigns against the

---

[36] M.P. Curran, The Life of Patrick A. Collins (1906), 201.

[37] American, I (1880), 42.

[38] O'Brien, Parnell and His Party, 2.

British, indicated their state of readiness when the battle reopened in the fall of 1879. The Irish in Ireland were no longer poor, no longer without powerful allies.

While the ex-peasant gained a measure of political power and material affluence, he did not forget his past nor the memories of English oppression. Even the children of the original immigrants remembered the sordid tales relayed from one generation to the next in the form of family legends.[39] The fact that their parents had been "frozen out" by the despised British landlord resulted in the creation in the later generations of "an affection for Ireland as ardent as the most national[istic] native born inhabitant of Cork, the very capital of Irish nationality."[40] Many a British traveler in America during this period recognized the Irish-American's "deep feeling of resentment against England,"[41] the ever-burning hatred of England which the organs of Irish-American nationalism never permitted the ex-peasant or his children to forget.[42]

While all this reorganization and preparation occurred in America, Irish nationalism itself experienced similar change. After the failure of O'Connell the Irish people wandered across the political stage without an effective leader. Neither the Young Irelanders nor the Irish

[39] Curran, Patrick Collins, 1.

[40] Bagnell, The American Irish, 124.

[41] James Eckman, "The British Traveler in America, 1875-1920." Unpublished Doctoral Dissertation. Georgetown University (1946), 134.

[42] Ibid., 278.

Revolutionary Brotherhood produced a voice capable of capturing the imagination of the Irish nation as a whole, or of dominating Parliament for the good of Ireland. Then in 1872 Sir Isaac Butt organized the Home Rule League and two years later this infant party faced its first general election with considerable success.[43] In the following year a rather obscure descendant of the Ascendancy, Charles Stewart Parnell, won his first seat in the House of Commons as a Home Ruler. Within two years he had emerged as the leader of that small group of active members, known as the "obstructionists."[44] It was obvious to some that a new light had appeared. Ireland was about to receive the guidance of a dynamic leader capable of simultaneously capturing the minds of the Irish people and disrupting the quiet calm of the House of Commons.

While Parnell slowly emerged as the dominant Irish parliamentarian, other Irish nationalists in both Ireland and America awoke to a desire to organize a concentrated effort to destroy England's control of Ireland. In August 1877 J.J. O'Kelley suggested that some means of uniting the many factions of Irish and Irish-American nationalism would have to be found if Ireland were ever to be free.[45] Unaware of O'Kelley's views, Michael Davitt—at the time in prison for his part in 1867 uprising— struck upon the one thing that would serve to unify Irishmen the world over, the hated Irish land system. He realized that an attack upon this

[43] Edmund Curtis, A History of Ireland (1937), 374.

[44] Ibid., 375.

[45] O'Brien, Post Bag, I, 266, O'Kelley to Devoy, August 5, 1877.

system, if successful, would not only remove much of Irish suffering, it would mark the beginning of the end of British rule.[46] However, the task of organizing the peasants and supporting a continued attack upon the very foundations of English rule would consume enormous funds which Ireland alone could not provide. Consequently, when he was released from prison in December 1877, he took his ideas, not to Ireland, but to America, where John Devoy and the Clan-Na-Gael financed his lecture tour during the summer of 1878. The plan he proposed received wide support through Devoy's efforts, as Ford's and O'Reilly's papers urged Americans of Irish blood to follow Davitt's lead. With this kind of backing Davitt virtually united all Irish-American factions behind his plan for a full-powered attack upon the land system. Yet the Irish parliamentary movement remained outside the picture; so, when Davitt returned to Ireland, he arranged for a meeting between Parnell, the most active parliamentarian, and John Devoy. This took place in Paris in early March 1879, when both agreed in general terms that the new movement, although basically agrarian, would establish a national public organization in which the extremes as well as the moderates would have an opportunity to arouse public opinion.[47] By emphasizing the agrarian aspects they hoped to capture the minds of both the peasants in Ireland and the ex-peasants in America, whose bitter memories of the land system remained so strong. By creating a national public organization they not

---

[46] Michael Davitt, The Fall of Feudalism in Ireland (1904), 150-171. The whole original idea is discussed in detail.

[47] O'Brien, Post Bag, I, 371, 401.

only would provide for the integration of those who advocated secret means
with those who abhorred such means, but also would avoid any possible
criticism by the Catholic Church. Thus by March 1879 a strange union
of forces emerged—one that eventually rocked the very foundations of
the Anglo-Irish Ascendancy. Oddly enough, however, the real strength of
the organized resistance rested upon forces beyond Davitt's or anyone
else's control.

The Irish land system that operated during the 1870's had a number
of peculiar characteristics that made its maintenance extremely difficult.
In the first place it provided the sole means of subsistence for over
90% of the people, the vast majority occupying small holdings without
right of tenure except that based upon the payment of rent.[48] Once the
tenant lapsed in this respect, the landlord could evict him and lease
the land to someone else, usually at a higher rent. In a rich country,
where little threat of famine existed, such a system might not have been
too harsh on the individual tenant. As long as the soil produced healthy
crops, he paid his rent and had no fear of being without a home or means
of subsistence. But in a poor land such as Ireland, where the fear of
famine and starvation constantly harried her people, this system proved
impossible.[49] The size of the holding and the relative poverty of tho
soil forced the peasant into a dual economy, one to feed his family, the
potato almost exclusively; the other to pay the rent. This latter sum

---

[48] Norman D. Palmer, The Irish Land League Crisis (1940), 2.

[49] Oscar Handlin, Boston's Immigrants, 1790-1865 (1940), 43-45.
An excellent short summary of the whole system can be found here.

he would earn either by planting and selling a money crop, or by traveling to England to work as a laborer in agriculture industry between the planting and harvesting of the potato. If catastrophe struck either side of his economy, the peasant usually faced an unpleasant winter. If it struck the potato, as it often did in the damp climate of Ireland, he faced the choice of eviction, if he used his rent money to purchase food for the family, or starvation, if he did not. Thus, it would be bad enough if only the potato failed, but, if agricultural prices fell at the same time, the peasant faced an utterly hopeless situation. He could neither eat nor pay. This double evil occurred at various times during the nineteenth century. One of these immediately preceded the final formation of Davitt's plan.

As one modern historian said:

> the fear of famine, or rather to choose between starvation and eviction, was the underlying political reality of the late seventies and early eighties of the nineteenth century in Ireland.[50]

The partial failure of the potato crop in 1878 and the falling prices of other crops united to produce a situation that threatened a recurrence of the pattern of the forties and fifties. The total value of all Irish crops fell from about 36,000,000 in 1876, to about 22,000,000 in 1879--an enormous loss of 38% in itself, but the more startling when one considers that the potato crop's value alone fell from 12,464,000 to only 3,341,000, a 75% decrease. In the midst of the economic unrest which this situation created, Davitt organized his attack upon the whole

---

[50] O'Brien, Parnell and His Party, 1.

Land system, not knowing what the future held, but confident of success, since he had already tied the parliamentarians under Parnell to the powerful and wealthy Irish-Americans.[51]

Davitt first organized his home county when he formed the Mayo Land League. On June 5, 1879 Parnell addressed this organization at Westport. By mid-summer Davitt, riding the tide of unrest, was organizing branches throughout the country and, finally, in October Parnell accepted the Presidency of the National Land League. He became the leader of a growing wave of agrarian agitation and promised to travel to America to seek funds and to establish permanent branches of the League.[52] The Irish-American once again became intimately involved in a domestic English issue.

As the decaying economic situation in Ireland strengthened Davitt's plan, aroused the old bitter memories of the Irish-American, and prepared the groundwork for Parnell's leadership during the 1880's, American politics closed a relatively unique period. In 1872, in spite of numerous handicaps, U.S. Grant and the Republican party won a decisive victory (55.8% of the votes cast) which enabled them to take 1,342 counties to 834 for the Democrats. However, the victory was dependent upon Democratic abstentions in the north and Republican reconstruction in the South.[53] These considerations, plus the depression which followed

---

[51] Michael Davitt, The Fall of Feudalism, 168.

[52] R.B. O'Brien, The Life of Charles Stewart Parnell, 2 vols. (1898), 195.

[53] W. Dean Burnham, Presidential Ballots, 1836-1892 (1955), 118.

the Panic of '73, led to the Democratic capture of the House of Representatives in 1874 for the first time in sixteen years. Interest immediately shifted to the election of 1876 with the Democrats expecting victory. Their chances were excellent. The South, all but Florida, Louisiana, and South Carolina, had already emerged from the carpetbaggers, while their nomination of Samuel J. Tilden offered the greatest opportunity to campaign against "Grantism." The struggle resulted in the well-known disputed election which was eventually settled in favor of the Republican, but the cheers did not last long as the settlement came at the cost of Reconstruction.

If the election of 1876 closed an era, it also opened one, "the period of no-decision." From 1876 to 1896 the relative strengths of the two major parties were almost equal. Elections turned on mere handfuls of voters. California went Democratic in 1880 by 22 votes out of 164,392 cast, while in the nation as a whole the Democratic presidential candidate polled only 7,368 less than his Republican opponent.[54] In the same year the Republicans won Connecticut by 2,660 votes, Indiana by 6,625, New York by 23,033, and the Democrats took New Jersey by 2,010. Maine voters elected a Democratic Governor by 200 votes, while giving the Republicans three of the five Congressional seats. In the Forty-Seventh Congress the Republicans controlled the House, but had to rely upon the aid of William Mahone, a Virginia Readjuster, in order to organize the Senate. In the following Congress they lost control of

---

[54] Ibid., 34, 130. 80% of those eligible voted in election of 1880.

the House, but managed to increase their control of the Senate.[55]  The
election of 1884 continued to reflect this even distribution of power.
Cleveland won all important New York with only 1149 votes to spare,
while capturing Indiana (6,527), Connecticut (1,276), and New Jersey
(4,358).[56]  The Indiana Congressional elections of 1886 were so close
a change of merely 15 votes would have given the Republicans two additional victories.[57]  The election of 1888 failed to deviate from the
pattern of previous years.  Benjamin Harrison, the Republican Presidential
candidate, won the state of New York with 13,002 votes, while the Democratic candidate for Governor won by 19,171.  Connecticut went Democratic for the third Presidential election in a row, but this time, by
only 344 votes of 153,798 cast.  Grover Cleveland went on to win the
popular vote by over 90,000, but lost the election, 233 electoral votes
to 168.  He had lost the all important New York State without which a
Democrat could not win the White House.

The numerical equality caused a static equilibrium to develop in
politics.  The politicians ignored the pressing problems of the times
and tended to rely for victory upon "the waving of the bloody shirt" or
upon personal attacks upon the candidates.[58]  The avoidance of issues

---

[55] The American, V (1882), 65.

[56] H.C. Thomas, The Return of the Democratic Party to Power in
1884 (1919), 228.

[57] Harry J. Siever, Benjamin Harrison:  Hoosier Statesman, 2 vols.
(1959), I, 300.

[58] Herbert J. Clancy, The Presidential Election of 1880 (1958), 162;
Thomas, The Return in 1884, 15.

became an obsession, for the politicians owed their elections, not
to their ability to present ideas to the voters, but to their ability
to manipulate party machinery. They merely desired to perpetuate office holding by their own party and elections became ends in themselves.
Innovations scared the "pro," since they generated ideas and forced
people to take positions on issues which in turn would possibly cause
an uncontrollable shift in political power.[59]   Only two issues were presented to the voters during these years, the tariff and government reform, but even here both major parties were split evenly and no real
differences existed.[60]  As a result the period from 1876 to 1896,
characterized by the close balance of political power and the avoidance
of issues, increased the possibility of pressure group influence upon
the politician.

American political life assumed the unique characteristics of the
"era of no decision" because, among other things, both major parties
could rely upon certain sections of the country with virtual absolute
certitude. The Democrats could expect to win at least the 153 electoral
votes of the southern and border states of Alabama, Arkansas, Georgie,
Louisiana, Maryland, Mississippi, Missouri, South Carolina, Tennessee,
Texas, Florida, Delaware, North Carolina, West Virginia, and Virginia.[61]
They could concentrate their forces, consequently, on the few northern

---

59 Robert E. Brooks, Political Parties and Electoral Problems, 3rd
ed. (1933), 75.

60 James Bryce, The American Commonwealth, 2 vols. (1888), I, 653,
657, 658.

61 The American, VII (1883), 310.

states that would give them the necessary votes for victory in a presidential campaign.[62] The Republicans in turn based their hopes upon the northern and western states of Colorado, Illinois, Iowa, Kansas, Maine, Massachusetts, Michigan, Minnesota, Nebraska, New Hampshire, Ohio, Oregon, Pennsylvania, Rhode Island, Vermont, Wisconsin, California and Nevada which accounted for 182 electoral votes.[63] Victory or defeat usually turned on the results in New York (36), New Jersey (9), Indiana (15), and Connecticut (6). If the Democrats won all but New York, they would fail of victory by 18 votes. The Republicans could win by taking this all important state—provided, the Democrats made no inroads into their bloc.

As these facts indicate, New York assumed a position in national politics far out of proportion to its size or population and the professional politician realized this throughout the era. Before the election of 1880, the first presidential canvass after the Era of Reconstruction, Democrats around the country demanded the end of the New York struggle between Samuel Tilden and "Honest" John Kelley which had erupted into an open election battle in 1879. In that year Kelley ran himself against Tilden's choice for Governor, captured the city by 77,566 votes and, consequently, gave the State to the Republicans.[64] The Cincinnati Commercial stated that the split would have to be resolved for "without

---

[62] Gail Hamilton, Biography of James G. Blaine (1895), 577.

[63] Walker Blaine, "Why Harrison Was Elected," North American Review (1888), 686.

[64] Clancy, The Election of 1880, 61.

New York, the Solid South is useless for national purposes," while the New Orleans *Times* told Kelley and Tilden to settle their differences, "then the Democratic Party of New York and the country would win the election."[65] Some Southerners were even hoping that Tilden would receive the Democratic nomination, since he had captured New York by over 30,000 votes in 1876 and Indiana by 5,000. Along with the Solid South these amounted to victory. The fact that reform would again enter the campaign merely increased his likelihood of receiving the nomination.[66] However, Kelley and others, refusing to settle the split with Tilden, boomed Delaware's Senator Thomas F. Bayard, but many Democrats complained that Bayard would never carry New York.[67] The Atlantic *Constitution* stated, "it was folly to nominate men who can not carry New York."[68] When the Convention met, the delegates passed over Tilden and picked Winfield S. Hancock, "After they heard that awful threat of Kelley,"[69] who claimed he would not vote for Tilden. In order to gain the important state of Indiana, they nominated William H. English as Hancock's running mate.[70]

Meanwhile the Republicans also indicated a concern for New York. Early in the year George W. Curtis, the editor of Harper's Weekly, stressed the importance of the state and the need to gain Roscoe Corkling's

---

[65] *Ibid.*, 66, 70.

[66] Alexander C. Fleck, *Samuel J. Tilden: A Study in Political Sagacity* (1939), 250.

[67] Charles C. Tansill, *The Congressional Career of Thomas F. Bayard, 1869-1885* (1946).

[68] Clancy, *The Election of 1880*, 124.

[69] New York *Times*, July 2, 1880.

[70] Clancy, *The Election of 1880*, 146.

approval of the ticket.[71] The Republicans took this advice after they nominated James A. Garfield as a compromise candidate when neither Blaine nor Grant, even with Corkling's support, were unable to gain a majority. To placate the "Boss" in New York, they gave the Vice-Presidency to Chester A. Arthur, his trusted lieutenant. The Republicans were willing to nominate a man who had just left the office of Collector of the New York Port under the stigma of corruption, for as William Chandler believed, New York was "important, probably vital and it might be worthwhile to stoop a little to conquer much."[72] Once the election campaign started, both parties flooded Indiana with money and workers. After a $500,000 battle the Republicans won and Ohio followed. With these results Arthur pleaded that all possible aid to be rushed to New York,[73] since the Democrats could still win if they took it. Unfortunately for them they failed. "Honest" John Kelley had tricked the city professionals into nominating William Grace for Mayor. This Irish-Catholic's candidacy raised the whole Catholic question and although he won his contest, the Democrats took the city by only 3,045 votes, hardly enough to offset the upstate Republican lead.[74]

Republicans looked with apprehension to the next election, since their 1880 victory came with such a slim measure of success. Then in

---

[71] Ibid., 206.

[72] Ibid., 184.

[73] Sievers, Benjamin Harrison, I, 180.

[74] Gibson, The New York Irish, 319.

1882 they lost control of the House of Representatives, while the Democrats captured three New England, three mid-western, and three far-western states, picking up six Governorships.[75]  If the Democrats made such inroads into Republican strongholds in 1884, New York would become indispensable for a Republican victory.  The fears of many increased, when Blaine appeared on the list of candidates for the Republican nomination, since the old independent wing of the party voiced disapproval on the basis of Blaine's record of opposing reform in government.  One source estimated that this group could muster 80,000 votes in New York State.[76]

In spite of the opposition from this quarter the Republicans nominated Blaine and the Democrats countered with the reform-minded governor of New York State, Grover Cleveland.  The New York World predicted that Cleveland would receive the dissident Republican vote which would enable him to carry the state.[77]  Both parties gave the Vice-Presidential nominations to mid-westerners, John Logan of Illinois for the Republicans and Thomas B. Hendricks of Indiana for the Democrats.  As predicted the Mugwumps bolted their party and publicly campaigned for Cleveland. At the end of the battle professionals from both camps concentrated upon New York.  In late October Blaine arrived on the battle field only to face the reaction to the "Rum, Romanism and Rebellion remarks" and the dinner of the industrialists at Delmonico's.[78]  Before he could

---

[75] The American, V (1882), 65.

[76] Frederick Bancroft, ed., Speeches, Correspondence and Political Papers of Carl Schurz, 6 vols. (1913), V, 201, Plumber to Schurz, May 12, 1885.

[77] Thomas, The Return in 1884, 181.

[78] Allen Nevins, Grover Cleveland: A Study in Courage (1932), 182.

correct the damage Cleveland took New York by 1149 votes out of over
1,150,000 cast. Why Cleveland won will be forever debated, but the why
or how did not bother the professionals of that day. They were more
amazed that he won by so small a margin. In fact a change of a mere
575 votes would have given the election to the "man from Maine"—a sum
any good ward leader could provide even today.[79]

With this thought in mind the professionals started early for
the next battle. In December 1887 Cleveland determined what the issue
would be when in his Annual Message he asked for a reduction of the
tariff.[80] Of course he received the Democratic nomination, while the
Republicans, after Blaine refused to openly battle for the nomination,
picked Benjamin Harrison of Indiana and Levi P. Morton of New York.
The election, like the preceding campaigns, turned on New York, Indiana,
New Jersey, and Connecticut. Matthew Quay of Pennsylvania engineered
the Republican strategy and literally flooded the critical state of
Indiana with the vast sums collected by John Wanamaker. When the Republicans won Indiana by 2,352 votes of 537,008 cast, the Democrats had
to take Connecticut, New Jersey, and New York.[81] Connecticut was theirs,
but by only 344 votes and New Jersey also. They failed in New York and
Cleveland was forced to leave the White House even though 90,000 more
Americans had preferred his continued residency to that of Harrison's.[82]

---

[79] Carleton Putnam, Theodore Roosevelt: The Formative Years, 1858-
1886 (1958), 504.

[80] Nevins, Cleveland, 379.

[81] Eugene H. Roseboom, History of Presidential Elections (1957), 283.

[82] Baron Rosen, Forty Years of Diplomacy, 2 vols. (1922), I, 75;
Walker Blaine, "Why Harrison Was Elected," 686.

For the third straight election New York determined the outcome.

While the political climate of the 1880's was being shaped, events occurred in the world of Anglo-American diplomacy that foreshadowed a trend which eventually led to the famous Venezuelan controversy in 1895. The trouble did not begin until after Rutherford B. Hayes entered the White House. In the years immediately preceding his election Anglo-American relations were rather peaceful and calm, the result of the Treaty of Washington, British statesmanship under Gladstone, and the wise diplomacy of Hamilton Fish. However, in 1874 Gladstone left office and Benjamin Disraeli returned only to lead England on the road to a new imperialism. Three years later Fish left his office and turned the keys over to William M. Evarts, a much less qualified and gifted statesman. In addition, the good will generated by the Treaty of Washington suffered a serious blow in November 1877. The Halifax award was announced.

The reaction of Americans to the announcement that the United States would be asked to give $5,500,000 to Great Britain as the monetary difference between the American use of the Canadian inshore fisheries and Canadian rights to ship duty free fish into the American market, was only the first of a series of problems which led Carl Fish to entitle this section of his general study of American diplomacy, "Baiting the Lion, 1877-1896."[83] Even though the American Commissioner E. A. Kellogg refused to sign the final award, the United States paid, but under

---

[83] Carl Fish, American Diplomacy (1916), 370.

protest. Meanwhile, leading figures bitterly complained. James G.
Blaine, at the time a leading Republican Senator, declared, "we should
utterly refuse to pay a single penny,"[84] since he believed with many
Americans that the award was both excessive and unfair.[85] Senator Edmunds agreed, while even Fish himself was quite upset.[86]

Before the effect of this could wear off the Fortune Bay incident
occurred. In January 1878 an angry mob of British citizens drove a
group of American fishermen from the Canadian shore and damaged American property. Evarts protested the incident and demanded an investigation by the British. After an exchange of notes he eventually claimed
over $100,000 in damages and asked the British to settle the question
as soon as possible. The British were in no rush, however, and the question lingered into the next decade.

The British return to imperialism which began with Disraeli's second ministry created another problem, but this time in the South Pacific.
In 1875 the United States, England, and Germany had interests in the
Samoan Islands. A struggle for control of these developed after the
United States signed a treaty in which the Samoans gave the Americans
the right to use Pago Pago harbor (the best in the South Pacific) as a
coaling station in return for an American promise to use its good of-

---

[84] James G. Blaine, Political Discussions (1887), 176-185.

[85] James M. Callahan, American Foreign Policy in Canadian Relations (1937), 362-363.

[86] Allan Nevins, Hamilton Fish (1936), 889; Selig Adler, "The Senatorial Career of George Franklin Edmunds, 1866-1891." Unpublished
Doctoral Dissertation. University of Illinois (1934), 319.

fices whenever the Samoans became involved with a foreign power.[87]
Both the British and Germans managed to secure similar rights, and it
soon appeared that an open struggle over the islands would commence at
any moment. Yet this was avoided in September 1879 when the three
consuls agreed to cooperate in the administration of the Island.[88]
Not until Grover Cleveland's first administration did the question re-
emerge.

By 1879 Latin-American questions appeared which later caused some
difficulty for Anglo-American harmony. In February the War of the
Pacific erupted with Peru and Bolivia on one side and Chile on the
other. By June Americans pictured the whole thing as a British inspired war and for four years the United States remained involved in efforts to settle it.[89] At the same time Americans became quite concerned
with the question of a French built and controlled canal across the
isthmus of Panama. This problem eventually generated a movement to
abrogate the Clayton-Bulwer Treaty which had regulated American-
British relations in that area of the world from 1850.[90]

As if these were not enough, other problems arose concerning Canadian-American relations. On numerous occasions Indians under the leader-

---

[87] George H. Ryden, The Foreign Policy of the United States in Relation to Samoa (1933), 13.

[88] Ibid., 257.

[89] Herbert Millington, American Diplomacy and the War of the
Pacific (1948), 60.

[90] Bailey, Diplomatic History of the American People, 432.

ship of Sitting Bull had crossed the border from Canada, only to swiftly return after destroying American property. In 1879 Evarts made an official diplomatic complaint that something be done to prevent such attacks.[91] But the problem was not easily settled and it continued into the administration of Chester Arthur.

While these basic Anglo-American struggles tended to stir the diplomatic waters, a question foreign to such basic differences appeared as a forerunner of what was to occur in the 1880's. In 1866 the British arrested a number of Americans of Irish birth for inciting the people of Ireland to rebel. One of those captured, Edward O'Meagher Condon, was still in prison in 1875 when Colonel Ricard Burke brought his case before the State Department through friends in Congress.[92] In 1878 after the Department intervened in Condon's behalf the British permitted him to return to the United States, where the Republicans gave him a job in the Washington office of the Treasury Department.[93] Two years later the same Condon played an active role in the arrangements for Parnell's visit to Washington. In this way Irish-American influence upon Anglo-American relations reappeared and the Irish Question returned to America's shores.

While Irish power in America increased in its own right in addition

---

[91] United States Foreign Relations, 1880, 486. Evarts to Thornton, August 9, 1879.

[92] O'Brien, Post Bag, I, 104. Ricard Burke to Mortimer Moyanhan, April 20, 1875. Burke had participated in the 1866 Canadian fiasco.

[93] Ibid., 476. Condon to Devoy, January 2, 1880.

to the increase due to the peculiar political situation, events in Ireland progressed to a point which they afforded the Irish-American the possible opportunity to use this power for Ireland's cause. At the same time Anglo-American relations headed in the direction of renewed difficulty. Everything was ready for an Irish-American attempt to increase Anglo-American tensions. Whether or not they accelerated the general trend remains to be seen.

Chapter I

The Irish-Americans and American Politics

As a result of the considerations which made New York the pivotal state, politicians sought issues to attract the voters that would gain for their respective parties that all conclusive prize. In their search they focused their attention on Irish-Americans, among other groups, for three reasons, numbers, voting habits, and sentiments.

From 1845 to 1891 over three million Irishmen came to the United States,[1] about seventy-five percent of the Irish immigration to the new world.[2] In the 1870 census 1,855,827 of the 29,000,000 Americans were born in Ireland. Ten years later Irish-born Americans numbered 1,854,571 with an estimated 2,756,054 children.[3] In 1890, when children of foreign parents were first counted, the Irish-American population numbered 4,913,238, either Irish-born or children of parents, one of who was Irish-born.[4] In addition many Americans, more than one generation removed, considered themselves members of the Irish nationality, and these were "in reality, often more Irish in sentiment than their

---

[1] Brown, "Origins and Character," 328.

[2] MacDonagh, "Irish Emigration to the U.S.," 376.

[3] William R. Grace, The Irish in America (1886), 19; Joseph Edgar Chamberlain, "The Foreign Elements of Our Population," Century, N.S., VI (1884), 756.

[4] Jameson, "Irish-Americans, The Irish Question," 3.

own fathers and mothers."[5] Even without this latter group the Irish-born and their children hovered between four and five million through-out the 1880's.

These figures alone would have attracted the attention of even the budding politician, but they impressed the professionals especially because of their geographic distribution. In 1880 sixty-three percent of Irish-born Americans lived on the Atlantic Sea Coast north of North Carolina, and formed the most numerous foreign element in the states of Virginia, New Jersey, New York, Pennsylvania, Rhode Island, Massa-chusetts and Delaware,[6] three of which remained critical for political purposes throughout the decade. Even within these states they tended to gather in the great cities, "being victims of their own poverty."[7] In 1890 the Irish born and their children amounted to 36% of the popu-lation of Boston, 34% of Philadelphia, 27% of New York, and 25% of Brooklyn. Two mid-western cities, the railheads of the west, also con-tained large concentrations, Chicago with 16% Irishmen and Saint Louis, 15%.[8] New York State had the largest concentration in terms of pure numbers. In 1880 the state had a population of 3,871,482, of which

---

[5] Bagnell, The American Irish, 33; Grace, Irish in America, 24. "Fenianism appealed to the sentimental side of the Irish character and fanned a flame of patriotism which burns strong in the Irish breast even to the second and third generations of those who have left their native land forever."

[6] Chamberlain, "The Foreign Element," 763.

[7] Brown, "Origin and Character," 328.

[8] Jameson, "Irish-Americans, the Irish Question," 5.

499,445 or 13.7% were Irish born.[9]   In the city numbered 198,595 of

1,206,299 or 17.4% of the population.  One student of the Irish in

New York claimed that approximately 87,685 Irish-born citizens could

vote in 1880, an estimate which did not include the second generation.[10]

In 1890 of the 5,923,952 persons living in the state 483,375 claimed

birth in Ireland.  However, when the children are included this figure

jumps to over 1,178,000 or almost 20%, while parents and children amounted

to 27.5% of the city population.[11]   From such figures Florence Gibson

concluded that:

> by 1882 the New York Irish represented the balance
> of power in the state. The fact that the electoral vote
> of New York was so large gave the Irish an undue influ-
> ence on national affairs as well.[12]

One visitor from England reflected a similar conclusion when he stated:

> The fate of a Presidential election depends upon
> the vote of a single state, New York, which is almost
> entirely governed by the Irish vote.[13]

Whether this was true or not made little difference to the professional

politician.  That it was possibly true was enough.

In addition to their numbers the Irish-Americans possessed a sec-

ond attention gaining characteristic, that peculiar brand of nationalism

which lived on an intense hatred of England and everything English.

---

[9] Gibson, The New York Irish, 321.

[10] Ibid., 323.

[11] Ibid., 428.

[12] Ibid., 375.

[13] Bagnell, The American Irish, 60.  It is interesting to note here
that the same was said for the Independent Republican who also could
muster an estimated 80,000 votes.

All their poverty, degradation, and every insult to the Irish pride the Irish in America laid at the doorstep of England and as Phillip Bagnell stated in 1880, "this grudge is the deepest of all."[14] As the Anglo-Irish struggle revived during the decade, Irish-Americans received ample opportunity to recall their bitter memories, and they soon learned to appreciate those who spoke out against that evil English nation. For that very reason the politicians played upon this nationalism and few Irish-Americans failed at least to listen.

The voting habits of the Irish also attracted the politician. When they first arrived, they tended to support the party that "stood for easy naturalization, the Democratic party,"[15] and later continued to vote Democratic because the Republican party recalled the old Know-Nothing label which equated a vote for Republicanism to one against the Catholic religion.[16] Some observers who recognized this tendency in the Irish-American character held that they so voted because the Democrats were "more radically opposed to the principles of the English political system."[17] But again the why is not quite as important as that they did. This fact caused Republicans to appeal to the Irish after the Civil War, as was indicated, but their success was not very

---

[14] Ibid., 129.

[15] Grace, The Irish in America, 14.

[16] Maurice Francis Egan, Memoirs of a Happy Life (1924), 38. "My mother did not believe that a man could be a good Christian and not belong to the Democratic party."

[17] Bagnell, The American Irish, 128.

great. The vast majority continued to vote Democratic, according to most observers, at least down to the decade of the 1880's.[18] Then, as a number of scholars have indicated, there appeared among the Irish-Americans a greater tendency to shift party labels.[19]

The election of 1880 did not at first produce any great rush on the part of either party to attract Irish-Americans to their respective banners, but the politicians increased their interest as the campaign progressed. This initial failure to gauge the role of the Irish voter was due probably to two things. First of all, neither party knew exactly how the emancipation of the South would effect the election. Although the Republicans realized that "the aim of the Democratic party is to conjoin the electoral vote of New York and Indiana with the electoral vote of the sixteen southern states," they did not know how close the Democrats would come.[20] Secondly, in the initial phase the Republicans fought the election merely by waving the "bloody shirt" which meant that they did not have an issue specifically attractive to the Irish, that is, one based upon purely Irish interests.

Although no great effort appeared, the Republicans did attempt to capture the Irish by establishing special organizations. On July 18, 1880 an Irish-American Republican Convention opened at Indianapolis.[21]

---

[18] Gibson, The New York Irish. The author states they voted Solid Democratic until 1882, but this does not seem to be true.

[19] James P. Shannon, Catholic Colonization of the Western Frontier (1957), 133; M. Justille McDonald, The History of the Irish in Wisconsin in the Nineteenth Century (1954), 157. She holds that the Democrats fought to retain the Irish vote while the Republicans fought to capture it during the 1880's.

[20] Hamilton, James G. Blaine, 580.

[21] Donahue, Irish Catholic Benevolent Union, 23.

The speakers accused their fellow countrymen of blindly following a single party which gained them little, while that same party discriminated against Irish-Catholics by not offering them important governmental positions. The second Vice-President of this organization was none other than James Lewis Brady, an ex-Confederate Army colonel and the principal speaker at the first Convention of the Irish Catholic Benevolent Union in 1869.[22] At the same time Irish-Americans in New York formed the Irish-American Republican Association with Thomas R. Bannerman as Corresponding Secretary,[23] who had just completed six years as the secretary of the Clan-Na-Gael and had served on the Reception Committee for Parnell's tour in early 1880.[24] Similar associations were organized in Brooklyn, Buffalo, and Syracuse, while attempts were made in Chicago and Boston. A New York State Convention convened at Saratoga on September 27, 1880, and Colonel Ricard Burke, who had interceded on Condon's behalf with the State Department, took "the stump for Garfield."[25]

Such efforts under the direction of Republican Irish-Americans were strengthened when party leaders found an issue that would appeal to the Irish. On October 16 Wharton Barker published the first issue of his protectionist magazine American under the editorship of Professor Robert Ellis Thompson of the University of Pennsylvania. Both were to play con-

---

[22] Ibid., 16.

[23] New York Tribune, August 4, 1880.

[24] O'Brien, Post Bag, I, 477.

[25] New York Tribune, September 29, 1880; John Devoy, Recollections of An Irish Rebel (1929), 351.

spicuous roles in the 1884 and 1888 attempts to tie the Irish-American

to the banner of Republican "Protection" but in this first issue Thompson

merely stated the policy of the magazine, Republican and protectionist

in politics and pro-Irish in the Anglo-Irish struggle.  In the October 23

issue, however, he noted that "it was never so easy to convert Democrats,

and especially Irish voters to the Republican party."  He went on to

say that this was so because all the issues that had attracted the

Irish to the Democratic party no longer existed and that "the only is-

sue of this campaign for which the Irish vote can be made to really

care, is that between American Protection and 'British Free Trade.'"[26]

At the same time Blaine in an open letter to a prominent Irish citizen

used the same argument to capture Irish votes.

> . . . the course of yourself and other Irish voters is one
> of the most extraordinary anomalies in our political
> history . . . the great mass of Irish voters in the United
> States will, on Tuesday next, vote precisely as English-
> men would have them vote—for the interests of England . . .
> the Irishmen of America use their suffrage as agents of
> the Tories.  The Free-Traders of England desire nothing
> so much as the defeat of Garfield and the election of Han-
> cock.  They wish to break down the protective tariff and
> cripple our manufactures . . . [27]

Thus as the campaign closed, the Republicans found an issue that they

could "pitch" to the Irish and Thompson returned to it on October 30.

> English Free Trade policies have ruined Ireland . . . .
> To Irishmen in America these facts should appeal very
> strongly.  They have voice and vote as regards the
> financial policy of their adopted country.  Shall it
> be cast so as to give their condonation of the wrongs
> which have blighted the country of their birth?  Shall

---

[26] American, I (1880), 19.

[27] Bangor Whig and Courier, October 29, 1880, quoted in Hamilton,
James G. Blaine, 489.

it be cast to expose the rising industries of the new
world and the treatment which destroyed those of
Ireland? This is the issue of the present political
campaign and it is an issue that should not be over-
looked nor despised. If American Irishmen follow the
blind leadership of former years, they will but assist
and perpetuate the essence of the very wrongs of which
they so loudly, so justly complain. If they but reason
out their peace, their power and their interests, they
will vote for those principles and that party which
realizes to them the best measure of their hopes in the
wisest legislation for the industries and labor by
which American Irishmen live.[28]

The fact that such passionate appeals came on the eve of the election

indicates that, first, the Republicans, finally aware of the nearness of

the political balance, sought to detach the Irish and, secondly, they

hoped to accomplish this by connecting the Irish-American sympathy for

Ireland to the protectionist band wagon.[29] The Republican appeals to the

Irish during the early stages of the battle in all probability equalled

their attempts in earlier elections, since they felt no need to expand

these and because they had no specific issue. Only after they realized

the importance of the Irish did they discover that protectionism had

such a direct appeal to the Irish masses, but then it was too late.

---

[28] American, I (1880), 41.

[29] There seems to be little hope of explaining why the Republicans
waited until the end of the campaign to use the very pointed argument
that tied the Anglo-Irish struggle to the protectionist issue. I
have looked at Professor Clancy's work on the election and Professor
Muzzey's biography of Blaine but in neither could I even find a men-
tion of it. Walter Poulschock failed to do so in his recent study
of the tariff issue, "The Politics of the Tariff in the United States,
1880-1888," unpublished Doctoral Dissertation, University of Pennsylvania, 1962. That the Republicans failed to use this argument can be
seen in the statement of Thompson when he wrote "And if the Republicans
take the pains to put these facts before the voters of the Eastern
States, they fairly may look for a great accession of strength from a
quarter from which they have had in previous years but little strength."
See American, I (1880), 19.

This interpretation is supported by the activities of the Democratic bosses. There is little evidence that they were concerned with a possible mass exodus of Irishmen from the party. Patrick Collins was safely in their ranks, as was John Boyle O'Reilly.[30] The Democrats did make one important concession, Daniel Dougherty of Pennsylvania nominated Hancock, but there seems to be little indication that Irish Democrats did anything but normal campaigning.[31]

In the years following the election this was not true, however, for both parties increased their efforts to appear attractive to the Irish voter. Visiting Englishmen constantly referred to the "growing power of the Irish in American politics,"[32] while the English minister in Washington continued to inform his superiors of this reality. On March 7, 1882 Sir Lionel Sackville-West, while informing the British Foreign Minister concerning speeches made by various members of the House of Representatives in memory of Robert Emmet, cautioned that these violent speeches were meant only to capture the Irish vote.

> The fact is that no member of the House who depends for election on the Irish vote, and there are many who do so depend, shrinks from seeking to secure it at any price regardless of what they know to be the true interests of the country and the circumstances which may result from doing so. Under these circumstances it is better perhaps to treat their proceed-

[30] Clancy, The Election of 1880, p. 36.

[31] Roche, John Boyle O'Reilly, 263.

[32] James Eckman, "The British Traveler in America, 1875-1920." Unpublished Doctoral Dissertation. Georgetown University (1946), 133.

ings with indifference and as coming from their
peculiar political organization.[33]

The tempo of the political interest in the Irish increased as Congress
debated the British arrest and imprisonment of Irish-American citizens
in Ireland.  In the middle of this agitation a great Irish-American
protest meeting was held in Cooper Hall, New York.  Three Democrats,
Senator Charles William Jones of Florida, Representative Samuel S.
Cox of New York, and Representative Samuel Randall of Pennsylvania, attended.  The Democrats projected this whole question into the 1882
congressional campaign when their platforms in New York, Indiana and
Illinois condemned the Republican administration for permitting American citizens to remain in English jail.  The Democrats, in effect,
openly used specific issues that appealed to the Irish for the sole
purpose of gaining their votes.

A few voices began to caution against such attention being shown
to the Irish.  John Gilmary Shea, a leading Catholic intellectual,
cautioned politicians concerning their efforts to capture a "Catholic
vote" by raising questions and issues that would arouse Catholic reaction.  He reminded them that no Catholic political organization existed,
but that as a whole Catholics were conservatives.[34]  At about the same

---

[33] Paul Knaplund and C.M. Clewes, eds. "Private Letters from the
British Embassy in Washington to the Foreign Secretary, Lord Granville,
1880-1885," American Historical Association Annual Report 1941 (1942),
164. West to Granville, March 7, 1882.

[34] John Gilmary Shea, "The Anti-Catholic Issue in the Late Election—
the Relation of Catholics to the Political Parties," American Catholic
Quarterly Review, VI (1881), 36.

time Robert J. Creighton faced the subject more squarely, when he wrote:

> the American Irish party has become an important fac-
> tor in American politics, and may, if it pleases, hold
> the balance of power in the coming presidential elec-
> tion. It is thoroughly organized, perfectly disciplined,
> skillfully led and, above all, it knows its own mind
> and purpose. And these purposes are paramount. American
> politics will be made subservient to them, and compacts
> will be forced upon party leaders, however, distasteful
> such alliances may be. . . . A great country like this
> can not afford to make its government the plaything of
> popular caprice, or the prize of a reckless political com-
> bination.[35]

To a large extent, Creighton reflected the bitter thoughts of many
"old-fashioned Americans when they found the election of a president
virtually in the hands of a race whom for years they have looked upon
as alien and inferior."[36] But the politician failed to heed these warn-
ings for the "shrewd Yankee-caucus man has long since appreciated the
big battalions of the Irish at the ballot boxes and votes are facts in
America, often more potent than even dollars."[37]

The Republicans started to reap some benefits from their efforts
by 1882. Joseph Murray, an Irish-born Catholic, bolted Tammany Hall
to become a Republican and in 1882 nominated Theodore Roosevelt for his
first political office.[38] In the same year John J. O'Brien, another old
influential Irish Democrat, was chosen Chairman of the Republican Committee of New York county.[39] Meanwhile, John Sherman remarked how easy

---

[35] Robert J. Creighton, "Influence of Foreign Issues on American
Politics," International Review, XIII (1882), 185.

[36] Bagnell, The American Irish, 60.

[37] Ibid., 59.

[38] Putnam, Theodore Roosevelt, 244.

[39] Gibson, The New York Irish, 374.

it was to convert intelligent Ohioan Irish voters to break with the Democratic party on the question of free trade.[40]  In spite of this success the Democrats still won control of the House of Representatives but, as West informed Granville:

> I do not think that their accession to power will in any way affect our relations.  They will pander the Irish vote as did the Republicans and the retributions of Cox and Robinson will probably continue.[41]

Even after the elections the Republicans continued to cater to the Irish.  In early 1883 a rumor appeared that Captain Edward O'Meagher Condon was to be fired from his post in the Office of the Supervisory Architect of the Treasury Department on the ground "that his public utterances were disrespectful and offensive to the British government."[42] When questioned on this point Secretary of the Treasury denied the rumor and Condon retained his position.  The Republican administration refused to fire this prominent Irish-American extremist, even though his bitter anti-English speeches were causing some embarrassment in official circles.[43]

Such activities on the part of Republicans indicated that a concentrated effort would possibly be made to win the Irish-American in 1884.  In early May of that year, even before the nominating conventions,

---

[40] _American_, IV (1882), 385.

[41] Knaplund, "Letters to Foreign Minister," 172.  West to Granville, November 14, 1882.

[42] _American_, VII (May 12, 1883), 77.

[43] O'Brien, _Post Bag_, II, 299.  Condon was released from prison in 1878 and in 1880 he had this position.  He worked for the Republican National Committee in 1884 and remained active in Irish affairs at the same time.

Thompson opened the campaign with a warning to the Democrats that a large number of Irish-Americans had turned toward protection. "It will be an ill day for the Democratic party when it finds the Irish-American arranged against it by some of the most powerful motives which govern those who cast it."[44] Next the Irish Republican National League met in Chicago with representatives from twenty-five states in attendance.[45] When the party met in its national convention Reverend Charles O'Reilly of Detroit offered the invocation on the opening session. He was the first Catholic priest to receive this honor at a National Republican Convention, but, strangely enough, he was at the time the Treasurer of the Irish National League of America, the American branch of the Parnell movement.[46]

In the course of the convention, one of Blaine's followers argued that he should receive the nomination, since he would capture the New York Irish on two counts:

> It is said his ancestors were of the faith . . . and the dynamite wing of the Irish will go for him because they know he would resist British arrogance and pretensions and protect American citizenship abroad.[47]

When West heard that Blaine won the nomination, he informed Granville that, if he had to win New York "by pandering the Irish vote, he would not

---

[44] American, VIII (1884), 67.

[45] New York Irish-American, May 17, 1884. It is interesting to note the similarity of this name to that of the organization that supported Parnell, the Irish National League of America.

[46] Thomas V. Cooper, Biographies of James G. Blaine and John Logan (1884), 79.

[47] Knaplund, "Letters to the Foreign Minister," 178. West to Granville, June 10, 1884.

scruple to do so, nor indeed would any other political leader with whom
I am acquainted hesitate to take such a course."[48]  Thompson felt that
it would not be necessary to pander to the Irish, since many would vote
for Blaine because others would attack the fact that his mother was a
Catholic, while the Irish nationalists would support him because his
election would promise "a vigorous foreign policy and a disposition to
make England recognize the existence of America in the world's politics."[49]
The New York Tribune, a constant friend of Blaine's for years, ridiculed
the opposition by stating that he was a "bad man" because he did not
favor "British free trade, having Americans punished for words they
had spoken in the United States, and because he deserved to lessen
British influence on the South American continent."[50]

The British reaction to Blaine's nomination was one of open hostility and the Blaine men continued to call attention to this in order to
increase the Irish attraction for him.[51]  The Saturday Review accused
him of relying upon the Irish vote "which must be purchased . . . by
professing ill will to England," but this would drive other voters
from his ranks, since he proposed "to disturb international relations
for his own sake."[52]  Such attacks did not go unheard by the Irish, in

---

[48] Ibid.

[49] American, VIII (1884), 147.

[50] New York Tribune, June 21, 1884.  Whitelaw Reid, the editor of
the Tribune was a staunch advocate of Blaine.  For the second remark,
see Chapter V.

[51] Gibson, The New York Irish, 378.

[52] Saturday Review, LV (1884), 167.

fact, they only enhanced Blaine's effort to appeal to this group, as many English visitors noticed at the time.[53]

After Blaine's nomination the focus turned to the Democratic Convention. The Independent Republicans had virtually bolted the party even before the Democrats met and Carl Schurz, one of their leading figures, indicated that he would like to see Senator Bayard selected. He felt Bayard could defeat Blaine, since many Republicans would not support Blaine's candidacy, but the man from Maine "would have the support of Irish dynamite faction,"[54] which he obviously felt was an important consideration.

If the Mugwump leaders wanted a Democratic candidate who would appeal to their followers, the old professional Irish-American Democrat did not. Once the boom for Grover Cleveland, reforming Governor of New York, who would clean up the national administration, gained momentum, these old pros reacted. Patrick Collins intimated that, if the Democrats were so set on Cleveland as to make his nomination assured, he would not even attend the convention. He argued that the Democrats had proven in 1876 and again in 1880 that they controlled at least fifty percent of the voting population, and, therefore, he did not think it good policy to "unite with a combination that might drive away more votes than it would attract."[55] He did not want the party to nominate Cleveland merely

---

[53] Eckman, "The British Traveler," 136.

[54] Bancroft, Letters of Carl Schurz, IV, 205, to Thomas F. Bayard, June 28, 1884.

[55] Curran, Patrick Collins, 23.

to gain the support of the Independent Republicans since for every
Republican gained the Democrats would lose twenty. Honest John Kelley
and his Tammany machine carried their opposition to Cleveland to the
floor of the Convention, even to the extent of spreading rumors that he
had lost his influence with Catholics and the Irish.[56] At the same time
Ford's Irish World proclaimed that Cleveland's nomination would drive
thousands of Democrats to vote for Blaine. According to Ford, the only
way the Democracy would retain the Irish vote was by nominating "Ben"
Butler.

The Democratic Convention ignored these voices, nominated Cleveland
and gave the Republicans their opportunity to appeal to the Irish.
The Republican bosses reminded Irishmen that their candidate's mother
was of Irish ancestry and a member of the faith, that his cousin was
a mother superior in a Catholic convent, and that Cleveland was nothing
more than a religious bigot who hated Catholicism. In between such
crude statements the Republicans tried to take advantage of the Irish-
American's hatred for England. Blaine's record as Secretary of State
was constantly painted as one which championed American interests
against those of England in the Halifax Award, the Canal issue, and the
War of the Pacific. They continued to emphasize that Republicanism
stood for protection of American industries, while Cleveland and the
Democracy wanted to destroy the tariff. Cleveland, the British candidate or the "Cobden Club" nominee, received the support of the Free

---

[56] Thomas, The Return of the Democrats, 177; Gibson, The New York
Irish, 380.

Trade Mugwumps "under the pay of British gold."[57]  Finally, they tried
to show that Blaine had defended Irish-American citizens imprisoned by
the British during 1881 and 1882 by writing this plank into the platform—"We believe that everywhere the protection of a citizen of American birth must be secured for citizens of American adoption."[58]

Such attacks obviously took their toll of Democratic voters as
important Irish leaders shifted to Blaine's support.  Shortly after his
nomination Alexander Sullivan, the then President of the Irish National
League and virtual dictator of the Clan-Na-Gael, openly supported Blaine
and used his influence to gain the support of the Irish National League.[59]
Thomas Fennell helped to organize a new Republican Irish-American club
in New York, while others formed an Association for the Protection of
American Industry.[60]  Ford's New York Irish World and Devoy's New York
Irish Nation vigorously supported Blaine, while Congressman John
Finerty personally changed his party label and took the Chicago Citizen
with him.  In August the annual convention of the Irish National League
elected Patrick Egan, an open and strong supporter of Blaine, as its
new president and, consequently, Republican Irishmen, retaining control
of this organization, permitted a number of pro-Blaine speakers to address

---

[57] Ibid., 205.

[58] Gibson, The New York Irish, 358.

[59] O'Brien, Post Bag, II, 247.  Sullivan to Devoy, June 10, 1884.

[60] Ibid., 250.  Fennell to Devoy, August 2, 1881.

the delegates.[61]   James L. Brady, an old campaigner for Garfield,
"took the stump" for Blaine, while Patrick Ford and others organized
an Irish-American rally for him in New York, where the speakers condemned the very thought of reducing the tariff and reminded the audience
that Blaine was the great potential enemy of Great Britain.[62]   Irish-
American Blaine-Logan Associations appeared as large numbers of Irish-
Americans flocked to his banner.

That this revolt among Irish Democrats was real can easily be seen
from the reaction on Cleveland's part, as he and his advisors tried to
marshall their own Irish forces.  John Boyle O'Reilly kept his Boston
Pilot on the Democratic side, while the New York Irish-American fought
to make its readers aware of the lies spread against Cleveland.  The
Democratic daily papers attacked Blaine's record as Secretary of State
which they said would lead the country to war.  The New York Evening
Post accused him of failing to liberate a single Irish-American citizen
arrested by the British.  The Post even went so far as to publish one
man's story of neglect at the hands of the "man from Maine."[63]  The
papers recalled that Cleveland had Irish blood since his mother's name
was O'Neil.[64]  But all these efforts did not seem to stem the tide.
The Democrats were forced to play their last card.

---

[61] David Saville Muzzey, James G. Blaine: A Political Idol of Other
Days (1934), 118.  Egan eventually received ample reward for his work.
See page 68.

[62] Hamilton, James G. Blaine, 577.

[63] Gibson, The New York Irish, 389.

[64] New York Irish-American, October 18, 1884.

Cleveland decided to come to terms with Patrick Collins. He summoned the Boston leader to the Executive Mansion in Albany. What was said has never been disclosed but two days later Collins delivered his famous "Albany Speech," one million copies of which were distributed among Irish-Americans. His biographer claims that this speech checked the stampede of Irish Catholics to the Republican side.[65] Whether this is true or not, need not be debated here. It is significant that Cleveland would come to terms with the man who had originally opposed his nomination.

The Collins speech is a classic attempt to refute the Republican arguments in one quick sweep. He denied that Cleveland was a religious bigot, accused the Republicans of never appointing Catholics to high office, offered a long list of those whom Cleveland had appointed while Governor of New York, and reprimanded the Republicans for permitting American citizens to linger in British dungeons, while pervading under the guise of standing for a vigorous foreign policy. Collins closed his address by declaring that "His friends will ever promise that his first act as President will be to free Ireland—for votes."[66] Those Irishmen who already had accepted Blaine's candidacy condemned Collins for these remarks, predicting his political demise because he dared to attack the "great and only friend of the Irish."[67] The effect of his

---

[65] Curran, Patrick Collins, 88.

[66] Ibid., 223.

[67] Ibid., 89.

speech can not be adequately determined; however, that he gave it does indicate that the Republicans had made inroads into what was once a sure thing for the Democrats.

The Republicans maintained the pressure and emphasized two issues which they felt would appeal to Irish-Americans. Alexander Sullivan continued to imply that Blaine's election would guarantee the success of the plans supported by the Clan-Na-Gael. Thompson, Devoy and others reminded their fellow Irishmen that the Republicans stood for protection, while the Democrats were servants of the English free traders. Such issues attracted at least the more violent class of Irish nationalists, those who believed in the use of force to gain Irish freedom. This is evident from a notice which appeared in Washington.

> Politics of the Joe Brady Club. There will be no meeting of the Joe Brady Emergency Club tonight. All dynamiters who favor the election of James G. Blaine for President of the United States will meet here on next Tuesday night. Blaine is the true friend of Ireland.[68]

It seems obvious that in 1884 both parties attempted to gain the Irish vote—the Republicans to balance the loss of the Mugwumps, the Democrats to couple their traditional Irish allies to their new friends—and that New York would decide the final outcome. Many students of history and politics have offered many explanations for what happened there on election day and the final Democratic victory. Some attribute the result to the work of the independents; others to the fact that neither Roscoe Conkling nor Senator George F. Edmunds campaigned for

---

[68] Knaplund, "Letters to the Foreign Minister," West to Granville, July 8, 1884. Joe Brady was executed for his part in the Phoenix Park murders. This is explained in Chapters II and IV.

Blaine in New York. The question of bad weather which hampered the up-
state Republicans has been offered for consideration, while still others
focus their attention upon the unfortunate remark of "Rum, Romanism and
Rebellion" and the dinner at Delmonico's. A few even hold that the Pro-
hibition party which captured 25,000 votes, mostly Republican, decided
the issue. In reality, however, anyone of the above mentioned factors
could have determined the outcome, especially when one considers that
only 1149 votes were involved. The politician did not have to determine
the exact cause. He only had to accept the fact that it happened and
then to remove the possibility of a reoccurrence.

While the real answer to the 1884 riddle will probably never be
known, two Republicans at least felt that the Irish had shifted to
Blaine's side in considerable numbers. Wharton Baker, the publisher of
American, was convinced that the Republicans had accomplished this and
would have won but for the unfortunate remark "Rum, Romanism and Rebellion."[69] Gail Hamilton, Blaine's biographer, argued that the New
York State election of 1885 proved that Blaine had split the Irish
vote. In the year the Republican candidate for Governor refused to
permit Blaine to campaign for his election and ran 15,000 votes behind
Blaine's presidential vote. This happened in spite of the fact that
the Republicans had nominated an Irish-American for Lieutenant Governor,
specifically to split the Irish vote. Since he gained only 8,000
more votes than the remainder of the ticket, even with the support

---

[69] Sievers, Benjamin Harrison, 262.

of the New York Irish World, Hamilton concluded that the Republicans failed to split the Irish. She implied that, if Blaine had campaigned, his popularity with the Irish would have led to a Democratic defeat.[70] However weak her argument is, it is important since it reflects the thinking of someone close to Blaine.

Once the results became known the Irish flocked to Washington for their reward. A strong delegation supposedly submitted Collins' name for the Cabinet post that was to go to New England, but this was too high a price for the "Albany Speech."[71] Cleveland did appoint other Irish leaders to rather responsible positions, however; William K. Roberts, the old Fenian leader, became Minister to Chile; S.S. Cox, an old New York Irish friend, became Minister to Turkey; Michael H. Phelan, the brother of Father David Phelan, the editor of the Saint Louis Western Watchman, received the consulship at Halifax.[72] A large number of Irish members of the I.C.B.U. received appointments to the Post Office Department and the Internal Revenue Service, so much so that the great bulk of the membership "came into power on a national level with the election of Governor Cleveland."[73] Anthony M. Keiley's reward was the most difficult to find. He had served in various Irish-American organizations before 1880, as Mayor of Richmond, Virginia

[70] Hamilton, James G. Blaine, 591.

[71] Curran, Patrick A. Collins, 103.

[72] Donahue, Irish Catholic Benevolent Union, 22.

[73] Ibid., 16.

and as the principal force in the reorganized Democratic party that
defeated Mahone's Readjusters. Cleveland first offered him the job
of Minister to Italy which he gladly accepted, but the Italians did
not. Next Cleveland offered the post at Vienna; yet the Austro-
Hungarian government also declared him to be persona non grata. The
Cleveland administration continued to search, and in 1886 finally discovered a position as judge at the International Court at Cairo. Keiley
received his appointment on August 1, 1886.[74]

While Cleveland fulfilled his oblications, both parties continued
to pamper the Irish vote. In the spring of 1886 the Irish in New York
organized a mass meeting to endorse the recently proposed Home Rule
Bill that Gladstone offered as a solution to the Irish Question. The
Democratic Mayor, William Grace, and Governor, James Hill, attended
along with the Republican Senator from Ohio, John Sherman.[75] Not to
be outdone by anyone Blaine addressed the question in early June when
he condemned the English for exploiting Ireland and warned them that
Americans stood as her friends.[76] In the same year the Chairman of the
Republican State Committee of Pennsylvania and the Democratic nominee
for Governor of Pennsylvania addressed the Annual Convention of the
I.C.B.U.[77]

---

[74] The Nation, August 19, 1886.

[75] New York Tribune, May 27, 1886.

[76] James G. Blaine, Political Discussions (1887), 478-484.

[77] Donahue, Irish Catholic Benevolent Union, 23.

Blaine's decision to campaign for his Republican friends in the
1886 congressional elections raised the whole question of his part in
the 1884 election, his following among the radical Irish, and his possible candidacy in 1888.  In his speeches he stressed the two issues
which had appealed to the Irish in 1884, protection and Anglophobia.[78]
This emphasis caused one editor to accuse him of working with the "war
faction—the Finertys, Sullivans and Fords—of the Irish National
League."[79]  Some people felt that his campaigning merely indicated his
interest in the 1888 election and the thought of his running again
caused many Democrats to attack him.  Some felt he was so weak polit-
ically he would fail of election "even with the aid of the dynamiters."[80]
One paper tried to embarrass Blaine by demanding that he state his position on the Irish dynamite attacks in London, but reflected that he
would never publicly take a position since he would fear losing American
votes if he indicated he was in favor of harboring dynamite refugees
like Patrick Ford.[81]  Blaine's attacks upon Democratic foreign policy
and his increasing demands concerning the fishery dispute caused some
papers to caution him not to start a "jingo campaign . . . like the one
that had captured a number of hot-headed Irishmen, but that alienated

---

[78] Public Opinion, II (1886), 428.

[79] Nation, August 19, 1886.  The Irish National League was holding
its annual convention at the time in Chicago.

[80] New York Times, September 1, 1886; Public Opinion, I (1886), 467.

[81] Public Opinion, II (1886), 409.  This whole question of dynamite
criminals is clarified in Chapter V.

some business interests which did not want the tail of the British Lion, twisted."[82]   In spite of such criticism Blaine continued to appeal to the Irish,[83] so much so that the Saint Louis Post Dispatch felt he would angle for the Apache Indian vote by discovering "a streak of Indian blood in his veins" as soon as they would register as citizens of Florida.[84]

Blaine's activity caused the London Times to publish an interesting article on the whole question of the Irish in American political life.  From a statistical study the article claimed that, whereas the Irish numbered about 33.3% of the foreign born in America in 1870, they had slipped to only 27.7% in 1880.  The author happily concluded that, since Irish numbers in America were dwindling, American politicians could no longer afford to pander to the dying force.  An American attacked this naive thinking in a letter to the Times which was subsequently published in a British magazine under the title, "The Power of the Irish in American Cities."  The author immediately denied that the Irish would lose political control of certain cities and offered several reasons for his position.  In the first place, the Irish in America were concentrated for the most in the northeastern cities where they were highly organized into various societies and nationalist organizations.  In addition, since the Irish controlled the Catholic Church and at the same time spoke the

---

[82] Ibid., I, 487, 508; II, 63.

[83] New York Irish World.  This is shown in a number of issues from August to November, 1886.

[84] Public Opinion, II (1886), 506.

English language, they could learn to control other Catholic immigrant groups which would tend to continue their power into the foreseeable future.  Finally, American politicians pander

> to the ruling celtic class among us, and I can per-
> ceive no emancipation from such rule in the near future.
> Just enough Irish act with the Republican party or constant-
> ly promise to do so, to prevent the Republican leaders and
> press from saying anything disagreeable about them.  A
> considerable number of Irish in New York, Chicago, Albany,
> Buffalo, and a few other cities voted for Blaine (while vot-
> ing the rest of the Democratic ticket) and talk about doing
> it again in 1888 in still larger numbers, and this hope makes
> the Republican leaders smile on the Home Rulers, and causes
> Democratic politicians to hug the Celtic nationalists all
> the closer to their bosoms lest they may lose them in the
> next Presidential struggle.[85]

The truth of these statements was often recognized by traveling Englishmen.  For instance, one tourist noticed that "the Irishman pure and simple is a real power in America," and again, wherever "there is any reference to 'that terrific British blister, the 'Irish Question,' great numbers of Irishmen in America unquestionably will take the side of Ireland."[86]  Fearing such talk would harm Catholicism, John Gilmary Shea appealed to all Catholics to vote as independents and not as groups.[87]  But the politicians had already forecasted that the Irish role in the election of 1888 would be similar to that of 1880 and 1884.  The close vote would recreate a situation in which a last minute unexpected switch would determine the outcome.

---

[85] An American, "Power of the Irish in American Cities," The Living Age, CLXXI (1886), 384.

[86] Eckman, "British Travelers," 135, 268.

[87] John Gilmary Shea, "No Actual Need of A Catholic Party in the United States," The American Catholic Quarterly Review, XII (1887), 705.

The Democrats seemed especially concerned with the Irish vote in
the spring of 1888. In March Chief Justice Morrison P. Waite of
Supreme Court died and rumors developed to the effect that Edward J.
Phelps, then Minister to England, would be appointed to the bench. Senator Edmunds, one of the Republican powers in the eyes of the Mugwumps,
spoke to Cleveland in favor of Phelps and left the interview with the
impression that Cleveland would appoint the New Englander.[88] However,
in April Patrick Collins, leading a group of Irish-Americans who despised
Phelps for his handling of the English post, informed the President that
he would lose Irish votes in the election if Phelps received the position.[89] Whether this changed Cleveland's mind or not can not be
definitely established, but Phelps was not appointed. Collins' role in
the case probably did carry some weight because by that time the party
chieftains had already decided to make Collins the permanent Chairman
of the National Convention.

While the Democrats indicated concern with the Irish vote, the Republicans mapped their basic strategy for the campaign. It was a simple
but sound program, to consolidate their own ranks while capturing
habitual Democrats. Initially the former aspect seemed unattainable,
since Blaine's public letter from Paris which answered the Democratic
challenge on the tariff as laid down by Cleveland in his Annual Address
in December 1887 indicated that he would again seek the nomination.

---

[88] Selig, "George Franklin Edmunds," 328.

[89] Curran, Patrick Collins, 80.

Then in January 1888 Blaine indicated to Patrick Ford that he would not
be a candidate for the nomination if he did not have unanimous support.[90]
Since Schurz and other Mugwumps continued their opposition to the "man
from Maine,"[91] he virtually eliminated himself from consideration even
though the New York Tribune and the Irish World supported him to the end.
When the Republican Convention opened on June 19, 1888, no one was sure
of the outcome, but eventually Benjamin Harrison of Indiana received the
first place on the ticket and the delegates felt compelled to give the
Vice-Presidency to a representative of New York, Levi P. Morton.[92] By
following this line they were able to close ranks for the most part and,
consequently, avoided one of the embarrassments of 1884. With respect
to the second part of their plan, they sought to appeal to a number of
groups, labor for one and the Irish for other. Their appeal began at
the Convention when the delegates approved a platform which called for
Home Rule for Ireland.[93] It was the first of many attempts.

While the Republicans completed their ticket and platform, the Democrats were hard at work forming a similar strategy. They also wanted
to solidify their ranks, and this desire was one of the main criticisms
of Cleveland's idea to strike the keynote of the campaign, the Tariff
Question in the Annual Message. The professionals feared that, since
the issue would cut across party lines it would possibly cost the party

---

[90] Hamilton, James G. Blaine, 603. Blaine to Ford, January 8, 1888.

[91] Bancroft, Letters of Carl Schurz, IV. Schurz to Bayard, April
3, 1888.

[92] Sievers, Benjamin Harrison, 355.

[93] Gibson, The New York Irish, 400.

votes. But Cleveland was determined to fight the battle on that issue—
a determination which only increased the Democrats' need to solidify as
much of the party as possible. This desire obviously led to the se-
lection of Patrick Collins as permanent Chairman of the Convention when
it gathered at Saint Louis. As Chairman Collins addressed the convention on the principles of the Democratic Party. His speech was re-
produced and used extensively in the campaign.[94] The delegates renom-
inated Cleveland and wrote a platform based upon the tariff issue, but,
interestingly enough, it also included one which pledged the party to
Home Rule for Ireland.[95]

While the Democrats catered to Irish pride, the Republicans opened
a two-pronged effort to capture the Irish. One side was organized by
Wharton Barker, an old friend of Harrison's. He contacted the Irish
through the editor of his magazine American, Robert Thompson, who in
turn had dealings with William Carroll and John Devoy.[96] By this time
Thompson had contributed articles on protectionism and Ireland to the
Irish World and, as his contribution to the campaign literature, he published a pamphlet, Ireland and Free Trade, An Object Lesson in Political
Economy. Over one hundred thousand of these were distributed in New York
and adjoining states in an effort to convince the Irish-American that
free trade of the British variety had killed the economy of Ireland.[97]

[94] Curran, PatrickCollins, 240.

[95] Gibson, New York Irish, 400.

[96] O'Brien, Post Bag, II, 252.

[97] The National Cyclopaedia of American Biography, X, 18.

At the same time Devoy and Carroll formed the Irish-American and Anti-Cleveland Protection League, while Devoy alone contributed a pamphlet, Cleveland and the Irish—A History of the Revolt of 1884.[98] Barker had originally committed $30,000 to cover the cost of the work, but early in July he found he could not rely upon his friends to help supply the funds, since they had already contributed to the war chest John Wanamaker was gathering.[99] When he contacted Matthew Quay, the National Republican Chairman, he discovered that funds were not available. In spite of these setbacks Barker continued to work through Thompson, Devoy and Carroll to the final tune of $40,000.

The National Committee's refusal to help Barker did not mean that the Irish had no significant role in their plans. On the contrary, the Irish were so important Quay did not want Barker to handle it.[100] This could possibly have resulted from a belief on the part of the professionals that Barker's Irish contacts did not control the Irish in America. Quay preferred to work through such men as Alexander Sullivan, John Finerty, Patrick Ford, and Patrick Egan, all of whom were well known for their more extreme positions on the Irish Question. At any rate the New York Irish World and the Chicago Citizen with their pro-Republican views were widely distributed in Irish communities.[101] Finerty himself traveled

---

[98] O'Brien, Post Bag, II, 252.

[99] Sievers, Benjamin Harrison, 362.

[100] Edward A. White, "The Republican Party In National Politics, 1888-1891." Unpublished Doctoral Dissertation. University of Wisconsin (1941), 192.

[101] Ibid., 191.

through Wisconsin's Irish counties in hope of winning these for Harrison.[102] Meanwhile, the National Committee organized a Republican League in New York which in turn established 22 clubs in 22 Irish districts and provided over 500 Republican workers on election day.[103]

The fact that both parties were interested in the Irish helped the tariff emerge as one of two main issues. The Republicans claimed that the American system of protection in reality saved the working man, since it closed America's market to goods produced by cheap foreign labor. In addition they claimed that Cleveland's programs, which they equated to the British concept of free trade, would in reality destroy America's economy as a similar British proposal had killed Ireland's.[104] The Democrats denied that they stood for English "free trade," but they had difficulty convincing the Irish. Consequently, Patrick Collins again addressed himself to the Republican appeals to the Irish at a mass meeting in Cooper Hall, New York.[105]

Collins' speech serves as a classic refutation of the basic Republican argument. He denied first of all that the Democrats stood for "free trade," or that their program was even a step in that direction, since it called for only a seven per cent reduction in the tariff. He next attacked the Republican contention that "free trade" destroyed Ireland by recalling the words of John Mitchell that the suspension of

---

[102] McDonald, The Irish In Wisconsin, 163-164.

[103] White, "The Republican Party, 1883-1891," 195.

[104] McDonald, The Irish In Wisconsin, 167.

[105] Curran, Patrick Collins, 244.

trade was the real cause for Ireland's economic decline. Since the Republicans had based part of their campaign upon the attempt to prove that Cleveland was a friend of England because of his tariff policy and his handling of Anglo-American relations, Collins ridiculed this by reminding his audience that the Republicans were responsible for the Halifax Award which cost the United States $5,500,000.

Collins' efforts to stem the tide were met with some realistic arguments by the leading Irish Republicans. Patrick Ford in August urged Irishmen to vote for the Republican party because only by exercising the American right to disagree over politics could Irishmen become true Americans. He later accused the Irish in America of blindly supporting British Free Trade which had destroyed the industries of Ireland and "forced her children to seek bread and a home beyond the sea."[106] To Ford the real issue was the tariff, "The American system versus the British colonial system."[107]

The Irish were important enough to cause even Harrison to enter the public debate, even though he conspicuously stayed on his front porch in fear of repeating Blaine's costly errors in New York (the Rum, Romanism, and Rebellion remark and the dinner at Delmonico's). When the Democrats accused him of being a bigot and a "slanderer of the Irish," however, he was forced to break his silence and publicly deny the rumor.[108]

The whole question of Anglo-American relations played a rather

---

[106] Patrick Ford, "The Irish Vote in the Pending Presidential Election," The North American Review, LI (1878), 187.

[107] Ibid., 189.

[108] Sievers, Benjamin Harrison, 398.

significant role in the election, but the most important incident occurred only a few days before the voting, when the British Minister to Washington, Sir Lionel Sackville-West, played into Republican hands by advising a supposed Englishman to vote for Cleveland because he was more pro-British than Harrison. The effect of this indiscretion has never adequately been measured and probably never will. It does, however, indicate Republican thinking on the significance of the Irish vote, since they were willing to use the issue as widely as possible and some claim they won the election because of it.

The constant interest in the Irish did produce some good. Senators in both parties were so keenly aware of the significance of the Irish that they were willing to settle a twenty-year old dispute between the War Department and a Catholic parish in Tennessee. During the Civil War the Union Army dismantled the parish church and used the materials without compensating the pastor. In 1866 the Senate recognized the legitimacy of the claim, but the money was never appropriated. Then in September 1888 the I.C.B.U. held its National Convention where the whole issue was raised on the floor. On the following day the delegates approved a petition which requested the Senate to appropriate the necessary funds. Within days the administration had a check for the proper amount in the hands of the parish priest.[109] Both the Republican controlled Senate and Democratic controlled executive wanted to please the I.C.B.U.

What effect all this activity had upon the Irish is difficult to

---

[109] Donahue, The Irish Catholic Benevolent Union, 201.

assess, if not impossible. Harrison won New York by 14,000 votes, yet lost the popular election in the country by over 90,000. By taking New York, however, he won the vote in the electoral college and he became President of the United States.

The debt Harrison felt to the Irish can be measured to some extent by the political appointments they received. The Ministership to Chile, the highest office conferred upon Blaine's Irish friends, went to Patrick Egan, the ex-treasurer of the Irish Land League.[110] A number of others received minor posts as a steady stream of Irishmen arrived in Washington for talks with Harrison. On May 22 Blaine arranged a meeting between Harrison and Patrick Ford who carried a list of names to the President. Blaine justified the meeting with the remark, "it will do much good in certain important directions."[111] At one time his Irish friends suggested to Blaine that William R. Grace, the first Catholic mayor of New York, who had entered that office as a Democrat, receive some position in Latin America, but Harrison refused. These requests continued long after the campaign and in 1891, Blaine appointed one Irishman as Secretary of the Legation at Bogota because the Catholic priest in Brooklyn who suggested his name controlled "many votes," and this "might be worthwhile in the next election."[112] Thus three years after the

---

[110] John Denvir, The Life Story of an Old Rebel (1910), 222.

[111] A. T. Volwiler, ed., The Correspondence Between Benjamin Harrison and James G. Blaine, 1888-1893 (1940), 64. Blaine to Harrison, May 22, 1889.

[112] Ibid., 186. Blaine to Harrison, September 16, 1891.

election the old professional still realized the significance of the Irish vote.

As a result of a unique political situation, evidenced in the election of 1880, where both parties possessed equality of voting strengths which increased the position of New York as the pivotal state, the politicians sought to win the Irish vote in 1884 and 1888. In the words of Gail Hamilton, someone close to the Blaine camp, "a divided Irish vote was second in importance only to a divided Southern vote."[113] However much of an exaggeration this was detracts little from the fact that both parties obviously sought the Irish vote. How this influenced Anglo-American relations is not quite as obvious.

---

[113] Gail Hamilton, James G. Blaine, 574. That they sought to capture Southern votes can be seen in a recent study, Vincent P. De Santis, Republicans Face The Southern Question (1960).

# Chapter II

## Irish-Americans and the Anglo-Irish Struggle

By the winter of 1879-80 conditions in Ireland had reached the famine stage and violence had become the order of the day. To live there was "like walking over a crater . . . where the foulest deeds of ferocity are executed without a scruple."[1] The great mass of agrarian misery gradually caused the Land League to extend its influence, but this alone could not guarantee the success of the movement. As Davitt had realized as early as 1877, money in large quantities would be indispensable and for this reason Charles Stewart Parnell agreed to travel to the United States.

Parnell's arrival in New York marked the real beginning of his ten year battle against the old Act of Union. Up to that point he was only the nominal leader of the peasants and the actual leader of only a small segment of the Home Rule party. Once in New York he became the symbol of struggling Ireland which permitted him to collect money and make contacts with all factions of Irish-American nationalism. His future rested upon this aid from America and, consequently, his success during this first official visit laid the foundation for his later assumption of leadership of both the peasants and the Irish parliamentary party.[2]

---

[1] Henrietta M.A. Ward, _Memories of Ninety Years_ (1925), 207.

[2] Bagnell, _American Irish_, 107; Grace, _The Irish in America_, 5.

Parnell arrived in New York on January 2, 1880 and sailed for England on March 11. Within this relatively short period he travelled as far west as Des Moines, Iowa; as far south as Richmond, Virginia; and as far north as Montreal, Canada.[3] He spoke in forty-one cities, seventeen states, and addressed legislative bodies in Virginia, Kentucky and Iowa.[4] At the various stops in the tour he was greeted by both national and local political figures. In fact William E. Robinson, a Democratic Representative from New York and a well-known Anglophobe, even served on the Reception Committee which welcomed him when he landed from Ireland.[5]

In the course of his tour he received an invitation to address the House of Representatives. On January 13, 1880 Edward Condon and Ricard Burke asked Samuel J. Randall, a Democrat from Philadelphia, to arrange for Parnell to address the House. Representative Thomas L. Young of Ohio, an American born in Ireland, offered a resolution to this effect on January 19, but "Sunset" Cox of New York, probably aware of the strength of the opposition to an invitation to address the House at a regular legislative session, suggested that the meeting be held in

---

[3] Kenneth E. Colton, "Parnell's Mission to Iowa," Annals of Iowa, XXII (1940), 312.

[4] Davitt, Fall of Feudalism, 199.

[5] New York Tribune, January 3, 1880. The committee included such well-known Irish leaders as John Devoy, J.J. Breslin, T.R. Bannermann, Michael Kerwin, Setphen J. Meany, and John E. Finerty.

the evening and only as a ceremonial one.[6] Some raised questions concerning the advisability of creating a precedent, but, when the roll
call was counted, 96 voted for the invitation while 42 voted against.
Parnell arrived on February 2.[7] Yet even before Condon made the initial
request, some Americans questioned the advisability of such action.
One Philadelphia editor agreed that Americans could freely discuss the
issue of Irish-British relations but that

> It is none of our business as a nation and we hope
> there will be no foolish action on the part of leg-
> islatures or Congress. Any action in that respect
> will be regarded in its true light as a bid for the
> political support of the Irish people in this country.[8]

When Parnell did address the House, the same editor said it was a "mistake to give Parnell a semi-official welcome."[9] This appraisal received support two years later, when Robert Creighton studied the
whole question of the influence of foreign issues upon American politics. He declared that Congressmen did not want a quarrel with the
British, but

> the 'Irish vote' is a powerful factor in American
> politics, and neither of the great national parties
> could afford to offend it by offering even a show
> of opposition to the questionable invitation to
> Parnell. To stand well with the 'Irish vote,' there-
> fore, the House did a most unwise act which may yet

---

[6] *Congressional Record*, 46 Congress, 2nd Session, XXII, Part II,
393. Young served in the Civil War and was active in Republican politics in Ohio.

[7] Davitt, *Fall of Feudalism*, 196. He said those who voted against
it were "pro-English," but they were "overwhelmingly defeated."

[8] Philadelphia *North American*, January 12, 1880.

[9] *Ibid.*, February 3, 1880.

make its influence felt upon domestic affairs in an
unexpected manner at an unlooked for occasion.[10]

While Americans debated the wisdom of the action of the House,

Parnell was more concerned with other problems. He was primarily inter-

ested in gaining the support of all factions of Irish-Americans, since

only in this way could he hope to receive sufficient financial support.

However, at the time of his arrival Irish-Americans were effectively

divided; the conservatives under O'Reilly, Collins and a Rev. Dr. Thomas

J. Conaty; one radical group under Patrick Ford; another tied to John

Devoy and the Clan-Na-Gael, and even within the Clan there had appeared

signs of friction by 1880.[11] In the words of one observer, Parnell had

to unite "the respectable lawyer, the affluent merchant, the local pol-

itician and the dynamite loving ex-Fenian soldier" and to a great extent

he was successful, at least while he remained in the country.[12] As if

this was not enough, he was also forced to defend his position against

attacks from Americans who intimated that he was collecting money, not

to help the peasants, but to finance political agitation.[13] James

Gordon Bennett, of the New York Herald, felt so strongly about this that

he formed his own relief fund to which he contributed a personal gift of

$100,000, while other Americans sent money direct to the numerous private

funds operating in Ireland.[14]

---

[10] Creighton, "Influence of Foreign Issues," 187.

[11] Gibson, The New York Irish, 336.

[12] Bagnell, Irish in America, 195.

[13] Philadelphia North American, January 22, 1880.

[14] Palmer, Land League Crisis, 99.

Although motivated partially by a desire to embarrass Parnell,
Bennett's action did reflect native American awareness of the seriousness of the Irish situation. Relief funds and Mayor's Committees sprang
up all across the country. Within a few days of its formation one such
fund amounted to over $3,000.[15] Resolutions for Irish relief appeared in
Congress[16] and on March 24 the U.S.S. Constellation sailed from New
York for Ireland with a shipment of food, purchased by the Herald fund.[17]
By August James Redpath, the New York Tribune's correspondent in Ireland, estimated that about $5,000,000 had been sent from the United
States, much of which came from native Americans.[18]

Meanwhile, Parnell received word that Parliament had been dissolved
and was forced to sail for Ireland on March 11. When he arrived, he
discovered that the election campaign in England centered around foreign
and colonial matters. Unlike in America, no one was interested with the
problems of Ireland, and William Gladstone, leading his Liberal Party,
won a smashing victory, capturing 353 seats to only 237 for the Conservative opposition, with an additional 62 seats controlled by Home
Rulers.[19]

---

[15] Philadelphia North American, January 20, 1880.

[16] Congressional Record, 46 Congress, 2nd Session, XII, Part II,
January 20, 1880, 397.

[17] Annual Register, 1880 part II, 27.

[18] Palmer, Land League Crisis, 104. Palmer accepts this figure
of $5,000,000.

[19] W.S. Churchill, Lord Randolf Churchill, 2 vols. (1906), I, 118.

For Parnell the campaign centered around the possibility of
gaining enough support in the Home Rule party to become its chairman. At that time William Shaw, the successor to Isaac Butt,
had remained aloof of the Land League and the whole question of agrarian
agitation. Parnell wanted to tie the party to the Land League, but he
could not do this as long as Shaw held the chairmanship. He campaigned
then to increase the size of his own following in the party and was successful, for on May 17, 1880, when the party met to elect a sessional
leader, he received 23 votes to 18 for Shaw. From that day forward
his party in effect became the Home Rule party. He had finally emerged
as leader of Ireland's parliamentary forces.[20] However, he remained
leader of the peasants only in name.

Before Parnell sailed from the United States, he called a hurried
meeting of all political factions among Irish-Americans, including the
"Fenians and the Constitutionalists."[21] For the most part it was a
successful meeting, since a broad base of Irish-American organizations
agreed to establish an American branch of the Irish National Land
League, but not everyone accepted Parnell's leadership. Dr. William
Carroll, a highly placed member of the Clan, openly broke with the
League and opposed the whole concept of a national organization. He
feared that such an organization would eventually overpower the Clan

---

[20] C.C. O'Brien, Parnell and His Party, 36.

[21] R.B. O'Brien, Parnell, 207. The term constitutionalist was
often used to refer to the more moderate elements which are referred
to as conservatives in this paper.

itself and many held similar views.[22]  Such opposition did not prevent
the fulfillment of Parnell's plans.  One of his aids, John Dillon, remained in America until May 1880 when with the cooperation of Devoy,
O'Reilly, and Ford he organized the American Land League.  Patrick
Collins became National President and almost at once branches of the
new organization appeared all over the United States.[23]  On the surface
the League united most Irish-Americans behind the land agitation in
Ireland; yet the unity was nothing more than an uneasy truce.

As the Irish in America forged a somewhat unnatural combination,
the British lawmakers returned to London for the opening session of
the new Parliament.  Most observers felt that, since only minor questions
would arise, the session would last for a short period and that legislation for Ireland would not even appear.  However, Parnell, well aware of
what was happening in Ireland, had already decided to press for a bill
that would compensate the evicted tenants.  T.P. O'Connor introduced such
a bill in late May, but the government felt it could not permit the Home
Rulers to gain credit for such an important measure and in June
William E. Forster, the Chief Secretary for Ireland, introduced his own
Compensation for Disturbance Bill.  The rising agitation in Ireland
plus the determined leadership of Parnell had forced the government to

---

[22] T.M. Healy, Letters and Leaders of My Day (1929), 95.

[23] Davitt, Fall of Feudalism, 241.  The scope of support can be in-
ferred by the fact that there were at the initial gathering delegates
from as far away as Richmond and San Francisco.

face up to the Irish problem,[24] but it was all to no avail, since, although passing the House of Commons, the bill failed in the Lords on August 3.[25] Joseph Chamberlain wanted Gladstone to call an autumn session in order to reintroduce the measure, but nothing was done to relieve the suffering of the Irish.[26] This was most unfortunate for the British because on June 1 the old Peace Preservation Act had expired without any new coercion measure being introduced. In effect, ordinary law returned to Ireland just when it was least desirable.[27]

When Parliament adjourned in early September, the Irish members under Parnell rushed to Ireland where they found the population in a potential state of revolution. On September 19 Parnell called for "peaceful picketing of landlords who evicted tenants." Meetings were held in various parts of the country as the parliamentarians combined with the Land Leaguers to fight evictions. By early October landowners urgently demanded coercion legislation.[28] Forster himself began to demand it by the end of the month, but Gladstone refused. Instead he authorized Forster to arrest Parnell and others who were inciting the peasants in the hope that this would stop the violence. This occurred

---

[24] Annual Register, 1880, part II, 82. Parnell and his party made excellent use of obstructionist tactics, speaking 599 times in the period from June 16 to July 9.

[25] C.C. O'Brien, Parnell and His Party, 49.

[26] J.L. Garvin, The Life of Joseph Chamberlain, 2 vols. (1932), I, 323.

[27] Ibid., 320.

[28] Annual Register, 1880, part II, 101, 104.

on November 2 on an indictment which included the name of James Redpath, the American correspondent of the New York Tribune.[29] But Parnell's arrest did not stop the tide of agrarian violence. Of the 2,590 agrarian crimes committed in 1880 1696 occurred in the last quarter, while of the 2,110 evictions only 198 occurred in the last quarter.[30] "A reign of terror had in truth commenced,"[31] and in late December Gladstone realized that some form of coercion legislation was indispensable. If he had any doubt, the trials of those arrested with Parnell in November dispelled it, for in January a Dublin jury, organized under ordinary law, freed the obvious offenders. Parnell had finally emerged as leader of the peasants in fact, as well as in name.

While Parnell's open fight for the peasants' welfare earned for him the actual leadership of the Irish masses, he never failed to realize that the success of the whole movement depended upon the uninterrupted flow of money from America. Davitt himself recalled that the foremost ally "on whom we counted in such a contest [to prevent evictions] was the Irish race in the United States,"[32] and in the summer of 1880 he returned to the United States for a lecture tour which he hoped would result in an

---

[29] American, I (1880), 33. Robert Thompson hoped for Redpath's arrest, since it would permit him to be better prepared to tell Americans about the real conditions in Ireland. He accepted the fact that the English might see in Redpath's reporting as interference in their internal affairs but argued that, since "the Cobden Club had interfered in the American presidential campaign by sending over pamphlets urging free trade," Americans could reply.

[30] J.L. Hammond, Gladstone and the Irish Nation (1938), 192.

[31] Churchill, Lord Randolf, I, 184.

[32] Davitt, Fall of Feudalism, 188.

increase in the number of branches of the American Land League. As he
traveled, he slowly discovered the reemerging divisions among Irish-
Americans. Shortly after the initial May meeting Collins and Ford
split over the question of control of the money collected. The conservatives wanted the money sent directly to Ireland, while Ford wanted
it sent first to the Irish World where it would be tabulated and then
sent to Dublin.[33] In theory Ford wanted the information merely to publish correct lists of contributors, but in practice it meant that he
would have served as a central treasurer with the power to force Parnell
and the Land League along a more violent direction if he so desired.
While these forces clashed, many members of the Clan followed the lead
of William Carroll and lost interest in the whole Land League question
especially after it came to dominate Irish thought in America.[34] Devoy
himself had his misgivings about the American Land League, mainly because
he had been unable to control it, but at least he continued to support
it.[35] Yet the money continued to arrive in Dublin in spite of these
differences.

Parnell must have worried about these during the fall and winter of
1880, especially after they and the agrarian situation widened. In
the fall of 1880 the American Land League under Collins called for a
convention to meet on January 12 in Buffalo, New York. Ford openly

---

[33] Ibid., 257.

[34] O'Brien, Post Bag, I, 533. Devoy to Reynolds, 21 June, 1880.

[35] Davitt, Fall of Feudalism, 257.

disavowed the call and ordered his league branches not to attend the
meeting.[36] When the conservative elements gathered in Buffalo, over
290 branches were represented, but only 120 delegates attended.[37] Collins
won reelection as President, but Ford would not recognize his leadership.
Parnell's fear of Ford's independent policy possibly prompted him to send
a telegram to the Irish World when Forster introduced a coercion bill in
January. After describing the situation in Ireland he assured Ford that
the Land League had sufficient funds to handle any temporary coercion
laws, but only "because of our American countrymen." He thanked the
"Irish World and its readers for their constant co-operation and substantial support in our great cause,"[38] and hoped that it would not cease.

Meanwhile, the Queen had addressed Parliament in early January and
had hinted to the need of a coercion policy. When Forster actually introduced the bill, Parnell first tried the old tactic of obstruction.
In this way the Irish party virtually stopped the functioning of Parliament in late January, but Gladstone struck back. On February 3 Michael
Davitt was arrested and on February 4 the majority in Parliament passed
a "closure resolution" which effectively eliminated Irish opposition as
36 members were suspended and ejected from the Commons.[39] The government
rapidly proceeded to pass the Protection of Property Bill on February 28

---

[36] Davitt, Fall of Feudalism, 365.

[37] Ibid., 366.

[38] New York Irish World, January 30, 1881.

[39] Hammond, Gladstone, 214-215.

and the Arms Bill on March 11.

Parnell faced one of many crossroads as a result of these events. He had to make a decision; either increase the agitation, which would mean virtual revolution; or decrease it, which would mean the end of the struggle. The disunity in America further complicated his decision since he had to consider the effects of his action upon both Anglo-Irish politics and the radicals in America. When Davitt was arrested, Parnell telegraphed to the American press that his arrest would not stop the work of the League, an implication that the agitation would continue.[40] Then Gladstone used the closure against the party, and the more radical element in America urged Parnell to secede from Parliament completely and make a new tour through the United States. Such action would have been revolutionary in nature, and Parnell privately decided against it. To a degree his failure to take a strong stand disappointed the radicals, but he kept the door open to America by sending Patrick Egan, the Treasurer of the Land League, to Paris and by hedging on any public statement to increase or decrease the agitation. In this way he kept the more violent element at bay while satisfying his own more conservative instincts.[41]

Meanwhile, the events of February increased Irish-American activity. A number of state legislatures passed resolutions condemning the British actions, while a number of newspapers followed a similar line.[42] Land

---

[40] Boston *Globe*, February 5, 1882, quoted in Davitt, *Fall of Feudalism*, 305.

[41] C.C. O'Brien, *Parnell and His Party*, 60.

[42] Davitt, *Fall of Feudalism*, 308.

League branches multiplied rapidly with New York and Philadelphia
supporting seventy separate units. Within a matter of days of the
passage of the coercion legislation the Irish World wired Egan
$25,000. By May 1, 1881 the league sent over $100,000 and by June
over 1200 branches existed, 800 of which Ford controlled.[43]

With the coercion laws passed Gladstone took up the question of
land reform. On April 6 he introduced his Land Bill. Although it had
many merits, Parnell refused to either accept or reject it. He continued to hedge, since his acceptance would have alienated the radicals
and his rejection would have caused increased agitation. Unfortunately, John Dillon forced Parnell to take a public position in relation to
the bill when his violent attacks upon it led to his arrest. Now Parnell
had two possibilities, issue a "no rent" proclamation which the radicals
demanded, or merely refrain from voting on the second reading of the
bill as the moderates urged.[44] Ford's enthusiasm for the whole Parnell-
ite movement cooled considerably when Parnell followed the latter path,
but Collins continued to lead his League branches behind the Irish leaders.
Once the bill itself passed the House of Lords in August, Parnell could
hedge no longer. He had to either order the League to accept it or reject
it.

The fall of 1881 witnessed the real end of Parnell's attempt to
combine the two extremes of Irish-Nationalism and the end came on the

---

[43] Palmer, Land League Crises, 284.

[44] C.C. O'Brien, Parnell and His Party, 66.

issue of this land bill. The radical Land Leaguers, such as Dillon and Egan, wanted Parnell to tell the peasants not to support the bill in any fashion. Patrick Ford telegraphed him an offer of renewed friendship if he would unfurl the "banner of no rent" and implied that, if he did not, America would become disinterested in the whole movement.[45] But Parnell, realizing the great merits of the bill, the fact that it provided for fixity of rent, tenure and improvements, did not want to deny these to the peasants.[46] Torn between the radical demands both in the Land League and in America and his better judgment of what was best for the peasants, he tried to take the middle path—he would test the act, that is, he would send a few select causes to the new land courts and give the British an opportunity to display their claims that just rents would result. Ford and the more violent members of the Clan expressed their deep displeasure, but before a real clash could develop Gladstone saved the day for Irish-American unity.[47] Taking Parnell's plan to "test" the act as a personal insult, he deliberately and violently condemned the Irish leader, threatened a tightening of British rule if the peasants did not support the Land Act and declared "the resources of civilization are not yet exhausted."[48] This bitter attack could not go unanswered and Parnell replied in a similar fashion at Wexford. This speech resulted in his arrest on October 13.[49]

---

[45] Ibid., 70; America, II (1881), 7. Americans in general accepted his bill.

[46] Hammond, Gladstone, 224.

[47] C.C. O'Brien, Parnell and His Party, 71.

[48] Hammond, Gladstone, 248.

[49] Annual Register, 1881, part II, 76.

The arrest of Parnell initiated a whole series of events which greatly influenced the Irish in America. On October 18 Parnell issued the "no-rent" manifesto from his jail cell and two days later Forster ordered the suppression of the Land League.[50] As a result of these moves and countermoves the whole movement teetered on the brink of failure, since its future depended upon two things which Ireland could not provide, money and some means of policing the enforcement of the "no-rent manifesto." Fortunately for Ireland, America furnished both.

When the news of the events of October reached Americans, the Irish-Americans realized the need to unify their support of Parnell and all elements issued a call for a great convention to meet in Chicago. T.P. O'Connor and T.M. Healy, two close parliamentary associates of Parnell, and Father Eugene Sheedy, an active Land Leaguer, arrived in early November to help stir the Irish-American interest in conditions at home.[51] When the convention opened, over 1,000 delegates had arrived from thirty-eight states and territories. John Finerty, the editor of the Chicago Citizen called the convention to order and the delegates pledged a special $250,000 fund to resist evictions.[52] Father Sheedy, Healy, and O'Connor were all present to answer questions

[50] Joseph Chamberlain, A Political Memoir, 1880-1892 (1953), 22.

[51] Healy, Letters and Leaders, 140; Bagnell, American-Irish, 222. Bagnell holds that at this time, November 1881, nothing could exceed their [Irish-Americans] interest and enthusiasm on the whole subject of Ireland.

[52] Davitt, Fall of Feudalism, 366; John Boyle O'Reilly, "Ireland's Opportunity-- Will it be lost," American Catholic Quarterly Review, VII (1882), 116. He said some Irish-Americans demanded revolution but the conservatives wanted only Home Rule not separation.

nd generally to generate enthusiasm.  But they had really little to do.

he British had solidified the ranks of Irish-Americans, for the ex-

remists of Ford's variety cheered the "no-rent manifesto" and con-

ervatives stood shocked at the arrest of Parnell and the suppression

f the League.

With the money problem solved by the generous support of the

hicago convention Irish-Americans turned to the second need, a tool

o enforce the "no-rent manifesto."  The Ladies Land League was

rganized originally in New York by Parnell's sister in the summer of

380.  It later spread to Ireland where it became a well-organized

djunct to the League itself.  With the suppression of the League it

merged as the only instrument capable of filling the breach.  Thus,

ran supplied the funds from Paris and the ladies campaigned for ad-

erence to the "no-rent manifesto."

Parnell had perceived early in February 1881 that a "no-rent"

ll would virtually open the door to actual revolution.  True to this

ediction the situation gradually slipped from the hands of the

dies into those of the radical agrarian Irish terrorist groups

ring the cold winter.[53]  Many of the increasing number of agrarian

imes were undoubtedly organized by the I.R.B. and the Clan, but most

sulted from the spread of what the Irish peasant called "Captain Moon-

ght."[54]  By February 1882 agitation appeared throughout the country

[53] O'Brien, Parnell and His Party, 74.

[54] Palmer, Land League Crises, 304; Chamberlain, Political Memoir,

and Forster reacted in a typical manner with mass arrests. By the end of March it became evident that the government was waging a losing battle. Forster with his 25,000 troops, 20,000 constables and thousands of spies was forced to make a public appeal to the people to maintain the peace, but who would listen to "Buckshot" Forster.[55] In the ten month period before Parnell's arrest 46 major crimes were committed in Ireland including nine murders and thirty-two attempts. In the five months following his imprisonment, the murders alone jumped to fourteen with an additional sixty-one attempts.[56] By April Gladstone had used "all the resources of civilization." He had to deal with Parnell.

Just when Gladstone decided to negotiate, the imprisoned "Uncrowned King" reached a similar conclusion. He saw the rapidly deteriorating situation in Ireland with power slipping more and more into the hands of uncontrollable "Ribbonmen" as a definite threat to his own position, his political future, and the future of the whole Irish parliamentary movement. If the agitation did not cease, it would cause his own political death.[57] Consequently, on April 10 Parnell opened negotiations with Gladstone, the result being the famous Kilmainham Pact. In return for certain additions to the Land Bill of 1881 and the possible abandonment of coercion Parnell promised to stop the peasant agitation.[58]

---

[55] Pomfret, Struggle for Land, 178.

[56] Hammond, Gladstone, 266.

[57] Chamberlain, Political Memoir, 41.

[58] Garvin, Joseph Chamberlain, 348.

On May 2 he left Kilmainham jail. The land question was played out, the tenants tired, and the world anxious for a rest.

The radicals in America, especially Ford, were shocked at the news of the pact and once again the Irish World openly broke with the united movement. Ford could possibly have known of Parnell's decision before-hand since his branches were not represented at the Fourth National Convention of the American Land League which opened in Washington in April. At that gathering Collins resigned and turned over the presidency to James Mooney. During his term in office he supervised the collection of almost a half a million dollars.[59] After such a successful two years the Land Leaguers must have looked upon the coming year with great expectations, but these were disappointed by the events of the following month.

If the Kilmainham Pact sent violent shock waves through the forces of Irish-American nationalism, with seemingly far reaching consequences, they did not last long, since within four days of Parnell's release the Phoenix Park murders completely overshadowed all aspects of the Irish question. On May 6 Lord Frederick Cavandish, the Chief Secretary for Ireland, the replacement for Forster who had resigned with Parnell's release, and his undersecretary Thomas Burke were murdered by a group of extremists, the "Invincibles."[60] Radicals in America cheered, but Parnell bitterly condemned the crime and felt that, since it came just when he had made some headway with Gladstone, all seemed lost again.[61] The American

---

[59] Curran, Patrick Collins, 60.

[60] P.J.P. Tynan, The Irish National Invincibles (1894), 407.

[61] Chamberlain, Political Memoir, 62.

conservatives called for Irish-Americans to meet in Boston to protest the crime. Those in attendance unanimously authorized the posting of a $5,000 reward for the capture of the criminals. O'Reilly and Collins rushed a telegram to Parnell to announce the reward and to promise their continued support of his program.[62] Such statements had little effect upon the minds of British statesmen, however, and in July Parliament passed another coercion bill.

The events of May and the British reaction to the Phoenix Park murders split Irish-Americans wide open, and Davitt returned in the summer of 1882 to reunite these forces. He announced a meeting to be held at the Astor House in New York for July 22, 1882.[63] Representatives of the conservatives and the Clan-Na-Gael, along with Patrick Ford, met with Davitt to solve their differences. How well they succeeded is unknown, but Davitt did return to Ireland where he claimed that Irish-Americans were again united but only behind some form of continued land agitation. Dillon, Egan, and Davitt probably used this to force Parnell into returning to the land question,[64] but the "Uncrowned King" absolutely refused. He was convinced that the land question was dead, that agitation of the 1881-82 variety was useless and that his political career demanded its avoidance. To enforce his views he cut off the flow of funds to the Ladies League, which killed that organization and called for a general meeting of the various elements of Irish

---

[62] Roche, John Boyle O'Reilly, 218.

[63] Davitt, Fall of Feudalism, 367.

[64] Ibid., 371.

nationalism. They met in Dublin on October 17, 1882 to hear Parnell declare that the Land League would be dissolved and replaced with the National League of Ireland. He clearly explained that the new organization would be a purely constitutional, parliamentary movement as opposed to the Land League which was virtually semi-revolutionary in nature.[65] Most of the old Land Leaguers and the Home Rulers accepted, including Davitt. Yet John Dillon retired for an extended vacation in Colorado, disgusted with the turn of events and Parnell;[66] Egan closed the books of the Land League, sent his report to Parnell and left Paris for the United States, arriving early in 1883. He too settled in the west, in Omaha, Nebraska.[67] With this victory Parnell returned to the task of quieting Ireland, accomplishing this by the end of the year.[68]

The abandonment of land warfare drove some radicals, those under Ford, into open opposition to Parnell. Ford himself refused to associate in any national unified organization until the summer of 1886. However, the Clan followed a slightly different course. By this time Alexander Sullivan had gained control of the Executive Board of the Clan with the help of Michael Boland and Dennis Feeley (this combination was known as "the Triangle") at the convention in 1881. Sullivan took immediate steps to organize violent attacks upon England.[69] In early 1882

---

[65] Pomfret, Struggle for the Land, 220.

[66] John Devoy, Recollections of an Irish Rebel (1929), 227.

[67] Davitt, Fall of Feudalism, 535.

[68] C.C. O'Brien, Parnell and His Party, 84.

[69] Henry Hunt, The Crime of the Century (1889). The complete story of the 1883-84 dynamite campaign is found here.

he went to Paris and received 20,000 in League funds from Egan.[70]
As will be shown later Sullivan used this money to finance numerous
dynamite attacks in English cities from 1883 to 1885. However, such
secret activities did not prevent the Clan under Sullivan's leadership
to publicly support Parnell's new movement. When the American Land
League met for its last National Convention in Horticulture Hall, sit-
uated in Philadelphia's renowned Fairmount Park,[71] Sullivan had already
ordered the Clan's membership to gain control of the various organizations
which sent delegates. At the same time Patrick Egan had invited Devoy to
a private meeting at which a platform for a new organization would be
formulated for presentation to the delegates.[72] Four of the seven men
invited to formulate this statement of aims were members of the Clan
and this same kind of domination was found on the floor of the Convention itself.[73] In the midst of the deliberations Parnell wired the delegates and asked that the new organization form a platform which would

> enable us to continue to accept help from America
> and at the same time avoid offering a pretext
> to the British government for entirely suppressing
> the national movement in Ireland.[74]

The committee and the delegates complied by dissolving the Land League
and creating the Irish National League of America, which closely re-

---

[70] O'Brien, Post Bag, II, 106.

[71] American, Il (1883), 45.

[72] O'Brien, Post Bag, II, 190. Egan to Devoy, April 18, 1883.

[73] O'Brien, Parnell, 207.

[74] Davitt, Fall of Feudalism, 392. This telegram clearly indicates
Parnell's fear that any attachment to radicalism would ruin his political
career.

sembled Parnell's constitutional, parliamentary movement in Ireland, at least on the surface. The new organization was controlled by the Clan, however, and Alexander Sullivan became its first President.[75] Some concessions were granted to the more moderate elements, since Father Charles O'Reilly of Detroit accepted the position of Treasurer. John Boyle O'Reilly had high hopes for the new organization, since he believed that it would serve as a rallying point for all Irish-Americans; but shortly after the convention, some of his friends felt that the Clan would only use it as a tool for their secret work.[76] Nevertheless, the public press reacted favorably to the convention,[77] especially because the extremists did not dominate the public proceedings.[78] Consequently, Sullivan had the advantage of serving as President of a relatively respectable organization, which he used as a cover rather than a tool for the active work. Thus, while Ford broke with Parnell, Sullivan and the Clan in public supported him, but in private started a secret war with England.

Parnell seemed satisfied with the April convention, since he believed that Irish-Americans followed his advice. Meanwhile, he continued to keep his part of the Kilmainham pact, offering mild solutions to Irish troubles whenever he appeared in public which was rel-

---

[75] Le Caron, Twenty-Five Years, 211.

[76] O'Brien, Post Bag, II, 194. O'Reilly to Devoy, April 28, 1883.

[77] American, II (1883), 52.

[78] Ibid., 36. There is some indication that Sullivan wanted the presidency to be in a better position to influence Irish voters in the presidential campaign of the following year.

atively rare in 1883 and 1884. Even the British press recognized the "moderate and almost cheerful tone" which the leader of the Irish party had adopted, and the relative calm that settled over Ireland.[79]

As a result the British devoted their energies to their own problems during 1883. Toward the end of the year Joseph Chamberlain convinced Gladstone that urgent reform in the franchise should receive first place in the 1884 legislative program. In January 1884 the cabinet agreed to include agriculture laborers in the voting population and devoted the entire year to the great struggle to push it through Parliament.[80] When the Lords held up its passage, Gladstone called a recess on August 14. For two months the Liberals cried "Peers against the people" and, when Parliament returned in late October, the battle was decided. The Lords accepted the bill, the Queen signed it, and millions received the right to vote. The reduction of agitation, accomplished by Parnell, had given the English the opportunity to take one more step on the road to democracy.

The British Liberals, especially Chamberlain, cheered when the news of the victory in the Lords appeared, but their cheers were short lived, because the victory itself laid the foundation for the renewal of the Anglo-Irish struggle. By January 1885 the Home Rule party had outlived the radical taint of the land war days—even the Irish Bishops had accepted them—and the new act guaranteed at least eighty-[81]

---

[79] Saturday Review, LVI (1883), 326, 329.

[80] Chamberlain, Political Memoir, 96.

[81] Ibid., 96.

five Home Rulers in the next Parliament. Parnell had patiently waited
for the time when his party had the numbers and prestige to become
the balance of power in Parliament. The extension of the franchise
virtually guaranteed that his time was near at hand.

The mere thought that the Home Rule party would win a balance
position in the next general election forced the Liberals to open negotiations with Parnell for a solution to the Irish Question.[82] Chamberlain wanted to establish some degree of local government along with what
he termed a "central board" which would represent all of the local
units. Parnell felt that the "central board" would form a kind of
Parliament for Ireland, and, consequently, refused, because he wanted
the question of an Irish Parliament kept separate from the question of
local affairs.[83] In spite of Parnell's refusal Chamberlain decided to
offer his plan to the Cabinet, maybe because he knew the Irish Bishops
would support it. Yet the Cabinet rejected it and even suggested coercion as the only effective means to pacify Ireland. This forced
Parnell to vote against Gladstone on a minor budget question on June 8,
1885. This defeat, coupled to widening differences within his own party,
convinced Gladstone that his best course would be to simply resign. Thus
the Conservatives formed a new government in late June.

While Parnell began to use his new power to disrupt English political life, events occurred in America that were to have far reaching
effects upon Parnell's whole movement. Alexander Sullivan had refused

---

[82] O'Brien, Parnell and His Party, 89.

[83] Chamberlain, Political Memoir, 88.

to call a meeting of the Clan in 1883, probably to avoid the possibility
of accounting for the money received from Egan.  As a result one section
of the Clan demanded Sullivan's resignation and began to bitterly crit-
icize his control of the Executive Board.  Consequently, Sullivan and the
Triangle agreed to call a convention for 1884, where they admitted the
expenditure of money for the dynamite campaign, but failed to account
for the funds spent to the satisfaction of what became known as the anti-
Sullivan faction of the Clan.[84]  After the convention this new element,
which included Devoy, spent the next four years trying to bring the
whole matter to light.

Sullivan's troubles were further magnified by the fact that he was
President of the Irish National League of America.  Some Americans had
attacked that organization on the ground that it was an association of
one race devoted to the creation of a foreign state.[85]  Sullivan defended the League against this opposition but, when the delegates to
the Second National Convention of the League met in Boston on August 13,
1884, he discovered critics within the organization itself.  They accused
him of trying to bring the League into active American politics.[86]  He
could not ignore the feeling generated by this accusation so he resigned,
but the Clan saw to it that Patrick Egan was elected to succeed to the
presidency.  At this time Egan was a close associate of Sullivan both in

[84] Le Caron, Twenty-Five Years, 231.

[85] Alexander Sullivan, "The American Republic and the Irish National League of America," The American Catholic Quarterly Review, IX
(1884), 35.

[86] New York Irish American, May 12, 1884.  This Democratic paper
continued to make this charge.

American and Irish-American politics.[87] Whether this change pleased
Parnell or not is hard to say, but his representative at the meetings,
John Redmond, did report that the delegates opposed the use of dynamite
and promised to support Parnell. He gave them an opportunity to prove
this when he asked the Irish in America to support a special parliamentary
fund which would finance the general elections. Within a few short
weeks the League responded with 14,000.[88] Parnell was not alone.

While the League appeared somewhat united, the struggle in the Clan
continued. In early October 1884 Devoy openly attacked Sullivan's
domination of the organization[89] and by December a movement had developed that called for the end of Sullivan's dynamite attacks.[90] Such
continued abuse caused Sullivan to threaten to resign his position,
but because he never did fulfill the threat the controversy raged for
another three years.[91] In this atmosphere of growing conflict in
radical American ranks, Parnell was reaching his height of power.

In the summer and fall of 1885 Parnell had two great interests,
the alliance with the Conservatives and the December elections. By voting with the Conservatives he had defeated the Liberal attempt to re-

---

[87] Le Caron, Twenty-Five Years, 227.

[88] O'Brien, Parnell and His Party, 138.

[89] O'Brien, Post Bag, II, 256. Burns to Devoy, October 8, 1888.

[90] Ibid., 259. Mulcahy to Devoy, December 28, 1884.

[91] Ibid., 261. Mulcahy to Devoy, April 3, 1885.

impose coercion, and, when the new government gave the Irish post to
Lord Henry H. Carnavan, well-known for his efforts to solve the Irish
problem, Parnell felt that he could gain even more from the alliance.[92]
However, the cabinet's refusal to accept Carnavan's conciliatory pro-
posals forced Parnell to break with the Conservatives.  At that moment
Chamberlain indicated a willingness to grant something more than the
local government plan, but Parnell refused to negotiate, content to wait
for the elections.  Meanwhile, Gladstone had hinted that he might con-
cede to Parnell's wishes, but he also was waiting for the election returns.[93]

In December the Conservatives dissolved Parliament and called for
a general election.  British voters went to the polls for the first time
in five years and for the first time under the recently extended franchise.  As the results arrived at the office of the London Times, it became evident that Parnell would play a major role in the coming parliamentary session.  The Liberals won 335 seats; the Tories, 249; and the
Home Rulers, 86.  Neither party could rule without Parnell.  He stood at
the pinnacle of his power.[94]

When Parliament met on January 21, 1886, Home Rule was in the air.
On that opening day the Irish listened to a call for coercion in the

---

[92] O'Brien, Parnell and His Party, 98.

[93] Chamberlain, Political Memoir, 161.

[94] John Boyle O'Reilly, "At Last," The North American Review,
CXLII (1886), 109.  "Ireland is saved by 20 million Irish-blooded
Americans."

Queen's speech and, when the Conservatives raised the bill, Parnell
and Gladstone turned them out of office. On February 1 Gladstone formed
a new government; six weeks later he offered his Home Rule Bill to the
House of Commons.[95] By then Chamberlain had resigned and started the
formation of what was later called the Unionist-Liberal Party.[96]
Gladstone forced his bill through its first reading, but by June Chamberlain had organized the opposition, and it failed to pass the second
reading on June 7, 341 to 311. Gladstone decided to take the issue to
the people, dissolved Parliament, and prepared for elections in July.
In a fierce campaign Gladstone and Parnell lost. The Liberal-Unionist
and Conservative alliance returned to London with a majority of 118
seats. Home Rule was dead.

The whole question of Home Rule and its failure had a decided effect upon the Irish-Americans. When the possibility of Parnell's gaining the balance of power first arose, the dynamiters were forced to
suspend their operations as Irish-Americans watched events in Ireland
with great intensity. Parnell kept Egan well-informed and the Irish
National League responded with continued support.[97] Even Americans,
as evidenced in their newspapers, hoped that Gladstone would succeed.[98]
When the bill suffered defeat in early June and the election returns

---

[95] O'Brien, Parnell and His Party, 165.

[96] Chamberlain, Political Memoir, 168.

[97] Davitt, Fall of Feudalism, 490.

[98] Public Opinion, I (1886). This can be seen in any number of
issues.

arrived, a great disappointment descended upon the Irish in America. However, as in former times they reacted with a call for unity and the Irish National League decided to hold its third convention in Chicago in the middle of August. All eyes in both England and Ireland turned to Chicago, for, as one observer stated, "without Irish-American support Parnell ceases to be a power and without the support of Parnell Gladstone is helpless."[99]

When the delegates arrived a struggle quickly developed between those who wanted to renew terrorism and dynamite, and those who wanted to follow the lead of Parnell. At the time Sullivan was organizing a new dynamite campaign and attended the convention with this in mind.[100] The fact that Ford agreed to return to the main stream of Irish politics strengthened Sullivan's hopes. Meanwhile, Parnell sent William O'Brien and Michael Davitt as his personal representatives, and instructed them to gain the support of the delegates without promising a renewal of the land war. Parnell had little room for maneuver, since he could not expect his Liberal allies to support the old breed of terrorism. The showdown came when O'Brien and Davitt met with Egan, Ford, and Sullivan for a backroom strategy session. Sullivan voiced his interest in terrorism, but O'Brien and Davitt were able to convince the others that this was not necessary. "Eviction would be resisted but not by terrorism."[101]

---

[99] O'Brien, Parnell and His Party, 195.

[100] Le Caron, Twenty-Five Years, 247.

[101] William O'Brien, Evening Memories (1920), 136-139.

With these assurances the leaders agreed that the convention would issue a moderate platform and promise complete faith in Parnell's leadership. Egan resigned his office which went to John Fitzgerald of
Lincoln, Nebraska, while Father O'Reilly continued as Treasurer.[102]

While O'Brien and Davitt arranged for American money, Parnell
turned his mind to the problem of Ireland and Parliament. The new lawmakers entered upon their duties on August 5, 1886 against the background
of an Ireland again on the verge of revolution. The old causes of dis-
content had reappeared. Agricultural prices had declined rapidly in
1885 and 1886 to a point far below the averages of the preceding years.[103]
As a result many peasants were unable to pay even the rents that had
been adjusted by the Land Courts. The Bishops of Ireland had advocated some form of temporary relief as the only way to avoid disaster,
while Parnell asked Parliament to suspend rents for two years. When
this was denied, he asked the Irish in America for a special anti-eviction
fund.[104] Although the situation resembled conditions in the fall of
1880 Parnell was unwilling to lead the peasants into a new struggle
for the land. He wanted the money merely to prevent foreclosures.

If Parnell was unwilling to actively fight evictions, others were
not. In October William O'Brien announced the famous "Plan of Campaign" on the front page of his United Irishmen. Advocates of the plan

---

[102] Davitt, Fall of Feudalism, 515.

[103] Pomfret, Struggle for the Land, 242.

[104] O'Brien, Parnell and His Party, 201.

felt that it would win the support of the peasants, while not alienating the Liberals. According to the plan the peasants on an estate would consult and determine the amount of rent they could pay, offer this to the landlord, and, if he refused to accept it, the money would be used to fight evictions through legal means and to feed those evicted.[105] Parnell supported the ideas at first, but, when it spread throughout Ireland during the winter of 1886-87, he began to fear its effect upon the Liberals. Then in January the government arrested five leaders, but a Dublin jury would not agree on a conviction and they gained their freedom.[106] The government had demonstrated the need for new coercion laws.

When Parliament met in early 1887, coercion and Ireland again appeared on the legislative program. Parnell and his Liberal allies debated the Queen's speech for three weeks, but they could only delay the Conservatives' program. The situation rapidly deteriorated in an Ireland under ordinary law. The government appointed Arthur Balfour as Chief Secretary and introduced a Crimes Bill on March 11, a rather unique document in that it imposed extraordinary law for an unspecified period of time. In the following month Balfour arrested William O'Brien and John Dillon for their activities in conjunction with the "Plan of Campaign," while on April 18 the London Times published the first of a series of articles entitled "Parnellism and Crime." In the midst of

---

[105] Hammond, Gladstone, 563.

[106] Blanche E. Dugdale, Arthur James Balfour (1937), 85.

all this Parliament debated the Crimes Bill and, although delaying
tactics were rather successful, Parnell could only prevent its passage until July. Balfour immediately suppressed the National League
and enforced the new laws with extreme severity, but he was unable to
break the boycott.

Ireland once again was attracting the attention of the whole world,
including the Vatican, in the summer of 1887. In July the Pope sent
a representative to Ireland in an effort to evaluate the "Plan of
Campaign" in concept and practice. After spending some time gathering
information he returned to Rome where his report was examined by the
Congregation of the Holy Office. While the idea itself continued to
prosper in spite of Balfour's efforts to the contrary,[107] the Congregation issued its findings, a condemnation on three counts: it was unlawful to break a contract freely entered into; the land courts were
available if rents were unjust; and boycotting was contrary to justice
and charity.[108] The news struck Ireland like a thunderbolt and a
bitter controversy ensued. In the final outcome the priest lost and
the Irish party emerged supreme.[109]

Before this ceased to attract Irishmen the world over, the famous
Parnell Commission opened. In early 1888 James O'Donnell opened a libel
suit against the London _Times_ on the ground that its series, entitled

---

[107] Ibid., 171.

[108] Ibid., 117.

[109] O'Brien, _Parnell and His Party_, 215.

"Parnellism and Crime," had implicated his name and damaged his reputation. When he lost the case Parnell felt compelled to ask the government for a commission to determine the truth or falsity of the original series. The government replied with a special commission to examine the whole range of Parnell's contact with radical Irish nationalists and agrarian crime. The hearing opened in October 1888, but the basis of the articles, a series of letters, were not proven to be forgeries until February 1889. This signaled a great victory for Parnell.

During these disputes Parnell continued his contacts in America but 1887 and 1888 witnessed the beginning of a temporary decline in Irish-American nationalism. The struggle within the Clan-Na-Gael broke into almost open warfare in late 1887 and two years later the whole image of Irish-American nationalism suffered from the disclosures made after the "Triangle's" murder of Dr. William Cronin, the leader of the anti-Sullivanites.[110] At the same time the unity of the Irish National League of America showed signs of weakening, probably because Parnell's domination relegated it to becoming a mere "collecting agent."[111]

Although the significance of the connection between the Irish in America and Parnell tended to break down in late 1887, the momentum of events carried Irish-American interest at least into 1889. In effect Parnell's leadership of Irish nationalism kept alive the Irish-American

---

[110] Henry Hunt, Crime of the Century (1889). The whole story is contained here.

[111] O'Brien, Parnell and His Party, 425.

bitter memories of the past and his belief that he could aid in the fight to defeat the hated English.  All this occurred just when the politicians of America enflamed this same Irish-American hatred. Whether her diplomats did the same will be discussed in the following pages.

# Chapter III

## Anglo-American Relations

The story of America's relations with England in the years from 1877 to 1895 has received many labels. As was stated before, Carl Fish described it as "Baiting the Lion, 1877-1897" and remarked that "never before had diplomacy been so much at the mercy of politics. . . . Particularly popular was the diversion of twisting the tail of the British lion."[1] Thomas A. Bailey in his more recent study agreed with Fish, when he admitted that "during the late eighties and early nineties Anglophobia was still a force to be reckoned with in American political life."[2] In itself this was not extraordinary, since "throughout the nineteenth century the path to Anglo-American understanding was a thorny one, for there was abundant anglophobia in the United States."[3] However, it had significance for the Irish-American, since it occurred within the framework of his increasing role in American politics and his aroused interest in the Anglo-Irish struggle. Did this deterioration of Anglo-American relations help the Irish-American use his political power to further the cause of Irish freedom? In other words, was the chance cluster of circumstances which characterized the period following the Civil War reemerging? Did Irish interests once again

---

[1] Fish, American Diplomacy, 370.

[2] Bailey, Diplomatic History of the American People, 477.

[3] John B. Brebner, North Atlantic Triangle (1945), 246.

coincide with those of America's diplomats as well as her politicians? To answer this one must discover how extensive and influential anglophobia was at the time and the thoughts of those directing America policy concerning American interests.

Many factors contributed to the American dislike of England during the nineteenth century, but the most important was the long history of diplomatic battles. As far back as the founding of the colonies Americans had cause to dislike England, and the constant contact between the two nations did little to alleviate the situation. The fact that England fought the United States twice was never forgotten,[4] while the numerous disputes concerning boundaries, fishing rights, etc., kept these feelings alive from 1815 to 1860. British actions during the Civil War especially intensified anglophobia, an intensification reflected in these words of James Russell Lowell:

> We know we've got a cause John
> That's honest, just and true
> We thought 't would win applause, John,
> Ef nowhere else, from you.[5]

Northerners especially condemned English construction of Confederate gunboats, which eventually led to the famous "Alabama Claims," but this and other disputes were officially settled by the Treaty of Washington, signed in 1871.

Anglophobia did not necessarily disappear after 1870, however; in fact,

---

[4] Stephen Gwynn, ed., The Letters and Friendships of Sir Cecil Spring-Rice: A Record, 2 Vols. (1929), I, 66. To Ferguson, June 17, 1887.

[5] Quoted in Bailey, Diplomatic History of the American People, 344.

for nearly half a century after the Civil War the
natural sentiments of friendship, based upon ties
of blood and a common heritage of literature and
history and law, were distorted by bitter and exaggerated memories.[6]

Other factors helped to strengthen the memories. "Hundreds of thousands

of Americans firmly believed that England was an arrogant and anti-

democratic land-grabber."[7] The protectionists in both parties disliked

England because of her stand for free trade, while the cheap money

advocates felt the same way because she represented the gold standard.

Many others resented the English for their superiority complex, re-

sentment best described in these words of Lowell, when he heckled Amer-

icans who imitated the British:

Perhaps one reason why the average Britain spreads
himself here with such an easy air of superiority may
be owing to the fact that he meets with so many bad
imitations as to conclude himself the only real thing
in a wilderness of shames.[8]

He went on to say that before the Civil War the English never thought

"that an American had what could be called a country" and, consequently,

"it will take England a great while to get over her airs of patronage

toward us, or even possibly to conceal them"[9] even though the United

States emerged from that war a powerful nation. At one point he of-

fered the English a word of advice, when he reminded them that

---

[6] E. D. Adams, Great Britain and the American Civil War, 2 Vols.
(1960), II, 305.

[7] Bailey, Diplomatic History of the American People, 475.

[8] James Russell Lowell, "A Certain Condescension in Foreigners,"
Fire Side Travels (1904).

[9] Ibid., 323.

> the only sure way of bringing about a healthy rela-
> tion between the two countries is for Englishmen to
> clear their minds of the notion we are to be treated
> as a kind of inferior and deported Englishman.[10]

This clearing of the mind occurred in the period from 1871 to 1900

as anglophilia gradually superseded the old animosity. The increase in

communication that followed on the heels of the transatlantic steam-

ship and the Atlantic cable contributed greatly to this change.[11]

Mutual friendships developed between prominent leaders of both countries,

for instance, that of Cecil Spring-Rice and Theodore Roosevelt, while

some of these developed into lifelong ties such as the marriage of

Joseph Chamberlain to Mary Endicott, the daughter of Grover Cleveland's

Secretary of War.[12] The fact that after 1867 England became more dem-

ocratic and less aristocratic added to this rising anglophilia.[13] At

the same time American literary endeavors were receiving wide acclaim

in England, while Americans learned to appreciate English literary and

scholarly works. James Bryce's publication of his sympathetic, but

honest, study of America indicated the trend of the future in this regard.[14]

Although all these signs pointed to a time when the majority of Americans

would like, rather than dislike England, the decade of the eighties was

still a time when the politician could profitably "twist the lion's tail."

---

[10] Ibid., 331.

[11] Eckman, "British Traveler," 275.

[12] Gwynn, The Letters of Spring-Rice, I, 64; H.C. Allen, The Anglo-American Relationship Since 1783 (1959), 111.

[13] Adams, Great Britain and the Civil War, 304.

[14] Allen, Anglo-American Relationship, 152.

Against the background of changing American attitudes Anglo-
American relations during these years fall conveniently into three
periods. The first, from January 1880 to January 1882, was one of
growing tension as William M. Evarts, Secretary of State under Rutherford B. Hayes, struggled with a number of problems, none of which he
was able to solve before James G. Blaine succeeded him in March 1881.
Blaine's short tour of duty, from March to December 1881, witnessed
an intensification of tensions. The second period began when Frederick
G. Frelinghuysen became Secretary of State. Within a month, he had indicated the policy he and his boss, Chester Arthur, would follow.
For the most part it was one of relaxing tensions, even though they
kept the canal and fishery issues alive. This period, the calm before
the storm, carried into the administration of Grover Cleveland, that
is until December 1885 when Congress reconvened. From that time until he left office, Thomas F. Bayard, Cleveland's Secretary of State,
in spite of his efforts to the contrary, suffered through one Anglo-
American dispute after another.

When Evarts returned to his desk after the Christmas holidays of
1879, he must have been somewhat dismayed by the growing number of problems with England. At the time the most important of these questions
did not even concern England directly. In the previous summer Ferdinand
de Lesseps had organized a company to construct a canal across the
isthmus of Panama. Almost immediately Senator Ambrose E. Burnside of
Rhode Island introduced a resolution in the Senate that strongly
condemned any central American canal, built by a foreign power. When

Congress reconvened in December, he reopened debate on the question.
Evarts, realizing how the issue had captured the imagination of the
people, worked Burnside's arguments into a report which he submitted
to the Senate on March 8, 1880. He clearly stipulated that the administration's policy was "An American canal under the control of the
United States,"[15] but such a policy obviously contradicted the terms
of the Clayton-Bulwer Treaty of 1850 which had provided for joint
British and American ownership of any such project. Evarts had added
a new margin to the original dispute with de Lesseps, and this resulted
in Representative William Carpo of Massachusetts introducing a resolution which called for the abrogation of the Clayton-Bulwer Treaty.[16]
It was sent to the House Committee on Foreign Affairs where it lingered
until the Committee reported it favorably in the following session. The
whole question generated much public debate as leading students of public affairs condemned the fact that such a canal could be built with
foreign money.[17] In effect a dispute with a private French citizen
eventually evolved into another Anglo-American battle which continued
until the end of 1883.

While this question absorbed Evarts' thoughts in the early months
of 1880, the Fortune Bay question quietly rested until the British
finally answered his August 1, 1879 note in which he had demanded

---

[15] Alice Q. Tyler, The Foreign Policy of James G. Blaine (1927), 26.

[16] Ira Dudly Travis, The History of the Clayton-Bulwer Treaty
(1900), 206.

[17] Dexter Perkins, Hands Off, A History of the Monroe Doctrine
(1941), 162, 163.

$105,305.00 for damages inflicted upon American fishermen. The British reply did not reach Evarts until the middle of April, when he discovered that they refused to accept the claim on the technicality that the American fisherman had used the shore in the direct act of fishing, an illegal act according to the Treaty of Washington.[18] By then, both Houses of Congress had requested the papers on the matter and Hayes admitted in his accompanying letter that a basic disagreement had arisen as to the proper interpretation of certain clauses of that treaty. Consequently, he asked Congress to approve the "suggested avenues of approach which the United States could take to secure the indemnity."[19] The suggested avenue, the Loring Bill, was none other than the reimposition of duties upon Canadian fish and fish oil—duties that had been removed by the terms of the Treaty of Washington in exchange for the right of Americans to fish in Canadian waters.[20] In reality the administration asked Congress to unilaterally change the terms of a treaty. The British Minister in Washington, Sir Edward Thornton, expressed his surprise at the extraordinary character of this proposal and feared that Congress would accept it, since "both parties would surpass themselves in order to use this as an aid in the election drive,"[21] as Americans were

---

[18] British and Foreign State Papers, LXXII, 1291. Salisbury to Hoffin, April 3, 1880. Hereafter referred to as B.F.S.P.

[19] A Compilation of the Messages and Papers of the President (1917), 4542. Hereafter referred to as Messages.

[20] John W. Forster, A Century of Diplomacy (1900), 424.

[21] Knaplund, "Letters to Foreign Minister," 101. Thornton to Granville, June 1, 1880.

"very sore over the question" mainly because they remembered the Halifax award which many felt was unjust.[22]  The mere threat that Congress would accept the Loring Bill possibly prompted the British to review the whole case, since in early June Lord George Granville asked his legal advisors for a ruling on the possibility of justifying the fact that the Canadians had taken the law into their own hands.  Shortly afterwards Congress adjourned without considering the Loring Bill, but Thornton urged Granville to settle the question as soon as possible, since it would undoubtedly reappear in the next session.  He reminded the Foreign Minister that, even though one "can not make as much political gain from a grievance with England as they used to during the Civil war," as long as the question remained open "it will be made use of as a grievance against us."[23]

As this question slipped out of the foreground of Anglo-American relations temporarily during the summer and fall of 1880, Evarts turned his attention to other problems.  When the Indians continued to cross the frontier he complained in strong terms but the British failed to answer in any satisfactory manner.[24]  At the same time he entered into negotiations with Colombia with the view of gaining for the United States virtual control of any canal built in that area.  It directly conflicted with the terms of the Clayton-Bulwer treaty, but Evarts never had to face

---

[22] Ibid., 95.  Thornton to Granville, May 4, 1880; May 25, 1880.

[23] Ibid.

[24] Edgar McInnis, The Unguarded Frontier (1942), 310.

this particular problem, since Colombia never ratified the treaty.[25]
By then the House Committee on Foreign Relations reported the old Carpo
resolution and called for the abrogation of the Clayton-Bulwer Treaty.
In the midst of these troubles Evarts was constantly harrassed by the
War of the Pacific. Many Americans saw the war as a British inspired
struggle and wanted the United States to intervene in order to prevent
an increase of British influence there.[26] Evarts followed a cautious
policy, however, until the fall of 1880 when he offered American mediation. After this failed in October, he avoided this problem until the
fall of Lima in February 1881 afforded another opportunity to settle
the war, but he accomplished little before he left office in the following month.

Meanwhile, the British studied the whole question of the Fortune
Bay incident and on the advice of the law officers Granville decided
to recognize in principle the legitimacy of the American claim on the
basis of the British inability to justify the mob action taken by the
Canadians.[27] Before Evarts could settle the amount of the claim he
was forced to complicate matters by protesting two additional instances
of mob action, only this time Americans were not permitted to purchase
bait, a right supposedly guaranteed by the Treaty of Washington. At
the time he implied that the British handling of the Fortune Bay question had encouraged such action and that "if such attacks continued,

---

[25] Tyler, Foreign Policy of Blaine, 28.

[26] Millington, The War of the Pacific, 66-67.

[27] B.F.S.P., LXXII, 1298. Granville to Lowell, October 20, 1880.

the United States would have to give up the fisheries or resort to
force which would threaten the amicable relations between the two
governments."[28]   When Granville received this note from Minister James
R. Lowell, he immediately expressed his fear of its strong language
and later informed Thornton that the government wanted an immediate
settlement based upon a fair estimate of the cost and not upon the deliberations of a special commission which he had suggested in the
previous month.  When confronted with this turnabout, Evarts asked for
$120,000 and Granville countered with an offer of $75,000.  This is
significant in light of an earlier statement by Thornton, made in a
private conversation with Evarts, that the British Cabinet would not
approve of any settlement over $10,000.

This sudden change could have resulted from the harsh note of
February 4, but it also could have been influenced by the fact that
James G. Blaine had accepted Garfield's offer of the State Department.
Thornton had informed Granville in December that the issue should be
settled as soon as possible "before a hostile successor is appointed"[29]
an obvious reference to Blaine, the leading candidate for the office,
whom Dexter Perkins has called a professional "twister of the lion's
tail."[30]

At any rate the whole matter of money was quickly settled within
seven days of Evarts' strong dispatch, when he accepted Granville's

[28] U.S.F.R., 1881, 496.  Evarts to Lowell, February 4, 1881.

[29] Knaplund, "Letters to the Foreign Minister," 112.  Memo to
letter, Thornton to Granville, December 28, 1880.

[30] Perkins, Hands Off, 248.

offer of $75,000. Before the money changed hands, however, a last
minute flaw developed. The British would pay only if Evarts would accept it as final payment against all claims, but Evarts refused to accept this condition, since he honestly did not know if additional incidents had occurred. A rash of telegrams did not erase the difficulty
before March 4 and Evarts was forced to leave another problem for Blaine.

When Blaine entered the State Department, some Americans anticipated
that his appointment indicated that the administration would take a
strong stand on the Canadian problems, especially the Fortune Bay case.[31]
This probably prompted Blaine to explain his position to Thornton, as
he could not accept what Evarts had refused without exposing the administration to attack.[32] When hearing this Granville made one further concession. He would pay the $75,000 if Blaine could accept it as full
payment for all claims prior to January 1, 1881.[33] Lowell telegraphed
this new offer to Washington, while he tried to get Granville to increase
the sum, since it looked "small to the United States" and "for another few
thousand pounds they could have amicable relations," to which Granville
replied that his government thought $75,000 was too much. However, he
hinted at the possibility of raising the offer, when he added that England "wanted friendship."[34]

[31] American, I (1881), 346.

[32] Knaplund, "Letters to the Foreign Minister," 121. Thornton to
Blaine, March 14, 1881.

[33] U.S.F.R., 1881, 510. Lowell to Blaine, March 9, 1881.

[34] Ibid. Lowell to Blaine, March 12, 1881.

With both sides seeking a solution to the problem Blaine shifted
negotiations from London to Washington where he could deal personally
with Thornton. Shortly afterward he informed the British Minister that
the United States would accept a sum of $80,000 in satisfaction of all
claims up to March 4, 1881.[35] When the British failed to answer, rumors
started to fly that Blaine would increase the claim to include the value
of the possible catch.[36] Thornton reminded the Foreign Office that "it
is very desirable that the question should be settled" and "not at all
to be desired that they continue into 1885 when the whole fisheries
question will be reopened."[37] But the British remained firm and Blaine
finally accepted the original offer of $75,000 for all claims up to
March 4. When the British paid, they did so, however, on the condition
that it would not prejudice the question of treaty rights. These they
felt were still open to debate.[38]

The Fortune Bay incident came to an end when the money actually
changed hands, but Thornton was not overjoyed with Blaine:

> I still think that he is an impulsive and dangerous man,
> and that in case of any serious question between us he will
> require very careful management. He complains that we are
> very sensitive upon any question with the United States, but
> admits at the same time that the Americans have inherited this
> defect. He himself is certainly not free from it. But there

---

[35] B.F.S.P., LXII, 1301. Thornton to Granville, April 4, 1881.

[36] Knaplund, "Letters to the Foreign Minister," 127. Thornton
to Granville, April 12, 1881.

[37] Ibid., 129. Thornton to Granville, April 19, 1881.

[38] B.F.S.P., LXXII, 1319. Granville to Thornton, May 27, 1881.

> is certainly no desire amongst them generally to
> quarrel with us for its own sake, and I trust that
> we shall be always able to deprive them of any ex-
> cuse for doing so.[39]

Thornton could see the underlying Anglophobia that existed in some
circles, but could see no real cause for alarm as long as the British
avoided any direct clash. His fears were substantiated only a few weeks
after the settlement, when in an official note Blaine complained that
Canadians universally refused to permit Americans to purchase bait and
that, since no adequate police force existed to guarantee American
treaty rights, the United States would possibly be forced into sending
warships to the fishing grounds.[40]

While the Fortune Bay negotiations absorbed some of his time,
Blaine also focused his attention upon the Indian problem. By May
1881 he had received reports of numerous boundary crossings and subsequent attacks upon isolated American settlements with great loss of
property.[41] He complained to Thornton and placed the responsibility for
the raids upon the Canadian government, but the English Minister denied
this on the ground that Canada alone could not possibly police the entire border. At another time Blaine implied that the United States
would use force to drive the Indians back over the boundary line and

---

[39] Knaplund, "Letters to the Foreign Minister," 133. Thornton to
Granville, May 17, 1881.

[40] U.S.F.R., 1881, 514. Blaine to Lowell, July 30, 1881.

[41] U.S.F.R., 1881, 588. Blaine to Thornton, May 14, 1881; B.F.S.P.,
LXXV, 58. Blaine to Thornton, May 10, 1881.

demanded that "the Canadians meet them at the border, disarm them and put them in a position where they will do no harm."[42] Thornton asked that force be used with caution and promised that the Canadians would try and prevent such crossings, but in late August Blaine again complained of new incursions and regretted the failure of Canadian authorities to adopt effective measures "after assurances the crossings would cease."[43] Again, however, the British would not be intimidated and in a lengthy report they placed the responsibility for the problem at Blaine's feet, since the United States had refused to accept a concerted plan for joint policing of the border and had failed to give information on the crimes committed to the Canadian authorities at the scene.[44] There the matter rested to be taken up by Blaine's successor.

During these months Blaine was not unaware of the possibility of reaping the benefits of the publication of the House report which called for the abrogation of the Clayton-Bulwer Treaty.[45] In anticipation of this, as was stated earlier, Evarts had negotiated a treaty with Colombia which, by giving the United States control of any canal built in the isthmus of Panama, violated the terms of the 1850 compact. However, since Colombia never ratified the treaty, the whole canal question was in a state of suspension when Blaine became Secretary of State. His

---

[42] U.S.F.R., 1881, 588. Blaine to Thornton, May 26, 1881.

[43] B.F.S.P., LXXV, 62. Blaine to Drummond, August 25, 1881.

[44] Ibid., 63. Drummond to Blaine, September 26, 1881.

[45] Mary W. Williams, Anglo-American Isthmanian Diplomacy, 1815-1915 (1916), 276.

position officially remained vague until June 1881, but at least as

early as April he unofficially intimated that the United States would

have to take steps to prevent any such canal from becoming a "back door

by which the enemy might gain an entrance."[46] He obviously referred to

the British as the enemy, since he stated that the "country with the

largest navy could control" the canal. What he had in mind was not clear,

but, when reports arrived in Washington that the Colombian government

had contacted European powers in an effort to gain guarantees that the

canal would be neutral, he decided to send his famous circular letter

of June 24, 1881.[47] In it he declared that there was no need for

European assurances of the neutrality of the canal zone, since such as-

surances were given in the 1846 treaty between Colombia and the United

States, and that, if anyone duplicated this guarantee, it would be con-

sidered "an uncalled for intrusion into American affairs . . . an al-

liance against the United States and an unfriendly act."[48]

Most of the nations of the world ignored the letter; a few at least

indicated that it did not interest them; but the British were interested.

They received the note in early July, yet Granville waited until November

10, 1881 to remind Blaine that the whole question of Anglo-American canal

relations fell within the terms of the Clayton-Bulwer Treaty.[49] The heart

---

[46] Knaplund, "Letters to the Foreign Minister," 172.

[47] Alice Felt Tyler, The Foreign Policy of James G. Blaine (1927), 30.

[48] U.S.F.R., 1881, 537. Blaine to Lowell, June 24, 1881.

[49] Ibid., 549. Granville to Hoffin, November 10, 1881.

of this note could very possibly have been transmitted to Washington by telegram. At least this would explain Blaine's sending a note on November 19, 1881 (he had yet to receive Granville's) in which he argued that the passage of years made the 1850 treaty obsolete and, consequently, asked for its modification. He particularly wanted the United States to have the right to fortify any canal built in the area, to hold political control of it, and to have sole right of protection of any railroad in the area.[50] When Blaine finally received the complete answer to his original letter, he sent a second dispatch, but, when it reached England, he was out of office.[51]

By this time the question had become a subject for much conversation. As early as November 1, 1881 the ranking British diplomat in Washington, Victor Drummond, reported that Americans were determined to carry out the neutrality scheme for the world in general. "It does not wish any power to be responsible for this but itself."[52] When President Arthur raised the question in his Annual Message, he mentioned that, since Great Britain had relied upon the provisions of the Clayton-Bulwer Treaty, the State Department attempted to abrogate "such clauses, thereof, as do not comport with the obligations of the United States toward Colombia or with the vital need of the two friendly parties."[53] The

---

[50] Ibid., Blaine to Lowell, November 29, 1881.

[51] B.F.S.P., LXXIII, 864. Blaine to Lowell, November 29, 1881.

[52] Knaplund, "Letters to the Foreign Minister," Drummond to Granville, November 1, 1881.

[53] Messages, 4645.

Senate requested the correspondence, but Arthur did not send Blaine's November letters, since the British had not yet answered them. In an obvious political move Blaine published the June note on the day after the Senate received the correspondence and three days before he left office.[54] The British Minister reported to Granville that the press was favorable to Blaine's arguments, yet he foresaw "no hard feelings" except if the discussions were prolonged.[55] Blaine had struck a national prejudice and the new minister, Sir Lionel Sackville-West, felt that Frederick Frelinghuysen and Chester Arthur would treat the question, not for any real desire to adjust the treaty, but for mere political gain.

This was not Blaine's only attempt to antagonize the British on the eve of his departure from office. Another centered around the War of the Pacific. As was indicated, Evarts had followed a rather cautious policy, but Blaine in characteristic fashion reversed this policy, when he recognized the puppet government of Peru which Chile had established after the fall of Lima. In a similar fashion he appointed new ministers to both Chile and Peru with instructions that emphasized America's interest in the settlement of the war without territorial change. Both men directly intervened in the peace negotiations and committed numerous indiscretions, news of which reached Blaine, but he refused to reprimand them until November 30.[56] Meanwhile, the British and

---

[54] He left office on December 19, 1881, and published the notes on December 16.

[55] Ibid., 160. Telegram from West to Granville, December 21, 1881. The use of telegrams always denoted a sense of urgency, since the regular channels took 12 to 20 days from Washington to London.

[56] Tyler, Foreign Policy of Blaine, 118-119.

French renewed their old offer to join with the United States in a joint mediation attempt; but Blaine refused, since, as members of a different state system, they had no right to interfere with an American program. He argued that the existence of a state system on this side of the Atlantic made it inexpedient for the United States to unite with European states to solve an American question.[57] This determination to end the war without European assistance, plus the bungling of the resident ministers, prompted Blaine to send William H. Trescott on a special mission with instructions to end the war. He had permission to be rather firm, if he felt the situation called for a strong statement of American desires, but he never really got a chance to act, since before he even arrived in Peru Blaine was out of office.

In December 1881 Blaine's "vigorous" policy did not reflect the mood of the country. Consequently, Hamilton Fish and other "stalwarts" recommended Frederick T. Frelinghuysen to succeed him. This appointment, plus that of J. C. Bancroft Davis as an Assistant Secretary, indicated very clearly the policy of Arthur's administration.[58] The business community and the country in general wanted Blaine's more vigorous policy converted into less dangerous action, especially in Latin-America,[59] and these new directors of policy gave the people exactly what they wanted.

---

[57] Ibid., 114.

[58] Allen Lawrence, "The Senate Foreign Relations Committee and the Diplomacy of Garfield, Arthur and Cleveland." Unpublished Ph.D. dissertation, University of Virginia (1952), 23.

[59] Ibid., 47; American, II (1881), 163. "Blaine's vigorous policy came to an end in time to save us from a state of war with the rest of the world."

Upon entering office Frelinghuysen applied the new philosophy immediately to the question of the War of the Pacific. He cancelled Trescott's original instructions and, although not recalling him, he effectively ended his mission. This reverse in policy led to a debate on the question in Congress where Blaine accused Arthur of instigating

> a policy which would destroy American commerce on the Pacific coast and build up English interests on its ruin [since he believed] that the steady moral pressure of the United States was needed to offset the heavy hand of England which Peru felt upon her at every turn.[60]

Later he described the war "as an English war with Chile as the instrument"[61] a description fully supported by numerous Americans in the area.[62] In spite of this testimony, however, Frelinghuysen was "determined to persevere in the non-intervention policy" and did all he could "to get out of the mess made by Blaine in Chile and Peru."[63] The United States withdrew and in the following year the belligerents signed a peace treaty. At that time the English, looking back on Blaine's policy of intervention and seeing it as an attempt to extend the Monroe Doctrine, happily accepted the settlement, since it ended the possibility and reduced "Mr. Blaine himself, if he were in office, to a condition of non-interference."[64]

---

[60] Hamilton, Blaine, 521.

[61] Tyler, Foreign Policy of Blaine, 113.

[62] Millington, War of the Pacific, 42, 43.

[63] Knaplund, "Letters to the Foreign Secretary," 105. West to Granville, March 21, 1882.

[64] "American Affairs," Saturday Review, LVI (1883), 721.

As one problem gradually disappeared the Indian question reemerged. On February 25, 1882 Frelinghuysen informed the British Minister that American troops had received orders to drive the Canadian Indians out of the country by force, if necessary.[65] In the following month he again intimated that "since there is no effective means of cooperation between the two countries, he had to use force."[66] Sackville-West refused to be intimidated and badgered, however, and countered by accusing the United States of creating the situation by refusing to answer the Canadian suggestion for a joint patrol.[67] Only then did Frelinghuysen reject the Canadian plan on the vague ground that "it does not meet the requirements of the situation" and substituted his solution, the principle of "hot pursuit."[68] In effect he wanted England to grant a blanket permission for American troops to enter Canadian territory. The British rightfully declined. There the matter rested as the Americans continued to complain and neither side would accept the other's solution. After 1883, however, the dispute gradually disappeared, when forces beyond the control of the diplomats caused the Indians to settle down.

Although these disputes caused Frelinghuysen concern, the real issue he inherited from Blaine was the question of the canal. Arthur had referred to the question in his First Annual Message as one "of grave

---

[65] B.F.S.P., LXXV, 66. Frelinghuysen to West, February 25, 1882.

[66] Ibid. Frelinghuysen to West, March 29, 1883.

[67] Ibid., 68. West to Frelinghuysen, April 5, 1883.

[68] Ibid., 74. Frelinghuysen to West, April 7, 1882.

national importance."[69]  What most Americans agreed was indicated by the

reaction which greeted the publication of Blaine's November 19 note.[70]

Sackville-West wrote a long letter to Granville, outlining the reaction

in some detail and reminding Granville that both "Frelinghuysen and

Davis are well aware that he [Blaine] has touched a national prejudice

which they can not disregard."[71]  The uproar must have moved Granville

because when he replied to the November 19 note his language was mild

although firm.  He felt that the cordial relations between the two na-

tions offered an opportunity to eliminate the disagreement, but he could

not see the need for modification of the treaty, although he could see

the need to join with other nations to guarantee the neutrality of the

canal.[72]  Sackville-West continued to recommend a soft policy throughout

January 1882 and was somewhat optimistic, but as he told Granville,

"much, of course, will depend upon the nature of my instructions."[73]

His optimism received some justification, when he interviewed Freling-

huysen, who hoped to drop the whole matter.  A few days later Davis in-

formed West that they

---

[69] Messages, 4628.

[70] Knaplund, "Letters to the Foreign Minister," 160.  West to
Granville, December 21, 1881.

[71] Ibid.  West to Granville, December 28, 1881.

[72] B.F.S.P., LXXIII, 873.  Granville to West, January 7, 1882.

[73] Knaplund, "Letters to the Foreign Minister," 161.  West to
Granville, January 17, 1882.

intended to entirely reverse Mr. Blaine's policy with
reference to the isthmus and South America, that
they had no fear of the British bugbear in these parts,
although the line they intended to take might cause
some excitement.[74]

By then the whole question had entered the Senate and the public arena.

One leading magazine accused Blaine of threatening the British if

they refused to abrogate the Clayton-Bulwer Treaty for the "domestic

stump."[75]

The reaction in the Senate and among the general public may very

possibly have changed the administration's attempt to drop the whole

matter. At any rate Frelinghuysen informed the British in May that the

President wanted the treaty revised but that he hoped that this "would

not interfere with the happy relations existing between the two

countries."[76] The news of the dispatch eventually leaked to the press.

Thompson felt that Frelinghuysen had definitely surprised him since

he "had indicated a desire to run American diplomacy according to the

desires of the foreign governments . . . but now he tears up the Clayton-

Bulwer Treaty."[77] The New York Tribune carried an extensive article of

praise on June 23 and most Americans received the message with similar

favorable reactions.

---

[74] Ibid., 163. West to Granville, January 31, 1882. As late as
February 6, Davis indicated this policy. West to Granville, February
6, 1882.

[75] "Another Chapter of Mr. Blaine's Diplomacy," The Nation, XXXIV
(1882), 93.

[76] B.F.S.P., LXXIII, 892. Frelinghuysen to Lowell, May 8, 1882.

[77] American, IV (1882), 130.

The British waited until after the opening of Congress in December to send their answer and Arthur was forced to include the topic in his Annual Message without benefit of knowing their position. Consequently, he took a very conciliatory approach, when he stated that

> time will be more powerful than discussion in
> removing the divergencies between the two nations
> whose friendship is so closely cemented by the in-
> timacy of their relations and the community of their
> interests.[78]

Granville accepted this tone of conciliation and incorporated it into his answer, but he stood firm on the question of not modifying the treaty. The debate continued through 1883. Then, when the English refused to accept the American position, Frelinghuysen decided to have the last word. He ordered the negotiation of a treaty with Nicaragua which ignored the British claims and granted the United States the right to construct a canal through that country. Arthur submitted it to the Senate on December 10, 1884 with Frelinghuysen's well-worn arguments as justifications.[79] Before the Senate acted, however, a new administration entered office.

While the canal dispute occupied a front stage position in Anglo-American relations in these years of Arthur's administration, the fishery question slowly reappeared to eventually replace the canal problem as one of the more important issues that separated the two countries. The memories of the Halifax award, the Fortune Bay incident,

---

[78] Messages, 4713.

[79] Ibid., 4843.

and continued harrassment of American fishermen by Canadians caused
Congress to pass a resolution that the President should terminate the
fishery articles of the treaty of Washington at the earliest opportunity.[80]  Arthur almost at once announced that he would terminate these
clauses as of July 1, 1885.  In January 1885 he issued the official
proclamation and reminded Americans that they would lose the special
privilege to work the in-shore fisheries off the Canadian coast.  However, the Canadians would also lose the right to sell their fish on
the American market duty-free.  But this would all occur in the middle
of the fishery season, and Sackville-West feared that, if the privileges
were revoked, a clash between Canadian and American fishermen would result.  Consequently, he asked Frelinghuysen if it would be possible
to extend both privileges until January 1, 1886, after the fishing
season.[81]  Frelinghuysen brought the question to the Senate Foreign
Relations Committee, since he did not think that the executive branch
could act on the matter unless Congress changed its earlier resolution,
but the Senators answered in the negative.  Consequently, the pressing
question greeted Thomas F. Bayard when he accepted the Secretaryship of
State under Grover Cleveland, the first Democratic president since James
Buchanan.

With the change of administration Sackville-West tried to sell his
idea for a second time.  He reexplained the problem and asked Bayard if

---

[80] Tansill, Foreign Policy of Bayard, 193.

[81] Knaplund, "Letters to the Foreign Minister," 181.  West to
Granville, January 8, 1885.

he would extend the deadline. After consulting with the Cabinet, Bayard said that he would not be able to extend the right of Canadians to sell fish duty-free in the American market, but that the President would be interested in asking Congress for a commission to solve the whole question, if the Canadians would extend to Americans the right to use the inshore fisheries. Thus, for nothing more than a promise the British agreed to get Canada to extend the deadline.[82] They wanted to avoid a conflict at all costs.

This concession on the part of the English helped to create a short period of very cordial relations between the two countries. Most of the earlier disputes no longer generated animosity; the Indian dispute, for instance, died a natural death, while the canal question ceased to exist after Cleveland's withdrawal of the Nicaraguan treaty in early 1885.[83] At the same time the two countries cooperated in preventing a German seiqure of the Samoan Islands.[84] Then, too, the election of Cleveland created a good deal of well-wishing in England for the continuance of good relations. This cordial feeling produced a very strong expression of affection for James Russell Lowell when he left the American Embassy, and his successor, Edward J. Phelps, continued to comment about the friendly spirit which characterized the relation of the two countries.[85]

---

[82] Tansill, Foreign Policy of Bayard, 197.

[83] Forster, Century of Diplomacy, 466.

[84] Ryden, United States Relations to Samoa, 293.

[85] Tansill, Foreign Policy of Bayard, 199.

Unfortunately, this was only the lull before the storm which broke in December 1885 when Congress returned to Washington. From that time until he left office Cleveland faced the ever-present thought of a possible clash between Americans and Canadians on three relatively significant disputes, the fisheries off the northeast coast of Canada, the fur seal controversy off the northwest coast of Canada and the boundary between Canada and Alaska. For three years he and his Secretary of State tried to solve these questions, but failed.

Bayard failed to settle these problems for many reasons, but one of the more significant was the peculiar political situation. For the first time in twenty-four years a Democrat occupied the White House and the Republicans wanted to dislodge him. In 1884 Blaine had attempted to paint Cleveland as a pro-English candidate and the whole Democratic party as a tool of British gold. The lesson of that attempt did not fall on deaf Republican ears, as they continued to exploit basic Anglo-American differences in order to reenforce their statements that Cleveland and the Democrats were pro-English. Throughout these years Bayard constantly complained about the partisanship of the Republicans in the Senate as they continued their efforts to use the diplomatic world to regain the political world until they succeeded in 1888.

The utilization of diplomacy to aid political causes began in earnest in December 1885 and for the first six months centered around the fishery dispute. On December 8 Cleveland asked Congress for authorization to convene a commission which would negotiate a new treaty on this problem.[86]    In the following month William P. Frye, Senator from

Maine, introduced a resolution which denounced the whole concept of such

a commission, and Sackville-West reported that the "New England Senators"

were against any agreement with England on the fishery question.[87]   Mean-

while, Bayard told Phelps that the temper of the Senate seems

> averse to the consideration of any public measure
> from a high or patriotic point of view, but that
> blind and obstructive partisanship seems to be
> the rule of their action.[88]

Phelps had already spoken to the British about how "the utterly unscrup-

ulous tactics of Mr. Blaine" would only cause trouble and, consequently,

the need "of clearing out of the way everything that could afford a

pretext for dispute."[89]   The Liberal Foreign Minister, Lord Rosebery,

(in Gladstone's third ministry) agreed to work for a speedy settlement,

but before anything could be accomplished the Senate passed the Frye

resolution, 35 to 10, on April 13.  The Republicans had indicated their

unwillingness to solve the problem.  As if this was not enough, in the

following month the Canadian authorities seized the American fishing

vessel, the David J. Adams.  Congress reacted immediately with resolu-

tions of retaliation as the public press debated the issue hotly.  The

Republican New York Tribune condemned the Canadian seizure, while the

Philadelphia Press noted that the incident would save Bayard, since

---

[86] Messages, 4917.

[87] Tansill, Foreign Policy of Bayard, 206.  West to Salisbury, January 20, 1886.

[88] Ibid., 208.  Bayard to Phelps, March 7, 1886.

[89] Ibid., xxxv.  Phelps to Bayard, March 22, 1886.

it would give him "a chance to vindicate his past mistakes."[90]  Even
the Nashville American, a Democratic paper, called for the closing of
all American ports to Canadian shipping.  Both Senator Frye and Blaine
demanded some form of retaliation.  Sackville-West, sensing the potential
seriousness of the problem, informed the authorities in London that "if
Blaine takes the issue up for electioneering purposes the Senate will refuse to sanction any arrangement simply in order to keep up the irritation."[91]  Later he was certain that Blaine wanted "some foreign question
for a platform and latches at any straw that may be laboring about."[92]
At the same time Bayard felt that his worst fears had been realized and
the Republican Senators would milk the anti-British sentiment dry.

By late June all responsible officials on both sides of the Atlantic expressed similar fears concerning where the agitation would lead.
Phelps had indicated earlier that, if the people wanted a strong stand,
Cleveland should give it to them, since such action "would take the
wind out of Blaine's sails, would place the administration in a strong
attitude with the country, and would be likely effectual."[93]  But this
possibility also arose in British minds and they wanted "to settle a
question which might easily grow into menacing proportions,"[94] especially

---

[90] Public Opinion, I (1886), 106.

[91] Tansill, Foreign Policy of Bayard, 229.  West to Lansdowne,
June 5, 1886.

[92] Ibid., 231.  West to Lansdowne, June 25, 1886.

[93] Ibid., 229.  Bayard to Phelps, June 9, 1886.

[94] Ibid., 230.  Phelps to Bayard, June 15, 1886.

as Bayard continued to complain of additional seizures. Once the document reached the Senate and debate opened, the Canadians lost hope of a fair and peaceful solution since the "American government, right or wrong, dare not yield in the face of their fierce democracy."[95] Phelps had indicated that irresponsible seizures would only prevent the Cleveland administration from opening negotiations on the whole question. Cleveland even became alarmed by August when he informed Bayard that the English had to be informed

> that a persistence in the present course touching this is furnishing aid and comfort to an element in this country hostile to everything English and glad of any pretext to fan the flame of hatred and mischief; that while the conservative people are endeavoring to stem this tide it is undoubtedly unfortunate that any conduct of any English neighbor should furnish a stumbling block to their efforts.[96]

But it was too late. On August 24, 1886 Blaine opened the campaign, made the fishery question his central issue, and lead other Republicans along the same path.[97]

If this was "one of the most important matters that occupied public attention in the United States in the year 1886,"[98] it was not the only Anglo-American problem. As early as May 1886 Bayard indicated a concern for the Hawaiian Islands and especially Pearl Harbor. This same concern for the future of these islands prompted discussions

---

[95] Ibid., 237. Sir John MacDonald to Lansdowne, July 29, 1886.

[96] Ibid., 242. Cleveland to Bayard, August 15, 1886.

[97] See Chapter I, page 8.

[98] Annual Register, 1886, part II, 467.

n the Senate Foreign Relations Committee. When the London Times pub-
ished an article which intimated that Hawaii and England would sign a
eciprocity treaty in the near future, the concern increased rapidly. [99]
n the following year the rumor that England would loan Hawaii
2,000,000 increased Bayard's interest in British expansionist ten-
encies. At the same time Americans became aware of growing collabora-
ion between England and Germany over the disposition of the Samoan
slands. As late as January 1886 England and the United States had
ooperated to forestall a German take over of these islands, but, when
ne Washington Conference opened on June 25, 1886, it soon became ev-
ient that the Germans and British had already arrived at an understand-
ng. [100] In the face of such cooperation Bayard refused to come to any
ettlement; the conference adjourned, but was never recalled, and Bayard
ontinued to complain about German encroachments. Such complaints were
seless in view of the British position, however, and the question was
ettled only temporarily in 1888 and not permanently until ten years later.

While the relatively minor problems appeared another Canadian-
merican dispute arose in the same summer of 1886, the question of the
ar-seals. From the time of America's purchase of Alaska by the United
ates in 1867 the government had taken steps to prevent the indiscrim-
ate slaughter of the fur seals who inhabited the shores of the Bering
a. At first this problem of protection for the seals was merely one

---

[99] Tansill, Foreign Policy of Bayard, 379.

[100] Ryden, United States Relations to Samoa, 366.

of enforcement against Americans, a relatively easy problem, but in 1884 the problem widened to include citizens of other countries, primarily Canadians. In that year the Canadian Department of Marine and Fisheries published information concerning these seals which explained how they spent most of their life on the shores of Alaska, and the little-known fact that in the course of each year they swam across the Bering Sea. Canadians discovered that they could slaughter the seals and gain their valuable furs on the high seas beyond the reach of American authorities.[101] In 1886 seventeen Canadian vessels hunted the open seas for the seals who were working their way across the Bering Sea. The Revenue Department ordered the U.S.S. Corwin to seize these vessels and three of them were taken into American ports in the summer and early fall of 1886. The United States justified their capture on the high seas as the only way to prevent the eventual destruction of the whole colony of seals.[102] The British complained bitterly, but the President did not order the release of these vessels until February 1887.[103]

With the end of the fur-seal season tempers cooled on the point. Then the fisheries problem returned dramatically to center stage on November 26, 1886, when Queen Victoria assented to a Canadian bill which permitted the seizure of American vessels entering Canadian waters for any purpose not permitted by treaty.[104] Cleveland voiced his disappointment at this

---

[101] J. Bell, "The Bering Sea Question," National Review, XCIV (1891), 28.

[102] McInnis, Unguarded Frontier, 303.

[103] Bell, "The Bering Sea Question," 29.

[104] Charles C. Tansill, Canadian-American Relations (1943), 49.

action in his Second Annual Address, but "the seriousness and the conditions of the question demand that he continue to seek a permanent arrangement." [105]    On the same day he sent the documents on the question to
the House and the Senate, and again asked for a commission

> to take perpetuating proofs of the losses sustained
> during the past year by American fishermen owing to
> their unfriendly and unwarranted treatment by the
> local authorities. . . . I may have an occasion here-
> after to make further recommendations during the
> present session for such remedial legislation as may
> become necessary for the protection of the right of
> our citizens engaged in the open-sea fisheries in
> the north Atlantic waters.[106]

The Senate did not wait for the President's recommendations, for Senator Edmunds introduced a resolution which gave the President power to
exclude "Canadian vessels from American ports whenever he was satisfied
that American rights were being violated."[107]    When Congress passed it
on March 3, 1887, Canadians became concerned with the trend of events
and indicated a willingness to solve the problem.

Before Bayard could take advantage of this change of mind he had
to contend with the old fur seal dispute. A Federal District Judge's
pronouncement that the Bering Sea was a "mare clausum" reopened the
whole question. [108]    On August 19, 1887 Bayard asked Germany, Norway, Sweden,
Japan, Great Britain, France and Russia to enter into an international

---

[105] Messages, 5084.

[106] Ibid., 5114.

[107] Tansill, Foreign Policy of Bayard, 251.

[108] Bemis, Secretaries of State, VIII, 65.

agreement to close the sea and save the seal. England refused on the ground that Canada would not agree. But Bayard could not press for a settlement, since the fishery negotiations had borne fruit.

By May 1887 both the Canadians and Americans wanted a solution to the fishery question. After some preliminary negotiations both sides agreed that a special commission should negotiate a new treaty and by late September the arrangements were completed. The commissioners met in Washington in the middle of November and continued negotiations until the signing of the Bayard-Chamberlain Treaty on February 15, 1888.[109] On the next day Cleveland sent the treaty to Congress, but 1888 was an election year and the question of its acceptance or rejection became completely tied to the political struggle in which the Irish were to play a prominent role.

When the original negotiations which resulted in the calling of a commission to settle the fishery question began, Bayard asked that the commission handle questions other than the fishery dispute. One of these centered around the Alaskan-Canadian border. When the United States purchased Alaska, it was assumed that the old boundary which both Russia and England had accepted could be surveyed. Then in 1885 both countries learned to their surprise that this was a geographic impossibility.[110] During 1886 both sides worked to discover a solution but none could be found except to chart a new boundary. Bayard wanted the

---

[109] Callahan, Canadian-American Relations, 376.

[110] Tansill, Canadian-American Relations, 142.

boundary surveyed, but the Canadians would agree only to a preliminary study.[111] This caused Bayard to incorporate this question into the agenda for the commission which met in November 1887. Although conversations on the subject were held, no solution was found and, as a problem separating Americans and Englishmen, it continued down into the twentieth century.

From the above discussion a number of conclusions can be drawn. In the first place, although many problems existed for the two countries, not one touched the national interest of either country with the possible exception of the canal issue. But even on this point the United States was obviously not interested in making a real issue of it. Secondly, those responsible for the conduct of foreign affairs were actively engaged in limiting disagreements. This was so especially true in the case of Thomas F. Bayard.[112] Thirdly, the growth of anglophilia, which continued in the course of the decade in spite of the anglophobia, tended to lessen the seriousness of these disputes. Even the anglophobia lost its impact as the British came to realize that, when used by politicians, it was meant only for domestic political effect.[113] As a result it is safe to conclude that this period, although witnessing violent activity in Ireland, which tended to increase the politician's use of anglophobia in his appeal to the Irish, did not

---

[111] Ibid., 145.

[112] Tansill, Foreign Policy of Bayard, vii.

[113] Knaplund, "Letters to the Foreign Minister." Here one may find many references to this fact.

see a merging of Irish interests with American diplomatic interests. The atmosphere which appeared following the American Civil War did not reappear during these years. In other words, Irish interests may have coincided with those of politicians, but they did not with those of diplomats.

Chapter IV

Coercion and Diplomacy

In May 1880 James Russell Lowell arrived in London to assume
the duties of his new position as American Minister to the English
Court after a rather successful mission in Madrid. For the first six
months he concerned himself with numerous diplomatic questions while
eyeing the developments in the Anglo-Irish struggle with some misgivings. When that struggle reached alarming proportions in December
1880,[*] his interest must have quickened, since it became obvious that
the government would ask for coercion when Parliament met in January.

When the Liberals proposed an "Additional Powers" bill at the
opening session, Lowell felt compelled to send a report to Evarts.
In it he stressed their call for coercion and the possible trouble it
could create for the State Department.[1] Evarts replied that the
British should be told that

> the United States could only watch with attention and some
> degree of solicitude the successive phases of a question
> touching the welfare of a population with which our own
> people have so many and close ties of blood.[2]

---

[*] See pages 77-80.

[1] U.S.F.R., 1881, 492. Lowell to Evarts, January 7, 1881. He
probably refers to the problems shouldered by Charles F. Adams in
1867. In 1866 (see pages 7-9) Irish-Americans returned to Ireland to
participate in the planned revolt. The British arrested many of them,
but they immediately appealed to Adams and demanded this intercession
because they were American citizens.

[2] Ibid., 496. Evarts to Lowell, January 20, 1881.

Lowell obviously wrote for some form of instructions in case problems
should arise, but Evarts failed to provide these. By the time Blaine
had succeeded to the office the first case had arisen and Lowell was
forced to make his own policy.

Shortly after the passage of the Protection of Property Bill,
a coercion measure, Lowell received word through the American Consul
in Dublin that Michael Boyton, arrested under the new law which denied
the right of trial by jury, claimed American diplomatic intervention
in his case on the ground of American citizenship. The Minister told
the Consul to determine first the validity of the claim and then the
nature of the crime. At the same time he reported the case to Blaine
and outlined his policy of protecting Americans; "I shall by no means
try to screen any persons who are evidently guilty of offending against
the criminal laws of Great Britain."[3]

Before Blaine received this statement of what Lowell considered
correct policy the newspapers carried the story. Robert Thompson demanded American intervention, but he had little real hope that the
State Department would act, since "the friends of Ireland in America
would have to pressurize Mr. Blaine to reenforce the energies" of
Lowell.[4] Others demanded at least a trial and condemned the arrest
under an "ex post facto" law. Meanwhile, when the American Consul in
Dublin noticed certain discrepancies in Boyton's statements, Lowell

---

[3] Ibid., 511. Lowell to Blaine, March 12, 1881 (received on March
25).

[4] American, I (1881), 365.

began his own investigation.[5]  At first Boyton based his claim upon his

father's naturalization, but, when he was asked to supply these papers,

he shifted his claim to the fact that he had served in the Civil War.

Lowell soon discovered that he had served in the navy and, consequently,

since the special laws which granted citizenship for military service

during the war were limited to those who served in the army, Boyton

would have had to take out papers and lived in the United States for

one year in order to gain citizenship.  Neither condition could he

prove.[6]  Lowell concluded that he was not a citizen and withdrew from

the case.

By then Blaine had received Lowell's original policy statement

which he generally supported, but reminded the Minister not to fail

"to protect American citizens" while not harboring criminals.[7]  When

he learned that there was some question as to Boyton's citizenship, he

unofficially spoke to Thornton about the case.  At the time Edward Condon

was calling for direct American intervention, but Blaine "at first

laughed at the idea of any interference on his part."  Thornton feared

that the great pressure "being brought to bear upon him," nevertheless,

would force him "to make some representation."[8]  As of April 5, however,

---

[5] U.S.F.R., 517.  Lowell to Blaine, March 21, 1881 (received April 3).

[6] Ibid., 521.  Lowell to Blaine, March 25, 1881.

[7] Ibid., 523.  Blaine to Lowell, March 31, 1881.

[8] Knaplund, "Letters to the Foreign Minister," 25.  Thornton to Granville, April 5, 1881.

Blaine had not mentioned the matter in any official dispatch.  Then

he received definite proof that Boyton was not a citizen, yet the

Senate had entered the question when it requested the documents in the

case.[9]  Meanwhile, Thompson continued to argue that England should not

be permitted to imprison Americans without due process of law, that is,

at least trial by jury.[10]  As the pressure mounted, Blaine spoke to

Thornton and mentioned the abuse he was receiving from the "Irish and

other Democratic" papers.  Although he personally felt that Boyton got

what he desired and "a public report" would be made to that effect, he

asked Thornton if his government, "as a matter of comity, would be will-

ing to give Boyton his liberty, on condition that he would return to the

United States and not be found again in Great Britain."[11]  While Blaine

in effect asked the British to back down, Boyton asked Lowell to accept

his passport as proof of citizenship, but Lowell refused.[12]  The Minister

held true to his original and correct policy; the Secretary attempted to

find a way out from under the public pressure.  Blaine possibly hoped

that the British would have some favorable reply to this request since

---

[9] Congressional Record, 47 Congress, Special Session of the Senate, XII, 192, 212, 328, 263.  On April 5 Senator John R. McPherson, of New Jersey, introduced a petition on Boyton's behalf and on April 6 it was referred to the Committee on Foreign Relations.  On the 12th Senator Burnside asked for the papers and four days later additional petitions were presented.

[10] American, II (1881), 1.

[11] Knaplund, "Letters to the Foreign Minister," 129.  Thornton to Granville, April 19, 1881.

[12] U.S.F.R., 1881, 524.  Lowell to Blaine, April 7, 1884.

he did not send the papers on the case to the Senate until May 20 after they asked for the second time.[13] These conclusively proved that Boyton was not an American citizen, but Blaine in a later dispatch to Lowell implied that, if he had been, the United States would have demanded a trial.[14] The tone of this last note was far removed from that of March 31 in which he followed a policy closer to Lowell's ideas. This must have been the result of public pressure. Thompson even went so far as to argue that "Boyton was near enough to citizenship" to entitle him to a very vigorous intervention on grounds of international comity.[15]

Within a week of his report to the Senate Blaine received an opportunity to apply this new policy. On May 27 he asked Lowell to inquire concerning the arrest of Joseph D'Alton who had proof of his American citizenship. A few days later Representative Samuel J. Randall informed Blaine that the British had arrested Joseph B. Walsh, another proven citizen. Blaine told Lowell to explain to the British that he realized their position in Ireland and the need for coercion laws, but that the United States "can not view with unconcern the application of the summary proceedings attendant upon the execution of these measures to naturalized citizens of the United States."[16] Although he did not want to defend Americans against violations of British law, he did want

---

[13] Messages, 4602.

[14] U.S.F.R., 1881, 530.  Blaine to Lowell, May 26, 1881.

[15] American, II (1881), 113.

[16] U.S.F.R., 1881, 532.  Blaine to Lowell, June 2, 1881.

those arrested to be informed of the crime committed and given a speedy trial.

Blaine must have sent a telegram to Lowell which contained the basic facts of this long dispatch, for on the very next day Lowell spoke to Lord Granville about the Walsh case. Granville recognized the concern of the United States, but he could not see how Blaine could possibly demand better treatment for Americans than that given to British subjects. Furthermore, he told Lowell that Walsh had lived as a liquor dealer at Castlebar, Mayo for some time and had indicated a desire to remain in Ireland as a British subject. When Lowell passed this information to Blaine, he added,

> I have reason to know that naturalized American citizens, trusting in their supposed immunity as such, have used language in public of extreme violence.[17]

Many of these Irish-Americans actually went to Ireland for the sole hope of preparing for a future revolution.[18] Boyton himself worked as a Land League organizer and at the same time of his arrest "was developing a more active policy."[19] Even Major Le Caron, the famous British spy in the Clan-Na-Gael, visited Boyton in his Dublin prison, a sign of his connection with the Clan. But these facts did not save the administration from attacks for its failure to pressure the British on Boyton's behalf and, consequently, for its abandonment of "an American

---

[17] Ibid.,533. Lowell to Blaine, June 4, 1881 (received June 16).

[18] O'Brien, Post Bag, I, II. In numerous letters statements appear to the effect that the Clan was preparing for a revolution.

[19] Le Caron, Twenty Five Years, 156.

sailor in an English prison, charged with nothing but a political of-
fence, for which he can get no trial."[20]

While Blaine tended to emphasize America's right to intervene in
cases of proven American citizenship Lowell indicated a more conciliatory policy. On June 8 he sent an official letter to the Foreign Minister on the Walsh case stating that the President did not want to
embarrass the British on delicate domestic questions, but, since Walsh
did have proof of his citizenship, the President had to act.[21] Two
days later in a letter requesting information on Daniel McSweeney, an
American citizen who had denied any role in inciting the populace,
Lowell again emphasized the fact that the United States did not wish
to embarrass Great Britain, but at the same time was anxious not to ignore just claims of American citizens for protection.[22] When Granville
answered this note, he gave Lowell the information on Walsh and stated
that McSweeney's case was then under consideration. At the time he took
the opportunity of assuring Lowell of Great Britain's appreciation of
the friendly attitude of the President and expressed the hope that this
friendly attitude would save him the trouble of explaining why England

---

[20] American, II (1881), 163. The question of public reaction has
been the subject of some discussion, that is, just how much information
reached the public press. Joseph B. Lockey stated that "So quietly had
the negotiations been conducted the public remained in ignorance of the
matter until Blaine had left the State Department." See "James G.
Blaine," The American Secretaries of State and Their Diplomacy, ed.
Samuel Flagg Bemis (1927), vol. VII, 290. This seems to be incorrect
in view of what Thompson published.

[21] B.F.S.P., LXXIII, 1223. Lowell to Granville, June 8, 1881.

[22] Ibid., 1224. Lowell to Granville, June 10, 1881.

could not accept any distinction between the liability of foreign and British subjects to obey the law.[23]

Next Granville decided to inform Thornton of Lowell's instructions. He indicated his surprise that Blaine would interfere, since both countries had arrived at an understanding in such cases during the American Civil War.[24] In a later dispatch he clearly explained the British position and instructed Thornton to inform official Washington that Gladstone refused to recognize any distinction between British subjects and foreign citizens in regard to crimes committed in Ireland. Granville explained that during the American Civil War, both countries agreed with respect to the suspension of habeas corpus that, assuming it was legally authorized, no complaint could be made if under its principles and subjects of foreign states received the same treatment as natives. This was based upon the right of every state to subject foreigners to laws passed for the maintenance of order and this included exceptional laws as well as ordinary ones. "Great Britain," he concluded "can not permit Irish-Americans to commit crimes which the act was passed to suppress."[25]

Granville wanted Thornton to pass this information to Blaine and others in an unofficial capacity. This was why four days after writing to Thornton he informed Lowell that he hoped he would not have to make his reasons a matter of record. Thus, when Blaine sent Lowell a second

---

[23] U.S.F.R., 1881, 542. Granville to Lowell, June 28, 1881.

[24] B.F.S.P., LXXIII, 1223. Granville to Thornton, June 19, 1881.

[25] Ibid., 1224. Granville to Thornton, June 24, 1881.

letter on Walsh, requesting more information,[26] Granville refused with

a statement that the British recognized no distinctions between foreigners

and British subjects.[27] This insistence on avoiding even a discussion of

the matter in official documents led Lowell to believe that a change in

tactics would help. He suggested that the United States should base its

case of Walsh on the ground that he was mistreated, and not on points

of law.[28] Even Lowell at this point sought a way out of a delicate sit-

uation.

The conviction that the British would not accept any legal argu-

ment remained with Lowell during August. The British had an air-

tight case, especially since both countries had solved the whole prob-

lem after a great deal of discussion in 1867 when Irish-American citizens

were arrested under a similar law. Such thinking caused Lowell to refuse

to help another American of Irish birth, John McEnery, since he believed

he could intervene "only when the individual has taken no part in

political activities."[29]

By late August the Walsh case reappeared when Lowell learned that

Walsh was critically ill, near death, and desirous of a medical examina-

tion to determine if he could remain in prison. Lowell, seeing a

possible approach that would save Blaine some embarrassment, informed

---

[26] U.S.F.R., 1881, 543. Lowell to Granville, July 1, 1881.

[27] B.F.S.P., LXXIII, 1228. Granville to Lowell, July 8, 1881.

[28] U.S.F.R., 1881, 540. Lowell to Blaine, July 15, 1881.

[29] Ibid., 545. Lowell to Blaine, August 11, 1881.

Granville that many well-known citizens of Pennsylvania had vouched for

Walsh's character and that they sought his release on the ground of

poor health.[30] Lowell also sent newspaper articles to Granville on

the case at the Foreign Minister's own request. This information ac-

cording to one author caused the British to release Walsh on October 21.[31]

The implication is that once Granville learned the reaction of Americans,

he freed Walsh, but this is hard to reconcile with the fact that the

British Minister in Washington kept Granville well informed on domestic

American developments. Walsh must have received his freedom for reasons

other than American pressure. The fact that he was sick and in this

condition could do no harm to Ireland, especially since Forster had

arrested Parnell and suppressed the Land League just prior to Walsh's

release, must have helped the British make their decision. In addition,

Granville did not want Walsh to die in prison and his condition created

this possibility.[32] Basically conditions in Ireland and British con-

siderations led to Walsh's release. Pressure from America possibly

served as one factor, but it did not cause the release.

Just as one case ended another arose. Patrick O'Connor of Baltimore

had approached Blaine in early December in an effort to gain State De-

partment intervention on behalf of his brother, Dennis, who was arrested

in Ireland on mere suspicion of being sympathetic with the aims of the

---

[30] B.F.S.P., LXIII, 1228. Lowell to Granville, September 1, 1881.

[31] Muzzey, Blaine, 202.

[32] B.F.S.P., LXXIII, 1229. Granville to Hoppin, November 11, 1881.

Land League.[33] When Lowell brought this case to Granville's attention, the Foreign Minister ordered an investigation which proved that O'Connor had been arrested on the ground of inciting and intimidating the peasants not to pay their rent. The arrest occurred on October 22, only a few days after Parnell had issued the "no-rent manifesto," and, consequently, it would seem logical to believe that O'Connor would commit such acts, especially since the Land League was unable to function. The British had a tight case as far as they were concerned, but Granville indicated a conciliatory attitude when he implied that O'Connor possibly would be freed on the one condition that his release would cause no "danger to the peace of the district."[34] This small ray of hope vanished within two weeks when Forster refused to order O'Connor's release, since to do so "would jeopardize the peace of Ireland."[35]

While these views were exchanged, Congress reconvened and Freling-huysen became Secretary of State. It was not long before both became involved in the whole question. In early January the editor of the Catholic Herald of Lawrence, Massachusetts, asked the new Secretary to look into the arrest of Michael Hart.[36] By publishing some letters he had received from Hart the editor aroused a great deal of interest among

---

[33] Ibid., 1229. Lowell to Granville, December 23, 1881.

[34] Ibid., 1230. Granville to Lowell, January 26, 1881.

[35] Ibid., 1230. Granville to Lowell, February 2, 1881.

[36] Congressional Record, 47 Congress, 1st Session, XIII, part 1, 764. The resolution was first reported by Representative Orth on January 23 and debated until January 31. Orth injected the party issue into the question on January 31. See pages 762-764.

the many Irish-Americans who lived in Lawrence. Meanwhile, some

congressmen also became interested. On January 31 the House passed a

resolution asking for the papers on the whole case. Sir Lionel Sack-

ville-West, the replacement for Minister Thornton, saw its passage "as

showing the importance attached to conciliating the Irish vote."[37] Two

weeks later Representative Robinson from Brooklyn introduced a rather

interesting resolution in the House which asked for an opinion by the

Attorney-General.

> If Joseph Warren Keifer, Speaker of this House, or
> Alonzo Cornell, Governor of the State of New York,
> or Charles B. Cornell, a laborer in the Department
> of Public Works in the City of New York, being a
> citizen of the United States, visit any part of the
> British Empire and should they be arrested without
> having committed any crime and without any charge
> of crime being alleged against him, could the Eng-
> lish government, by suspending the habeas corpus,
> or otherwise, lawfully detain him indefinitely on
> suspicion without trial or without any right in our
> government to demand his release.[38]

This resolution was sent to the Committee on Foreign Affairs, but, when

reported from Committee, the House voted to table it. It is interest-

ing, however, to note that 102 members voted against that motion.

While the House debated the issue, both Davis and West were inform-

ing their respective representatives in London of these developments.

Davis told Lowell of the January 31, 1882 resolution,[39] while West in

an effort to keep Granville informed sent newspaper clippings of the

---

[37] U.S.F.R., 1881, 250. West to Granville, February 1, 1882.

[38] Congressional Record, 47 Congress, 1st Session, XIII, part 1, 929.

[39] U.S.F.R., 1882, 198. Davis to Lowell, February 10, 1882.

reaction to the House Activities. One such clipping from the Baltimore American carried a story on O'Connor which identified him as the Treasurer of an Irish Land League unit.[40]

February rolled on and the question continued to occupy the attention of the House. Representative Campbell P. Berry asked the State Department to investigate McSweeney's case after the San Francisco Examiner published a number of his letters.[41] In early March Representative Abram S. Hewitt in the middle of the debate on the appropriations bill for the diplomatic corps raised the whole question of which party protected American citizens better, the Democrats or the Republicans.[42] For four days the question continued to dominate the debate as numerous representatives indicated a desire to appear as friends of the Irish.[43]

In the midst of this verbal battle Frelinghuysen rushed a series of telegrams to Lowell, reminding him of the actions in the House and urging him to use all "diligence, especially with McSweeney and Hart," to gain their release.[44] On the fourth of March he sent another telegram urging Lowell to seek prompt trials for O'Connor, Hart, McSweeney, Walsh, McEnery, and D'Alton "without discussing the applicability of the existing coercion statute to citizens of the United States."[45] It

---

[40] Ibid., 251. Consul Domahue to West, February 17, 1882.

[41] Ibid., 196. Davis to Lowell, February 1C, 1882.

[42] Congressional Record, 47 Congress, 1st Session, XIII, part II,1556.

[43] Ibid., 1611-1617. This was especially true on the Saturday session of March 4, 1882.

[44] U.S.F.R., 1882, 200. Frelinghuysen to Lowell, March 3, 1882.

[45] Ibid., Frelinghuysen to Lowell, March 4, 1882.

seems as if Lowell failed to grasp the urgency of these pleas, for in answering the first telegram he reminded Frelinghuysen that McSweeney and Hart were "no more innocent than the majority of those under arrest."[46] When the second telegram arrived, he waited two days to inform Granville that "the President hopes that the Lord Lieutenant will order early trials for cases in which Americans may be arrested."[47] Where Frelinghuysen said "prompt," Lowell said early. In the absence of any favorable news by the middle of March Frelinghuysen again telegraphed Lowell that "the President though desirous of not seeming unreasonable would be relieved if, without having to wait for general action regarding coercion act cases, he could inform Congress that this request regarding the Americans has been complied with."[48] The heat of congressional debate somehow filtered into the State Department.

The fact that the Republican administration was responding to congressional action only increased that activity. On March 9 the Senate requested the papers on McSweeney,[49] while Senator Nathaniel P. Hill of Colorado requested Frelinghuysen to investigate the arrest of James L. White.[50] On March 20 the President sent the papers on McSweeney

---

[46] Ibid., Lowell to Frelinghuysen, March 6, 1882.

[47] B.F.S.P., LXIII, 1232. Lowell to Granville, March 6, 1882.

[48] U.S.F.R., 1881, 227. Frelinghuysen to Lowell, March 16, 1882.

[49] Congressional Record, 47 Congress, 1st Session, XIII, part II, 1734. Senator James T. Farley introduced a petition concerning McSweeney and the resolution.

[50] U.S.F.R., 1881, 227. Frelinghuysen to Lowell, March 17, 1882.

to the Senate,[51] only days before an outcry for Lowell's recall arose
in the House.  Robinson of New York again led the fight with such words
that English visitors later testified their "blood boiled."[52]  West
immediately reported the incident to Granville, but felt that it would
have no real effect on Lowell's remaining in London.[53]

At this time Irish-Americans worked to arouse public support.
Mayor Grace of New York, Charles C. Dana, Patrick Ford and others pub-
lished a call for a mass meeting to protest the administration's handling
of the whole question.  On the evening of April 3 a large gathering at
Cooper Hall cheered the speakers as Senator Charles Jones, Samuel
Randall, and S. S. Cox shared the stage with other prominent New
Yorkers.[54]  Still feeling the pangs of Americanization, the New York
Irish-American declared that the actions of Lowell and Blaine implied
that "we can never become genuine American citizens."[55]  But such protests were played down by the Arthur administration as merely Democratic
outcries against the Republican party.[56]

In the middle of this congressional activity and the public agitation the administration worked feverishly for some kind of settlement.

---

[51] Messages, 4674.

[52] Eckmann, "British Travelers," 135.

[53] Knaplund, "Letters to the Foreign Minister," 165.  West to
Granville, March 21, 1882.

[54] Gibson, The New York Irish, 348.

[55] April 1, 1882.  This is a most interesting comment in view of
what was discussed in the Introduction.

[56] Knaplund, "Letters to the Foreign Minister," 166.  West to
Granville, April 4, 1882.

On March 25 Frelinghuysen tried to bargain with the British when he
offered information and a speedy trial for William Lane, a British citizen arrested in Detroit.[57] Two days later in another telegram he ordered Lowell to inquire concerning the arrest of James L. White. Senator
Hill had said that if the arrest was a mistake, he wanted White released; if not, he wanted a speedy trial.[58] Meanwhile, Lowell spoke to
Granville about the President's earlier request for speedy trials for
all those arrested, but the Foreign Minister said it was under consideration.

As Lowell reported this fact to Washington Granville was composing
a long note to West, and, for the first time, implied that the British
might authorize the release of the prisoners on the condition that they
leave the country.[59] He based this expectation upon the fact that the
coercive acts were designed to prevent crime, not to punish it. Thus,
anyone arrested could be freed upon reasonable proof that their release
would not disturb the peace of the country. He added, however, that,
if the United States agreed, the settlement would have to be final, and
West impressed this upon Frelinghuysen.[60] In other words, it would serve
as the solution to all future disputes on this point.

In effect, by authorizing West to discuss this idea unofficially

[57] U.S.F.R., 1882, 228. Frelinghuysen to Lowell, March 25, 1882
(telegram).

[58] B.F.S.P., LXXIII, 1232. Lowell to Granville, March 28, 1882.

[59] Ibid., 1233. Granville to West, March 31, 1882.

[60] Knaplund, "Letters to the Foreign Minister," 166. West to
Granville, April 4, 1882.

with Frelinghuysen, Granville was bypassing Lowell. He could have taken this step for many reasons, maybe because he felt Lowell had not communicated the true tone of the American position. At least this was the impression that West had received from Bancroft Davis on March 29. The Assistant Secretary felt that Lowell had not impressed the British with the unique situation in the United States and had given the British the mistaken notion that they could treat the dispatches on the "suspects" as "American 'bluster.'" Consequently, Davis tried to impress upon West the position in which Congress could put the President and the peculiar circumstances which prompted such congressional action.[61] Lowell himself later implied that he had not been as forceful in his presentations to the British as he could have been.[62] This failure did not prevent the presentation of additional requests for speedy trials, however.[63]

The result of all this agitation and sending of telegrams came on April 6 when Granville officially replied to Arthur's request for speedy trials. He first refused to make any distinction between foreigners and British citizens in the operation of the law. He further remarked that, since the coercion law suspended the right of trial by jury, the Lord Lieutenant of Ireland had no authority to order speedy trials for those who claimed American citizenship. In conclusion he argued that

---

[61] Ibid.

[62] Charles E. Morton, ed., Letters of James Russell Lowell, 2 Vols. (1894), I, 272, to C. E. Morton, April 22, 1883; 293, to O. W. Holmes, December 28, 1884.

[63] B.F.S.P., LXXIII, 1234. Lowell to Granville, April 3, 1882.

It is impossible either for Her Majesty's government
or for the government of the United States to be ignorant that the present disorders in Ireland have been
and are still, to a great extent fomented by Irish em-
igrants in the United States and by subscriptions of
money and publications hostile to British rule proceed-
ing from that source. As you are aware, Her Majesty's
government found it necessary last year to address a
friendly representation on this subject to the government
of the United States, and Her Majesty's government cannot
doubt that the President and his ministers must be
desirous of discouraging all such proceedings to the
best of their power. Under such circumstances it is
obvious that the efforts of Her Majesty's government
of the British Parliament for the vindication of law
and the restoration of order in Ireland would be liable
to be frustrated, if aliens in Ireland were in any respect treated as exempt from the operation of laws which
Parliament has found it necessary to enact for that purpose.[64]

He then played his ace; he offered to free the Irish-Americans, if they

agreed to leave the country. After stating their original position and

in theory holding to it, the British were willing to give to the United

States the practical satisfaction of seeing the prisoners freed. This

would permit the President to pacify Congress.

Some would hold that Irish-American pressure, as applied to Congress

and the State Department, caused the British to change their attitude,

but to attribute this exclusively to the influence of Irish-Americans

would fail to take into consideration native American attitudes. In

all probability the State Department would have intervened even if

those arrested had not been Irish-Americans, since, as the Nation said,

"we can not admit of imprisonment for long periods without a trial."[65]

---

[64] U.S.F.R., 1882, 317. Granville to West, April 6, 1882.

[65] March 31, 1882.

But the British could not possibly have given the American citizens

trials and still maintained control of the country. As has already been

indicated, even with such laws Forster could not maintain law and order

in April 1882. Thus, the very extreme situation in Ireland caused the

British to pass an act which permitted imprisonment of American citizens

without right of trial by jury. This action generated genuine American

support for State Department intervention on behalf of those arrested.

Consequently, the credit for forcing the British into offering those

arrested their freedom must go to native Americans as well as Irish-

Americans.[66]

Those who would say that conditions in Ireland caused this change in

the British position would possibly attack this view. They would argue

that agitation in Ireland over the land issue was waning at this time,

but this is not correct. Ireland remained in a state of constant terror

at least until after the Kilmainham Pact, which was arranged one month

after the British offer. In fact, that offer was sent four days before

the Kilmainham negotiations commenced, and Granville had already informed

West of the proposal a week before the note was sent. The one condition

of the proposal in effect confirms the fact that Ireland was in a state

of turmoil since Forster felt that, if they were released without that

condition, they would only jeopardize the peace of the land. If con-

ditions in Ireland did not produce the change, American pressure is

---

[66] Gwynn, Letters of Spring Rice, I, 62, 63. The author of these
letters often mentions the problem of American sympathy with the Irish
cause.

the only explanation.

Unfortunately for the Republican administration, this British offer was sent two days after Arthur delivered the papers on the case to the House.[67] On the day before Senator John T. Morgan of Alabama, a member of the Senate's Foreign Relations Committee, introduced a bill that defined the rights of Americans while resident in foreign countries.[68] Although the Senate thus entered the dispute, the real debate occurred in the House. It centered around Lowell's March 14, 1882 report to Washington, in which he attempted to place the entire question in proper perspective. In that report he clearly stated that he would help only those who deserved it and would not permit the use of American citizenship as a shield for crime. The Nation enthusiastically supported Lowell's policy as the most realistic possible, but many congressmen bitterly condemned it.[69] Sackville-West saw the congressional agitation as a sign of how Congress was "tyrannized by the Irish vote."[70] Certain congressmen were driven "by the influence which the Irish vote exercises to hold language which in reality they are far from subscribing to."[71]

---

[67] Messages, 4678.

[68] Congressional Record, 47 Congress, 1st Session, XIII, part 3, 2512; U.S.F.R., 1881, 261. West to Granville, April 4, 1882. The bill demanded the right of a speedy trial by jury. Senator Voorhees even entered a resolution that the conduct of the State Department on the Irish cases was illegal.

[69] Nation, XXXIV (1882), 308.

[70] Knaplund, "Letters to the Foreign Minister," 166. West to Granville, April 4, 1882.

[71] Ibid., 167. West to Granville, April 18, 1882.

In the same letter he told Granville that the Democrats used the Irish case as a pretext "for a violent attack . . . on the foreign policy of President Arthur, and his present cabinet. . . ." so as to destroy Arthur in the public mind. As a result "Lowell is made the scapegoat." By then rumors had appeared that Lowell would be replaced.[72] In fact, on April 25 Representative Robinson demanded just that and further argued "the United States should go to war if necessary to save the prisoners."[73] The Chairman of the Foreign Affairs Committee bitterly disagreed with Robinson, arguing that American citizenship should be a shield, not a sword, and accused Robinson of being "more solicitous about the Irish in Brooklyn than the Irish in Ireland."

Five days before this exchange of views the House had passed a resolution asking for additional papers and on the day of the exchange, May 22, Frelinghuysen sent his reply to the British note of April 6. The circumstances surrounding the writing of this particular reply had a decided effect upon its composition. Frelinghuysen and Arthur knew that it would be sent to the House and this knowledge must have caused them to compose a strong answer. Frelinghuysen informed Lowell that Arthur refused to accept the British position that there could be no distinction in the enforcement of laws in favor of foreigners. The President further felt that he had a right and a duty to inquire concerning arrested

---

[72] Ibid., 166. West to Granville, April 4, 1882. West first mentioned this possibility here.

[73] Congressional Record, 47th Congress, 1st Session, XIII, part 4, 3275-3286. The exchange was long and bitter.

American citizens and although Ireland was in a state of chaos this did
not justify the arrest of Americans without a trial or cause. Consequently, Frelinghuysen demanded that McSweeney be given the opportunity to return to the United States and that McEnery should be told why he was held
and when he would receive a speedy trial. Finally, he raised the case of
Henry O'Mahoney, who although not an American citizen, should get the
same measure of protection as that given to citizens of England.[74]
Thus, the conciliatory note of April 6, in which the British offered to
free the "suspects" on only one condition, prompted a series of demands
in return, one of which tried to tell the British how to treat those who
were not even American citizens. The only possible explanation for this
is the fact that Arthur and Frelinghuysen knew that eventually congressional eyes would read it. This in turn gives insight into the
impact and extent of congressional debate.

Oddly enough the British and Lowell had already taken steps to end
the whole dispute. On April 19 Lowell learned that the British had given
James White his freedom without condition.[75] Unfortunately, Frelinghuysen did not know this until May 3, two weeks after he sent his strong
note. At the same time, on the basis of Granville's offer to free all
the suspects, Lowell spoke to Forster to reassure himself that the offer
was correctly relayed. After getting the assurance he communicated the
terms to the prisoners, but they refused to accept them.[76] A few days

---

[74] U.S.F.R., 1882, 230. Frelinghuysen to Lowell, April 25, 1882.

[75] Ibid., 229. Lowell to Frelinghuysen, April 21, 1882.

[76] Ibid., 230. Lowell to Frelinghuysen, May 3, 1882.

later Lowell discussed the problem with Justin McCarthy, a member of Parnell's Home Rule party, and, when he mentioned the prisoners' refusal to accept their freedom on the one condition, McCarthy showed no real surprise, since in his words "they are there to make trouble."[77]  While Lowell worked to solve the problem, he failed to realize that the Irish did not want it solved.  When he discovered this, it must have increased his bitterness toward the Irish-Americans which had appeared in the previous month.  The editor of the Atlantic Monthly, T.B. Aldrich, had asked him to write an article for publication in his magazine, but Lowell refused because he was too busy.  In his reply he did state that he would be happy to do so, but "you must wait till I come home to be boycotted in my birthplace by my Irish fellow citizens (who are kind enough to teach me how to be an American) who fought all our battles and got up all our draft riots."[78]

Meanwhile, other problems continued to harass Anglo-American relations in the spring of 1882, in particular the question of Blaine's policy in Latin America, which occupied a great deal of the attention of the House Committee on Foreign Affairs.  During one of the lulls in the many congressional debates West spoke to Bancroft Davis who informed West that the President regretted interfering in certain diplomatic cases, but Congress forced him into acting.  When West relayed this message to Granville, he added his own observation, "it is always

---

[77] Morton, Letters of Lowell, I, 293, to O.W. Holmes, December 28, 1884.
[78] Ibid., II, 267, to T.B. Aldrich, May 8, 1882.

expected that we must understand that no offense is meant and that
such proceedings result from a peculiar political organization."[79]
In all probability these remarks included the Panama Canal issue
(Frelinghuysen sent that note on May 8) and the Irish "suspects," as
the case was known in the Halls of Congress.

All this activity resulted in a growing demand for Lowell's recall.
In early May the New York Herald raised the issue and justified it
with the statement that Lowell had lost the confidence of Irish-Americans.[80]  Needless to say the Irish papers raised the cry as often
as possible,[81] but here again there were purely American overtones to
the case.  The Nation defended Lowell by arguing that a diplomatic re-
resentative should try to serve the interests of the whole nation and
not those of only one segment.[82]  The New York Herald published a story
that Representative Orth, the Chairman of the House Committee of Foreign
Affairs, was being considered as Lowell's replacement.[83]  This indicated
that the whole campaign to have Lowell recalled may have been caused by
a desire to place a western politician in the London post.  Even the
violent protectionist, anti-English, pro-Irish Robert Thompson condemned

---

[79] Knaplund, "Letters to the Foreign Minister," 168.  West to Granville, May 1, 1882.

[80] Gibson, The New York Irish, 362.

[81] New York Irish-American, May 28, 1882; New York Irish World,
June 1, 1882.

[82] Nation, XXXIV (1882), 439.

[83] Gibson, The New York Irish, 365.

this.[84] Whatever the underlying motives may have been the issue did give Robinson an opportunity to gain additional publicity and to prove to his constituents his hatred for England. At one time he even accused President Arthur of "getting on his knee before Lord Granville, who refused to listen to the prayer, not the demand, of the President."[85] At another he accused some congressmen of sending messages to the British, advising them not to pay attention to the action of the House, since the Representatives did what they did only to curry favor with the Irish vote.

By the end of June the whole question began to lose its significance, at least for the English. The effects of the Kilmainham Pact began to reduce the peasants' agitation considerably, while Gladstone gave the peasants exactly what they needed. The political prisoners were slowly released from jail and on July 10 Lowell reported that only four of the original group remained behind locked doors.[86] However, the British passed a new coercion law on July 8 and Lowell decided to ask for instructions on future problems that might arise as a result of this law.[87]

The decline of agitation in Ireland did not cause a similar decline in the number of debates on the question in the House. In late July Congress again asked for additional information on the subject. On August 3, 1882 Frelinghuysen telegraphed Lowell and asked that the

---

[84] American, IV (1882), 113.

[85] Congressional Record, 47th Congress, 1st Session, XIII, part 5, 5451.

[86] U.S.F.R., 1881, 284. Lowell to Frelinghuysen, July 10, 1882.

[87] Ibid., 285. Lowell to Frelinghuysen, July 10, 1882.

remaining prisoners be released.[88]  Two days later he sent additional

papers to the House, while Lowell conferred with British officials.[89]

On August 8 Lowell reported that three of the four were offered their

freedom on the condition that they leave the country and that the other

one had already received his unconditional release.[90]  By then Congress

had adjourned but Lowell continued to send information.  In a series

of telegrams he informed Frelinghuysen that the remainder were freed

unconditionally, the last leaving prison on September 19.[91]  In late

September the matter came to an end.

Some would of course have us believe that the British finally

capitulated to the pressure of American politics, but upon a closer

examination of the sources it becomes evident that conditions in Ire-

land permitted the English to release the prisoners without demanding

that they leave the country.  By August it was evident that Ireland

under Parnell's strong will would move away from peasant agitation.

Once this underpinning disappeared, the radical Irish-Americans lost

their ability to arouse the masses, and, once this occurred, the British

could afford to release the "suspects," since their release would not

jeopardize the peace of the country.

Just when it seemed that the whole question would die a natural

death two additional cases arose which caused American officials to

---

[88] Ibid., 286.  Frelinghuysen to Lowell, August 3, 1882.

[89] Messages, 4699.

[90] U.S.R.F., 1882, 286.  Lowell to Frelinghuysen, August 8, 1882.

[91] Ibid., 300.  Hoppin to Frelinghuysen, October 3, 1882.

protest in strong terms. On August 16 Lowell received word that the
British had arrested Stephen J. Meany of New York, who at the time of
his arrest was a correspondent for the New York Star.[92] Two days later
he learned that Henry George, the advocate of the single-tax concept,
was also arrested.[93] These events caused Frelinghuysen to raise the
whole question of another Cabinet meeting and the President authorized
him to explain in detail his thoughts on the subject to the British
government. Arthur feared what effect "the new act would have upon
the business and social relations of American citizens, particularly
those of Irish birth," and he could not contemplate

> the enforcement of this measure on mere suspicion against
> American citizens without fear of its having an unhappy
> influence upon the good feeling which exists between two
> great nations of common origin and common language.
> I need scarcely add that this government has no
> sympathy with the motive or methods of the class of in-
> discreet individuals, insignificant, in number, in this
> country whose ill-directed zeal can neither serve the
> cause of Ireland nor reflect credit on the country of
> their adoption. The law abiding and peaceful American
> citizens of Irish birth should not be exposed to suf-
> fer on their account.[94]

In effect this dispatch served as a warning that the United States would
take a dim view of any arrests of American citizens on mere suspicion.
Before Lowell could communicate the message Henry George had been arrested for the second time, after the British had apologized to him
for the first arrest. Arthur felt that the second arrest indicated an
attempt by the British to harass George which could not be justified on

---

[92] Ibid., 287. Davis to Lowell, August 11, 1882.

[93] Ibid., 295. Davis to Lowell, August 18, 1882.

[94] Ibid., 293. Frelinghuysen to Lowell, September 22, 1882.

the basis of his questionable character. He did not want to believe the rumors that the British in Ireland constantly exhibited a strong prejudice against American citizens, but the case of George would tend to support such rumors.[95] Meanwhile, the British explained their position to Lowell. Stephen Meany would remain in jail, since he was a well-known radical, but they apologized for the arrest of George. They did ask that the American government take into consideration the conditions in Ireland while considering the case, and that it would not happen again.[96] By October Parnell had Ireland well under control and the case finally died.

The significance of the whole dispute revolves around the ability of the Irish to pressure Congress and the State Department. The question itself was integrated into the congressional campaign of 1882, and, when Congress returned in December, Arthur virtually claimed that his protests had forced the British to respect our rights by the release of those arrested.[97] Some Americans felt that the Irish had abused their rights of citizens in this case since "recent events in Ireland, and in this country also, very forcibly present the fact that American citizenship may be made use of for purposes widely at variance with those for which it is conferred upon aliens."[98] The fact that the Irish in America were able to pressure Congressmen and the State Department

---

[95] Ibid., 296. Frelinghuysen to Lowell, October 3, 1882.

[96] Ibid., 295. Hoppin to Frelinghuysen, September 29, 1882.

[97] Messages, 4713.

[98] Creighton, "Influence of Foreign Issues," 184.

.nto intervening in a domestic English issue (to some a misuse of cit-
zenship) does not alter the fact that in the final analysis they were
nable to influence the basic course of Anglo-American relations toward
he maintenance of at least an officially correct position. Their
ailure was due primarily to the fact that neither English nor Amer-
can diplomats wanted them to jeopardize those relations. Lowell him-
elf recognized the possibility that the "Irish subjects" coupled to the
ther more fundamental Anglo-American disputes of the spring of 1882
ould have led to some serious trouble, as he later told a friend, "a
ear ago it would have been easy for the wrong man to have made trouble
etween the two countries."[99]  Yet those in responsible positions did
ot really want trouble. Consequently, the Irish failed in their ef-
orts to use the "Irish subjects" case as a tool to generate bitter
eeling between the two countries.

[99] Norton, Lowell's Letters, 273, to C. E. Norton, April 22, 1883.
e could have possibly meant Blaine here. See page 287.

Chapter V

The "Physical Force" Men and Diplomacy

If Irish-Americans who traveled to Ireland gained the attention
of American legislators in the early eighties, their fellow countrymen
who remained behind in the quiet security of America attracted the attention of British officials. This latter group, the advocates of extreme violence as the means by which Ireland could gain her freedom,
troubled the British, because in the security of America they were
capable of planning anything from simple terrorist attacks, which
often endangered and on occasion took innocent lives, to outright guerrilla war against England. In such a situation the British desired the
active aid of the American government in the suppression of such activities, and, if this proved impossible, at least the prevention of actual
expeditions from America.

The extent to which Irish-Americans of this cast would go in order
to hurt England especially caused concern in official circles. For instance, in early January 1881 news of the Boer resistance to British
pressure in South Africa and the sympathy of Dutch citizens for that
cause prompted the Fenians (a name used by English officials to describe
all Irish nationalists) to offer a shipment of arms for the Boers, if
Holland officially supported their drive for independence. They believed
that this would help to tie down British forces that were urgently
needed in Ireland, then in the midst of the wild winter of 1880-1881.[1]

---

[1] Knaplund, "Letters to the Foreign Minister," 112. Thornton to
Granville, January 11, 1881.

The offer was made to the Dutch Minister in Washington, who promptly informed his British colleague.

If the Irish nationalists' tendency toward extremes troubled the British, their somewhat mistaken belief that the radical Irish in America formed a solid unified force only increased this fear. To an extent the British were correct, but the Irish were unified only as to aims. For instance, all Irish-Americans wanted Ireland freed, but only a few wanted to accomplish this by revolution, and even these tended to divide into three groups; those who only talked, those who mostly talked, and those who said nothing, in public that is. The first group would include Patrick Ford who continuously campaigned for terrorist attacks in the columns of his Irish World, but who never organized a specific act of terrorism. Ford did serve as an organizer and a director of the "Skirmishing Fund," which he collected through the use of his paper for the express purpose of attacking England, but he did not plan any such attacks.[2] His role was that of the propagandist. The second group included such men as O'Donovan Rossa, who used his United Irishman to urge upon Irish-Americans extremist plans of terrorism and was also able to organize some dynamite attacks.[3] The third group included Alexander Sullivan, and the "Triangle" section of the Clan.[4] These men said very little in public, but organized

---

[2] Gibson, The New York Irish, 330.

[3] Le Caron, Twenty-Five Years, 237.

[4] Henry Hunt, The Crime of the Century, 62.

a whole series of attacks in 1883 and 1884.

While the British tended to magnify the power of the Irish in America by failing to see the division within the radical ranks, the activities of the extremists did much to confirm their mistaken view. On January 14, 1881 a group of Irishmen attempted to destroy the barracks of an infantry unit stationed in Salford, Ireland with dynamite, but it failed with only minor damages resulting.[5] Within days Granville telegraphed Thornton to gather as much information as possible about Fenians, especially those in Philadelphia, since the British government believed that a Philadelphia contractor was building dynamite bombs for them.[6] Thornton tried to gain the necessary information and at one point felt that the contractor of the "infernal machines" (the label for dynamite bombs) would possibly accept a bribe, but nothing came of it.[7] Meanwhile, the English Consul in New York spoke to Allen Pinkerton, but the famous private detective felt even his organization would not be capable of gaining information on Fenian activities. This failure to discover Fenian plans intensified British precautions to guard government arms.[8] Then on February 10 considerable excitement arose as a result of a suspected attempt to "blow up Windsor Castle."[9]

---

[5] Annual Register, 1881, part II, 4.

[6] Knaplund, "Letters to the Foreign Minister," 114. Granville to Thornton, January 25, 1881.

[7] Ibid.

[8] American, I (1881), 246.

[9] Annual Register, 1881, part II, 11.

The continuous rumors of possible Fenian action prompted Thornton to increase his effects to gain information, but again to no avail.[10] These things, which indicated to the British a centralized planning board in America, occurred during the height of the debates on the Coercion Acts of 1881. The passage of these acts in the first week of March only served to intensify British interests in Irish activities in America.

In the spring of 1881 O'Donovan Rossa virtually dominated Irish-American radicalism. During the 1870's he had always associated with the more radical of the extremists and in 1876 had decided to raise a "Skirmishing Fund" which would finance a guerrilla war with the English.[11] Ford urged his readers to contribute and a sizeable sum was collected. Then, when the "New Departure" appeared and the Land League gained the attention of most Irishmen, Rossa broke with the Clan and demanded money from the directors of the "Fund" to finance dynamite attacks upon England. On February 5, 1881 the New York Irish-American called such talk the dreams of a mad man and such attacks as "acts of violence against humanity." In the following month Rossa claimed credit for the attempt at Salford, yet he only earned the animosity of the more moderate Irish nationalist for his violent speeches.[12] Even Robert Thompson, no conservative to be sure, publicly accused Rossa and his

[10] Knaplund, "Letters to the Foreign Minister," 117. Thornton to Granville, February 22, 1881.

[11] Gibson, The New York Irish, 337.

[12] American, I (1881), 333.

friends of actually "hurting the Irish cause by claiming credit for
every wild and criminal act done or supposed to be done by Irishmen
in the United States and by publishing decrees of death for English
rulers."[13]  In June Rossa started to publish his United Irishman, which
in the words of John Devoy "was the queerist Irish paper ever established.  It was a purely personal organ" in which Rossa gave his own
views and opinions, seldom devoting much space to actual news.[14]

The British read Rossa's paper with great interest, however.  In
fact the very violence of the language used caused Granville to make
an official complaint to Lowell, a copy of which he sent to Thornton.
The dispatch simply outlined the complaints against Rossa's United
Irishman, especially the numerous articles aimed at directly inciting
the Irish in America to "murder, incendiarism and outrages."[15]  Some
articles proposed plans to murder the Prime Minister and the Prince of
Wales, while others claimed the authorship of numerous dynamite attempts.  Granville felt that no country could permit secret societies
to openly advocate crime and wrote merely to keep the American authorities informed if they wanted to act in Rossa's case.  However, Lowell
remarked, when receiving the representation, that he would have recommended not making the complaint, since "he did not see how the government
of the United States could give effect to them in a judicious manner."[16]

---

[13] Ibid., II, 3.

[14] Devoy, Recollections, 328.

[15] B.F.S.P., LXXIII, 1179.  Granville to Thornton, June 24, 1881.

[16] Ibid., 1180.

The day before Granville sent his letter, Thornton had already spoken to Blaine in an unofficial capacity about the hostile language of certain New York papers. He tried this because he had received rumors that an official protest was on its way, and he hoped Blaine could stop the abusive language before this was necessary. Blaine said in effect that he could do nothing since "the habit of Americans is to allow the greatest freedom of speech."[17] However, he did say that most Americans had only contempt for such language, and it gained prominence only with the rumor that the British would protest. Furthermore, if the British could provide proof that armed expeditions were being organized on American soil, he would suppress these quickly. The burden of proof rested upon the English, of course, and in this respect they had accomplished very little. However, Granville viewed this conversation as an indication that American officials were "in complete harmony with Great Britain over the criminality of the designs indicated in those newspapers."[18] Victor Drummond emphasized this harmony when he explained that his government

> had been unwilling to make any official statement since this would cause trouble to the government, knowing as I do how large the Irish element is in your country, and its pecularity in making a hullabaloo.[19]

Unfortunately, Rossa did more than merely talk. On June 10 he organized an unsuccessful attempt to destroy the Liverpool Town Hall.

---

[17] Ibid., 1181. Thornton to Granville, June 27, 1881.

[18] Ibid., 1182. Granville to Drummond, July 28, 1881.

[19] Knaplund, "Letters to the Foreign Minister," 114. Drummond to Blaine, July 28, 1881.

The British captured James McKevitt and William Barton, convicted them, and sentenced them to penal servitude.[20] In the following month Sir William Harcourt, the Home Secretary, disclosed to Parliament the discovery of "infernal machines" (dynamite bombs) at Liverpool. On July 3 the Cunard steamship, Malta, arrived at Liverpool with a consignment of cement, but upon close examination by customs officials these contained a number of dynamite bombs. A few days later the Bavarian arrived with six additional barrels of cement which contained bombs and handbills carrying Rossa's name.[21] Since both vessels had sailed from Boston, those responsible for the bombs violated an American law which prohibited the shipment of dynamite on boats.[22] For this reason Drummond advised Granville that he should permit American officials to handle the question and no official note was sent on the subject.[23] However, the British press demanded that the United States close the New York Irish World and other violent papers, but this was impossible, since there was no connection between the papers and the deed. In early August American investigators discovered the manufacturer of the "infernal machines," but nothing was done.[24]

While the English public debated this issue, the government studied

---

[20] Annual Register, 1882, part II, 433; Le Caron, Twenty-five Years, 237.

[21] Annual Register, 1881, part II, 55.

[22] American, II (1881), 242.

[23] Knaplund, "Letters to the Foreign Minister," 114. Drummond to Granville, August 2, 1881.

[24] American, II (1881), 266.

another Fenian project. As early as February 1881 reports had appeared that indicated the Irish were capable of sending ships to prey upon English vessels.[25] On July 28 Drummond wrote to Blaine about a Fenian financed torpedo boat, built by the Delamatic and Company Iron Works of Jersey City.[26] He explained that John Breslin, a prominent Fenian had tested it in the New York Harbor. Since the tests were successful, Drummond asked Blaine if he would prevent the vessel from attacking British merchant ships and ships of war.

The whole question of the "Fenian Ram," as the submarine was known by contemporaries, has been clouded in mystery and confusion. A number of students have attempted to clarify the story, but these have only added to the confusion. At any rate, a few facts are certain. In 1872 John P. Holland arrived in the United States from Ireland with ideas on the construction of a submarine. After offering them to the United States Navy which rejected them, he turned to the Clan which offered to finance the construction, and the work began in 1876.[28] Three boats were constructed; the first failed completely; the second was successful, but too small for Fenian purposes; the third was finally completed under the supervision of Breslin in May 1881. "Number three" was about 30 feet

---

[25] Knaplund, "Letters to the Foreign Minister," 116. Thornton to Granville, February 8, 1881.

[26] Ibid., 144. Drummond to Blaine, July 28, 1881.

[27] Colby Rucker, "The Fenian Ram," United States Naval Institute Proceedings, LVI (1935), 1136.

[28] Rucker stated that the Clan spent $13,000 on the project, but Devoy stated it was closer to $60,000. See O'Brien, Post Bag, I, 470.

long, 6 feet wide, and weighed 19 tons.[29]  Under the circumstances one
would imagine that the Clan would keep the project secret, but this was
hardly true as many visitors from various countries observed the actual
progress of construction.[30]  The New York Sun published articles on the
whole project and clearly identified it as a torpedo boat.[31]  The American even published a denial that it was anything but a legitimate vessel of moral warfare and that it was not meant for anything inconsistent
with the law of war or American neutrality.[32]

Since the existence of the vessel seemed to be public knowledge,
the government must have known about it.[33]  This fact, coupled to the
general image of the Clan as the "chief repository of the physical force"
tradition,[34] should have placed American officials on guard to prevent
the violation of American neutrality laws.  However, no evidence exists
that such steps were taken until the British informed Blaine that the
boat was tested successfully, but even then Blaine informed the British
that he needed legal proof of its purpose.[35]  When the vessel disappeared

---

[29] "John P. Holland," Dictionary of American Biography, IX, 45.

[30] Robert P. Brooks, "John P. Holland and His Submarine," Proceedings of the New Jersey Historical Society, XIII (1928), 186.

[31] Rucker, "The Fenian Ram," 1138.

[32] American, II (1881), 266.

[33] O'Brien, Post Bag, II, 471.  Devoy claimed that Washington knew
all about the project.

[34] Jamison, "Irish-Americans, The Irish Question," II, 10.

[35] Knaplund, "Letters to the Foreign Minister," 143.  Drummond to
Granville, August 2, 1881.

from the New York harbor in early August, Blaine promised to do everything "Her Majesty's government wished in the matter . . . when there
was sufficient proof."[36] This was never forthcoming and the Irish kept
their vessel. On occasion it regained the headlines, as when the Irish
moved it to New Haven in April 1883 where it was stored for possible
future use.[37] At the time the New York papers speculated that it was
out at sea on an errand of destruction.[38] But the opportunity for its
employment never arose and it now rests in a public park in Patterson,
New Jersey, a monument to its inventor.

Even before this scare subsided the British returned to the problem of dynamite. On August 3 a group of revolutionaries gathered in
Chicago to hear Rossa demand the endorsement of an outright dynamite
policy.[39] The demand split the gathering, however, and some even walked
out. Those remaining did approve of a plan to study how the "Skirmishing Fund" could be employed, but this was about all that was decided.[40]
This event, plus the shipment of bombs from Boston, led Blaine to
impress upon the British the reaction of the American people against
such schemes. According to Drummond he stated that "if infernal machines
were used and any passenger ship with Americans on board was destroyed,

---

[36] Ibid., 147. Drummond to Granville, September 7, 1881.

[37] Brooks, "John P. Holland," 186.

[38] O'Brien, Post Bag, II, 189.

[39] Le Caron, Twenty-five Years, 187.

[40] Annual Register, 1881, part II, 60. The old fund collected
by Ford and others in 1876. See page 169.

the Irish would be exterminated."[41]  At the same time he believed that

the publicity given such ideas really showed that the Irish were not

serious.  Drummond refused to take such threats lightly, especially

after Parnell's arrest in October.  "The Irish here are very angry and

it is possible the dynamite party may take heart and use their devilish

inventions, when a good opportunity offers itself."[42]

This opportunity really did not present itself until after the

Kilmainham Pact.  On May 6 the "Invincibles" struck at England in the

famous Phoenix Park murders.  The American press denounced the crime

as did the Land League of America and most Irish-American papers.

Some Americans felt the crime had originated on American soil and feared

the effect this would have upon Anglo-American relations.[43]  The Nation

reported that the "irreconciliables or the Fenian section" of the Land

League actually planned the attack.[44]

Before this could be proven the British became so concerned with the

newspaper articles that they sent a second note, this time to Freling-

huysen.  The fact that neither Frelinghuysen nor Bancroft Davis was

fully aware of the contents of the original complaint caused West to

---

[41] Knaplund, "Letters to the Foreign Minister," 147.  Drummond to
Granville, Sept. 7, 1881.  In October Blaine attended the Yorktown
celebration where the British flag received a 21 gun salute.  Blaine
said this was done "to show the Irish . . . the true feeling of the
American government for England."  See page 151.  Drummond to Granville,
Nov. 1, 1881.

[42] Ibid., 148.  Drummond to Granville, October 18, 1881.

[43] Ibid., 158.  West to Granville, May 9, 1882.

[44] The Nation, XXV (1882), 384.

accuse Lowell of modifying the tone of the first complaint. If this was what happened, it could help to explain the conversation Davis had with West at this time over the "suspects" case. At any rate, once Frelinghuysen realized the British position he explained to West that most Americans hated the impunity with which these articles were published, but "the government is powerless to remedy the evil while they see at the same time the danger of persistently ignoring international comity."[45] He obviously realized that continued freedom of expression for the Irish would create in English minds the belief that the government sympathized with "the dynamite faction of the Irish conspirators."[46] When the London _Times_ made such an accusation, Thompson denied it, stating that both Americans and Irish-Americans had condemned the radicals but that the government could not arrest those concerned because they did not commit their crimes on American soil.[47]

In the summer and fall of 1882 the Anglo-Irish aspect of the Irish question tended to lose its vitality. This was the beginning of Parnell's two years of inactivity and the peasants no longer had any immediate complaints. At the same time the Clan-Na-Gael completed preparations for a concentrated attack upon England, however, and the British worked to unravel the mystery of the Phoenix Park murders.

---

[45] Knaplund, "Letters to the Foreign Minister," 169. West to Granville, May 16, 1882. He said that "it seems Lowell modified the first representations to Blaine in order to let it 'slide.' He was afraid of Blaine." On the "suspects case" see pages 154 and 155.

[46] _American_, IV (1882), 244.

[47] _Ibid._

Thus, while Ireland rested, Irish-American forces were at work to make 1883 and 1884 exciting years.

In early January 1883, after six months of intensive investigation, the Dublin police broke the Phoenix Park case. On January 13 fifteen suspects were arrested and seven days later twenty-one additional men were arraigned on the testimony of an informer.[48] Eight of those arrested eventually faced charges of murdering Lord Cavendish and the permanent Chief Secretary Burke on the basis of evidence supplied by James Carey, the informer.[49] In the course of the trial Carey disclosed the whole story of the "Invincibles" as a secret group of hardcore fanatics, dedicated to the assassination of high government officials.[50] He named P. J. Sheridan as one of the organizers of the society. Unfortunately, in February 1883 Sheridan was in the United States. Consequently, a number of English papers demanded his return to stand trial, but the Nation cautioned that "states have always been fearful of extraditing political prisoners."[51] In a later issue Godkin even questioned whether a warrant could be issued by the Secretary of State and, even if it were, Sheridan could claim the crime was political and, therefore, did not come under the terms of the extradition treaty.[52]

---

[48] Hammond, Gladstone, 331.

[49] Annual Register, 1881, part II, 6.

[50] Tynan, Invincibles, 478-486.

[51] Nation, XXXVI (1883), 180.

[52] Ibid., 200.

Meanwhile, the very possibility of such proceedings caused a great stir, especially as rumors appeared that Sheridan had hired ex-General Benjamin Butler, the then Governor of Massachusetts, as his lawyer.[53] Sackville-West cautioned Granville that little would be gained by officially requesting the extradition of Sheridan, since "the complete subserviency of the State Department to the Irish element in New York and the influence it will in this case exercise upon the decision of the Commissioner renders success extremely doubtful."[54] At the same time rumors appeared that the British had proof that "Number One" (the secret leader of the Invincibles) was an Irish-American officer of the Land League in America.[55]

In the midst of this excitement the Clan-Na-Gael under the leadership of Sullivan and the "Triangle" struck its first blow. Ever since Parnell's failure to lead a return to agitation in the summer of 1882, Sullivan had prepared for the renewal of warfare on his own terms. The money he had received from Egan (when he was the Treasurer of the Land League in Paris) served as the financial support for the project, and after eight months of preparation his agents attempted to destroy the office of the Local Government Board in London on March 15, 1883. At the same time nitroglycerine was discovered near the London _Times_

---

[53] The Nation, XXXVI (1883), 200.

[54] Knaplund, "Letters to the Foreign Minister," 174. West to Granville, March 13, 1883.

[55] Nation, XXXVI (1883), 225. This possibly referred to Sullivan but this is not true.

printing office.[56] Some damage resulted from the explosion at the government building but no one was hurt. It was later discovered that in October 1882 the leader of the group which executed the dual attack had arrived in London where he remained for two months. In early March 1883 eight Clan man left America and arrived by different paths in England. One of them established a nitroglycerine plant in Birmingham. According to one account on the night of the explosion the gang had sufficient material to virtually destroy London.[57] News of the attack led to the dispatch of troops to guard public buildings and prominent members of the ministry.[58] The explosions, coming in the middle of the disclosures of the trial of the "Invincibles," caused a near panic to spread through the city. The London Times asked that all remedial legislation for Ireland be dropped, while the Nation recognized that the explosions presented "a problem as English statesmanship has never before been called on to solve."[59]

Meanwhile, even before the attack the question of the Rossa articles had reappeared. On March 17 West again complained to Frelinghuysen about the newspaper attacks. Granville had sent an official complaint but West withheld it from publication at the request of the United States, since Frelinghuysen and Arthur feared that "if Congress got hold of the

---

[56] Annual Register, 1883, part II, p. 10.

[57] Le Caron, Twenty-five Years, 241.

[58] Davitt, Fall of Feudalism, 463.

[59] Nation, XXXVI (1883), 246.

correspondence just now, the Irish members would make political capital out of it and force Frelinghuysen to make a disagreeable answer."[60] Nevertheless, rumors of the complaint appeared in the New York Tribune on March 24 and the Nation attempted to explain the peculiar American position in one editorial that stated:

> the United States population is unwilling to legislate for the aid of foreign governments trying to stifle internal discontent or to restrict in so doing the right of asylum and political refugees. If it were tried it would end in a triumph for the 'assassination press' and in enlisting on the Irish side the sympathies of tens of thousands of Americans who now pay no attention to the Irish question whatever or are thoroughly disgusted with the Irish mode of agitating.[61]

Godkin did admit that the real power behind Irish agitation rested in America, that for the first time the Irish in Ireland have strong and wealthy allies, and that for this reason England has asked that the United States muzzle the Irish World and Rossa's United Irishman and prevent the collection of money to finance crime in England. Yet, as Godkin admitted the government would not act. Even James G. Blaine complained about this failure in a private conversation with West,

> it was a disgrace to permit the United States to be made the refuge for the scum of Europe. [There had been too much] demagoguery on the part of the Government in dealing with the Irish element in New York. . . . It must not be forgotten that although it dominated the state and city of New York, it was a foreign element and in no sense an American one.[62]

---

[60] Knaplund, "Letters to the Foreign Minister," 177. West to Granville, April 3, 1883.

[61] Nation, XXXVI (1883), 333.

[62] Knaplund, "Letters to the Foreign Minister," 175. April 1, 1883. Memo of conversation with Blaine.

These remarks can hardly be reconciled with his campaign for the White
House in the following year, but they were private, of course, and said
merely to gain information from West.  At least Arthur and Frelinghuysen
did not share this view, for in their answer to Granville's note on the
papers they simply refused to act.  West felt that their refusal reflected that "the President is afraid of doing or saying anything to offend the Irish faction."[63]

While this particular debate consumed time the British were engaged
in collecting Irish-American dynamiters.  On March 29 Dennis Deasy was
arrested in Liverpool.  This led to the arrest of another American citizen, James Featherstone at Cork, Ireland, on the charge of possessing an
"infernal machine."[64]  On April 5 the first of a series of arrests occurred in connection with the explosion of March 15.  Eventually seven
men were arrested for that attack upon the Local Government Board building.

These arrests did not reduce the state of fear and near panic that
gripped London, however, and Sir William Harcourt offered a new explosives law to Parliament.  He declared that the old law of 1875 failed
to meet the new emergency, since it did not prohibit the illegal manufacture of nitroglycerine.  The discovery of the plant in Birmingham
and the destructive capacity of the explosives produced stirred Parliament to rush into action.  Harcourt introduced the new measure on

---

63 Ibid., 177.  West to Granville, April 17, 1883

64 U.S.F.R., 1883, 465.  Pratt to Lowell, April 7, 1883.  Pratt was
the American Consul at Cork and he spoke to Featherstone on April 7, 1883.

April 9 and it became law within twenty-four hours.[65] The speed with which this bill passed through the normally slow grinding wheels of English officialdom must have delighted the dynamiters. Near panic had in reality struck London as rumors of more attacks constantly appeared and guards on all public buildings were doubled.[66] As the police continued to uncover connections between the plots and America, the British could only watch with amazement, the extremes to which the Irish would go.[67]

Meanwhile, the British discovered additional information on the connection between the violence in England and the United States. On April 10 the trials of the "Invincibles" opened in Dublin. Twenty persons were indited, but only five stood accused of the actual murder. During the trial of Joseph Brady (it lasted only three days), James Carey identified James Tynan as "Number One,"[68] a disclosure which involved the United States since Tynan was in America in 1883. By then Edmund O'Kennedy (alias Featherstone) and Dr. Thomas Gallagher, arrested for the March 15 attack, asked Lowell for American protection against English arrest.[69] Lowell replied that he could not interfere in their case

---

[65] Annual Register, 1883, part II, 84.

[66] Nation, XXXVI (1883), 311. Godkin published an article on the explosives bill and listed the penalties; causing an explosion would call for life in prison; merely attempting to cause one, 20 years and keeping dynamite, 14 years. It was a rather severe law to be passed in 24 hours, especially in England.

[67] Saturday Review, LV (1883), 455.

[68] Nation, XXXVI (1883), 333.

[69] U.S.F.R., 1883, 414. Lowell to Frelinghuysen, April 16, 1883.

because of the evidence the British had collected. In early May after
the execution of the "Invincibles" rumors appeared that England would
demand the extradition of Sheridan and Tynan for their part in the
Phoenix Park murders. When the State Department admitted reception of
overtures of this nature, Thompson cautioned that "the rights of national hospitality cannot be violated,"[70] and that these men could not be surrendered because the extradition treaty provides for the surrender only
of those who have been charged with specific offenses and not ac-
complices.[71]

The whole question of the extradition of radical Irish-Americans
which had generated debate for two years gained significance primarily
because both the British and the Americans were concerned about what
seemed to be a gigantic Irish-American conspiracy to destroy public
buildings in England.[72] This American concern prompted the introduction
into the Senate of Pennsylvania of a bill which would have prohibited the
"manufacture and sale of infernal machines and devices to destroy life
and injure property."[73] Other Americans wanted more than new laws; some
felt that the government should actively suppress this Irish conspiracy.
When such talk naturally led to the possible extradition of those who
organized and executed such dynamite attacks, the Nation reminded its

[70] American, VII (1883), 37.

[71] Ibid., 45.

[72] Nation, XXXVI (1883), 333.

[73] Ibid.

readers that such criminals could not be turned over to the British
because of the political offender clause in the existing treaty and,
if this were overcome, their actions would have to result in the loss of
lives before the British could even ask for them. According to Godkin
those who plotted in America were virtually free men. Neither the British,
nor the Americans, could punish them. In fact no law "could be pushed
through the Democratic House," to do this and, even if it could, it would
only provide for a trial by jury which in essence would be a political
trial, something unknown in America. Godkin concluded that the "chasm
between honest indignation held by Americans for these activities and
punishment of them in American courts," was too great to bridge.[74] The
Nation did state that these "Irish dynamite men [because they] propose
to blow up whole cities and large buildings . . . were enemies of the
human race."[75] However, it cautioned the government against suppressing
them since any such move would make them martyrs and "bring to their
support whatever dormant anti-British feeling there is in the country
among native Americans—and there is undoubtedly a great deal even among
those who now regard the conspirators with contempt and abhorrence."[76]

If the disclosures of the informer in the Phoenix Park case tended
to implicate Irish-Americans, those of the dynamite trials virtually
proved the connection. William Lynch, arrested for his part in the March

---

[74] Ibid., 356.

[75] Ibid. This became an important argument later concerning the
Extradition Treaty. See page 211.

[76] Ibid.

attempt under an alias of Norman, turned informer and described his

activities in New York. He was a member of the Emerald Club of New

York, a branch of the Clan-Na-Gael, and with the other members was ded-

icated to freeing Ireland by force. In the course of his testimony he

explained the whole operation of the club and in an interview published

in the Nation, officials of the club agreed that what he said was correct.

The Saturday Review believed that these disclosures, showing the definite

link between the dynamite plot and the Clan-Na-Gael would help to turn

American public opinion more to the British Side,[77] but the American

countered this with a denial of Lynch's testimony and defended the Irish-

American, claiming only a small minority take part in such activities.

In the same article Thompson claimed that the mere passage of Explosive

Bills would not cut the tie between the Irish-American and Irish na-

tionalists, since British law could not touch American citizens who

planned dynamite attacks upon England in the safety of America

> and it is the conspiracy of just this class of persons
> which constitutes the thorn in England's side. As the
> Irish-American gains in wealth and intelligence in Amer-
> ica it will continue to make them a far greater danger
> to England than if he had remained at home.[78]

The great interest aroused by the whole question in the spring of

1883 prompted more reflective Americans to question the whole role of

adopted citizens. One such American, Edward Self, contended that the

Irish used their citizenship, which was conferred upon them wholesale by

---

[77] Saturday Review, LV (1883), 515.

[78] American, VII (1883), 67. Even Godkin recognized the truth of
this statement.

both parties, to jeopardize the peace and quiet of the United States by
planning crimes that maintained the national feuds at home. He contended that these naturalized citizens had no right to embarrass the
United States government, yet politicians had refused to condemn these
crimes, since those who instigate them

> have been able to capture the Irish vote. Even now, if the
> reflecting portion of the community would assert itself and
> demand that American citizenship shall not be prostituted
> by the adopted citizen, nor by those who pander to him,
> the truckling political aspirant who plays with fire could
> very soon be taught that promotion does not come that way.[79]

In order to emphasize this point about politicians the author quoted a
statement by a New York Senator,

> It is the duty of all Irishmen in this country to bring about
> war between the United States and Great Britain. Put Irish-
> men in high places, into the state legislatures, into na-
> tional affairs, into the Cabinet of the United States and
> they will do their work well.[80]

Self reminded the younger politician of the relative decline of the Irish-
American population which indicated with certainty the eventual decay of
their political power. He did admit that many Americans sympathized
with the Irish cause but they "could not applaud the collection of money
under the guise of charity that was used in reality for political agitation." As if he read this article Frelinghuysen remarked to West, when
the British Minister delivered another dispatch on the Irish agitators,

---

[79] Edward Self, "The Abuse of Citizenship," North American Review,
CXXXVI (1883), 541.

[80] Ibid., 547.

he had always wished to avoid these discussions. Speaking generally he said that it was the game of the Irish faction to create an ill-feeling between the two countries by raising questions of this sort and he was desirous that they should not succeed.[81]

In June the first of the dynamite trials ended with the conviction of all involved except Lynch, the informer. They received life imprisonment for their attempt to create a panic in London.[82] So ended Alexander Sullivan's first attempt to terrorize the British, but he was not discouraged and the planning for additional attempts continued.[83]

With the end of these incidents leaders of both countries in all probability hoped that the radical element would lose its vitality and remove one source of embarrassment for both sides of the Atlantic. This dream evaporated on July 29. James O'Donnell murdered James Carey on the British liner _Melrose Castle_ as it steamed along the coast of Africa, carrying Carey to what he hoped was safety in New Zealand. Almost immediately after his arrest O'Donnell claimed American citizenship and asked the American Embassy in London to appoint a counsel for his defense. This caused some Englishmen to see the case as additional proof that the Irish-Americans were essentially a party of assassination and that a conspiracy to destroy England did exist in America.[84] Hoppin, the American charge de affairs, felt that there was

---

[81] Knaplund, "Letters to the Foreign Minister," 177. West to Granville, June 5, 1883.

[82] _Annual Register_, 1883, part II, 22.

[83] Le Caron, _Twenty-five Years_, 217.

[84] _Saturday Review_, LVI (1883), 133. Devoy and others said that O'Donnell had no connection with the Clan. See O'Brien, _Post Bag_, II, 229.

some doubt as to his citizenship, but, even if this could be verified,
he did not believe that the United States would have to appoint an at-
torney for his defense.[85] Even before Frelinghuysen received this official information the Irish in America had organized a movement to pressure the State Department into intervening. Early in September a large
meeting was held in Chicago where a committee was organized to present a
petition to the Honorable John F. Finerty, Congressman from Chicago's
Second District. Finerty received their request on September 25 and relayed the message to Frelinghuysen two days later. The petition asked
the Secretary to accept O'Donnell's claim for citizenship and "provide
for his defense." Frelinghuysen asked Lowell to determine whether
O'Donnell was or was not a citizen, and ordered him to do "whatever is
necessary to secure his defense."[86] Meanwhile, the Chicago Irish hired
William O'Brien and William J. Hynes to serve as assistants for O'Donnell's
defense, while John A. Logan, Senator from Illinois and later Republican
vice-presidential candidate in 1884, and four Representatives from Illinois asked Frelinghuysen to help O'Donnell as much as possible. By
this time the Secretary had received Hoppin's letter in which he implied
that O'Donnell was not a citizen, so he again asked Lowell to help
O'Donnell as much as possible, that is, "if he is a citizen."[87] Meanwhile, Hoppin had investigated the case and by October 18 had concluded

---

85 U.S.F.R., 1883, 452. Hoppin to Frelinghuysen, September 24,
1883 (he received this on October 8).

86 Ibid., 459. Frelinghuysen to Lowell, October 5, 1883.

87 Ibid., 460. Frelinghuysen to Lowell, October 12, 1883.

that O'Donnell was not an American citizen, since he failed to reside
for five years after taking out his papers, which was necessary, since
he deserted the Army during the Civil War and, consequently, had no
right to claim the one year residency privilege. Hoppin asked for
further instructions, although he could not see the correctness in starting a precedent of supplying legal counsel to arrested American citizens,
even if the department accepted O'Donnell's claim.[88] Two days later
Frelinghuysen ordered him to "immediately ascertain and report by telegram whether O'Donnell is an American citizen."[89] This prompted Hoppin
to visit O'Donnell, even though it was against his better judgment, and
on October 22 he informed Frelinghuysen that O'Donnell claimed citizenship on the ground that his father became a naturalized citizen while he
was a minor. For greater security he took out his own papers and voted
in the election of 1876 at Scranton, Ohio.[90] In an extensive letter
which Frelinghuysen did not receive until November 3 Hoppin explained
that O'Donnell, after driving a wagon train during the Civil War, settled in Ireland in 1871. He returned to the United States in time to
vote in the election of 1876, but shortly afterwards he again sailed for
Ireland. Since he virtually spent 13 years in England from 1870 to 1883,
Hoppin felt his claim for citizenship was not valid.[91] Meanwhile,

---

[88] Ibid., 467. Hoppin to Frelinghuysen, October 18, 1883. This was
not received until October 29 which explains the following telegram.

[89] Ibid., 468. Frelinghuysen to Lowell, October 20, 1883 (telegram).

[90] Ibid., 469. Hoppin to Frelinghuysen, October 22, 1883 (telegram).

[91] Ibid., 469. Frelinghuysen to Hoppin, October 23, 1883 (received
November 3).

Frelinghuysen in order to avoid a mistake asked Hoppin to determine "the regiment in which he had served, or the name of his captain."[92] Hoppin replied that he had never actually enlisted in the army and could not even name the place and date of his father's naturalization.[93] On November 1, 1883, Hoppin sent additional information by telegram which he had found in police records. O'Donnell had arrived in the United States in 1846 with his family and returned to Ireland in 1852. In 1860 he was back in the United States and served in the army as a hired substitute, "two or three times" never remaining long enough to join a regiment. In 1867 he returned to Ireland but left again in 1871.[94] Two weeks later he sent another telegram stating that O'Donnell's father had never completed the naturalization process.[95] In spite of this information which at least created grave doubt as to O'Donnell's citizenship Frelinghuysen informed Lowell on November 19, that "upon the facts before the Department, O'Donnell's naturalization appears established, and in the absence of proof to the contrary, he is to be regarded as a citizen of the United States."[96] He ordered him to ask the British to permit American counsel the right to appear before the British court in O'Donnell's behalf. American lawyers, hired by the Chicago Irish,

---

[92] Ibid., 471. Frelinghuysen to Hoppin, October 30, 1883 (telegram).

[93] Ibid., 473. Hoppin to Frelinghuysen, October 31, 1883 (telegram).

[94] Ibid., 474. Hoppin to Frelinghuysen, November 1, 1883 (telegram).

[95] Ibid., 475. Hoppin to Frelinghuysen, November 10, 1883 (telegram).

[96] Ibid., Frelinghuysen to Lowell, November 19, 1883.

traveled to England, but did not receive the right to address the court. Why Frelinghuysen accepted O'Donnell's claim can only be surmised, but Irish-American pressure was one factor he considered.

The case took a turn for the worse in early December, as far as American officials were concerned, when the British jury found O'Donnell guilty and sentenced him to death by hanging.[97] Two days later Congress reconvened and on December 10 Representative Robert Lowry of Indiana asked for the papers on the case while Abram S. Hewitt of New York entered a resolution which asked for a delay of the execution.[98] Meanwhile, a delegation of congressmen called on President Arthur to plead for his personal intervention on O'Donnell's behalf.[99] Samuel Cox of New York, a member of this delegation, later admitted that he went merely to please the Irish vote.[100] Lowell by this time had spoken to Granville concerning the possibility of commuting the death penalty, but the Foreign Minister refused.[101] Then on December 11 Arthur personally asked for a delay of the execution to permit further study of O'Donnell's case; however, Granville refused again and O'Donnell died on December 17, 1883.[102] While the British lived with rumors that the Irish nationalists

[97] Saturday Review, LV (1883), 717.

[98] Congressional Record, 48th Congress, 1st Session, XV, part 1, 71, 80.

[99] Tynan, Invincibles, 496.

[100] New York Tribune, December 9, 1883.

[101] B.S.F.S., LXXV, 614. Granville to West, December 10, 1883.

[102] U.S.F.R., 1883, 479. Frelinghuysen to Lowell, December 11, 1883; Lowell to Frelinghuysen, December 15, 1883. Both were telegrams.

would avenge his death, Thompson declared that the British had insulted
the United States by refusing to delay the trial and by not permitting
American citizens to serve on the jury since O'Donnell was an American
citizen.[103]

Shortly after the execution a rumor circulated in Washington to the
effect that Representative Hewitt had spoken to West after he had introduced his resolution of December 10. According to these stories Hewitt
had informed West that the resolution, which had passed the House unanimously was meant only for the Irish vote and that the British should not
take it seriously. The House of Representatives asked for an investigation of the case, but nothing came of it, or at least, nothing was published.[104] What actually happened was that Hewitt had told West that he
had offered the resolution in order to prevent the Irish members from
introducing one with stronger words.[105] At any rate the House asked
for documents on the O'Donnell case for a second time. When the Administration sent them on December 24, Samuel Randall declared that they
were important enough to be published, an obvious attempt to appear as
an Irish champion.[106]

While O'Donnell captured headlines the Clan executed two additional attempts to terrorize London. On October 30, 1883 at 8:00 P.M. two

[103] American, VIII (1883), 151, 163; Saturday Review, LVI (1883), 783.

[104] Congressional Record, 48th Congress, 1st Session, XV, part 2, 1431.

[105] Knaplund, "Letters to the Foreign Minister," 177. West to Granville, December 25, 1883.

[106] Congressional Record, 48th Congress, 1st Session, XV, part 1, 223.

explosions occurred in the "Underground Railroad" in London, causing damage to the trains, one station, and serious injury to a number of persons. Some British writers saw the attack as another proof of what the "Irish Home Rule party really is," while others attributed the whole problem to the Irish-Americans.[107] The Clan-Na-Gael, elated with their success organized a second attempt on February 26, 1884, the simultaneous destruction of four stations on the London, Chatham, and Dover railroad. Since only one device functioned properly, the others were discovered intact, and the British learned that the dynamite was made by the "Atlas" Company and that the clock mechanism was also of American manufacture.[108]

These disclosures forced repercussions to reverberate across the Atlantic. Some rumors appeared that the British Cabinet would demand that the American government prevent such attacks in the future before "public indignation reaches a point where friendly relations will be strained."[109] The British public recognized that American politicians were reluctant to do anything that would antagonize the Irish vote, that in other words, "the Irish were influential enough to be flattered, but by no means able to determine the policy of the United States."[110] Feeling this pressure both in England and in the United States President Arthur issued an order asking all government officials to enforce the

---

[107] Saturday Review, LVI (1883), 551; Annual Register, 1883, part II, 44.

[108] Annual Register, 1884, part II, 7.

[109] Saturday Review, LVI (1883), 303.

[110] Ibid.

existing laws with regard to the shipment of dynamite. In his message he recognized the fact that British authorities had publicly stated that the dynamite used in the February attack was of American manufacture, but that he did not believe this to be true. Nevertheless, the honor of the country, he felt, required him to act so that it could not be implied that the United States tolerated such crimes.[111] The proof that Americans were involved came on April 17 when the British arrested three Irish-Americans for the February attack and rumors appeared that they had admitted ties with America's radicals.[112] After the government officially charged that the explosives were produced in the United States, English papers demanded that the United States punish all those engaged in such activities.[113] But the United States could arrest only those who violated American laws and this meant only those who carried dynamite on a ship. This caused some embarrassment to American officials and Patrick Ford only compounded this when he announced the opening of a new collection fund to finance such attacks.[114]

Before the English could recover from the February attack the Clan organized a series of explosions for May 30. One of these detonated in Saint James Square, damaging a number of buildings; within minutes a more violent explosion occurred in Scotland Yard, but little damage re-

---

[111] Messages, 4815.

[112] Annual Register, 1884, part II, 12.

[113] American, VIII (1884), 21.

[114] New York Irish World, January 15, 1884.

sulted; while at about the same time a small boy discovered a black bag, containing dynamite, at the base of Lord Nelson's monument.[115] Fortunately, the American-made mechanism had failed to operate, and its discovery gave the authorities the opportunity to again accuse the Irish in America of plotting to destroy England.[116]

Americans in general sympathized with the Irish fight for freedom because they usually supported any such fight. The desire for Home Rule, for instance, received wide support among Americans, but this support did not mean that they sympathized with the more violent methods employed by the dynamiters. When it was obvious that a band of radical Irish-Americans were using American soil as a base for dynamite against England, many Americans in fact decried the situation. One author reminded Americans that they could not afford to let New York become "a store house for the political incendiaries of foreign states. The United States had the responsibility to prevent dynamite attacks and they could not avoid this as the Alabama case had shown so clearly."[117] In addition since such crimes were aimed at humanity itself, they should not go unpunished. However, he argued that the United States could not punish thes criminals, since they did not commit the crimes on American soil. In fact the only state with jurisdiction was England which meant that the United

---

[115] Annual Register, 1884, part II, 17.

[116] Saturday Review, LVII (1884), 733.

[117] Henry Wade Rogers, "Harboring Conspiracy," North American Review, LXXXVIII (1884), 523.

tates could contribute to their punishment by sending them to England.
onsequently, he concluded that a new treaty, which would make dynamite
rimes extraditable should be negotiated by the two countries.[118]

Just when some Americans realized their responsibility the Clan
nder Sullivan's leadership temporarily suspended operations for the
emainder of the year. He was busy on Blaine's election campaign and
as also under attack by the anti-Sullivanite section of the Clan.[119]
hese could have slowed operations to avoid embarrassment for Blaine and
o attempt to consolidate the Clan before moving again.

If actual operations ceased, planning did not, since within a month
f the elections, on December 13, an explosion occurred on the second
rch of the London Bridge. Little damage was done to the bridge, but
he culprits themselves were killed.[120] The leader of the gang, William
omasney, an American of Irish parents, had taken part in the events of
866 and 1867 in Ireland, and had returned to the United States where he
ecame active in the Clan. Some sources indicate that he had lost
nterest in the more violent means to gain Irish freedom by the early
880's and even restrained Edward Condon from organizing such attacks.[121]
et, in 1883 Sullivan's urging apparently had changed his mind and in
ugust 1884 he left the United States with his brother and John Fleming

---

[118] Ibid., 531.

[119] O'Brien, Post Bag, II, 256. Some people accused Blaine of not
ndemning the dynamite effects because this would have cost him votes.

[120] Mark F. Ryan, Fenian Memories (1946), 117.

[121] O'Brien, Post Bag, II, 26.

to destroy London Bridge. His death later led to the fight in the Clan when Dr. Philip Cronin claimed that Sullivan had not provided Lomasney's widow with the pension she desired.

This did not discourage Sullivan, however, and on January 24, 1885, simultaneous attempts were made to damage the Tower of London and the House of Commons.[122] At the Tower four people were injured, but the police captured James Cunningham before he fled the building. In the House the chamber was empty and the explosion caused little damage, but it did destroy Gladstone's chair. The public reacted violently and for two days London was on the verge of hysteria as soldiers and police guarded all public buildings. Stringent regulations on visitors to the House virtually excluded members of the press.[123] The reaction in America took a similar path. Godkin in a long and bitter editorial used the incident for an attack upon Blaine. He condemned the recent candidate for the Presidency for accepting the political support of Patrick Ford and his Irish World, since his acceptance signified the first time that Ford's radical ideas received any degree of recognition by decent Americans. Even during the election, Godkin complained, Ford had collected money for his "Emergency Fund" which he hoped to use to finance such attacks and supported Blaine because he felt he would permit these.[124]

---

[122] Annual Register, 1885, part 1, 17.

[123] Gwynn, Dilke, II, 128.

[124] Nation, XL (1885), 83. Ford did not organize any of these acts, he merely propagandized them.

The New York State Senate on the Monday following the attack debated a bill that would make the contribution of money for the sale, transportation, or use of explosive compounds a felony.[125] Senator Edmunds on the day after the explosion introduced a bill in the Senate that would make the manufacture, sale, or conveyance of explosives with intent to destroy life or property in any country a crime. Senator Bayard offered a resolution which condemned the twin attack in England, but, when this was debated on Monday, Senator Harrison H. Riddleberger asked that it be sent to committee. His attempt to kill the resolution was defeated and after some additional maneuvering the Senate passed it 63 to 1.[126] This attack had finally aroused American officials and public opinion as one state legislature debated a severe dynamite bill on January 28.[127] The British were thankful for this long overdue reaction.[128]

The British capture of James G. Cunningham and Henry Burton led to their conviction on May 18 with a sentence of penal servitude for life. By then twenty-nine men had been arrested by the British for dynamite crimes.[129] By then also the campaign had come to a close. Gladstone

---

[125] Ibid.

[126] Congressional Record, 48th Congress, 2nd Session, XVI, 1000. In the debate Senator Riddleberger implied that he was against the resolution because it "may be distorted into an expression of sympathy" with England. Republicans Ingalls, Hawley and Hoar wanted it to show the British that the American government had not neglected its duties as a friendly neutral by permitting the Irish to plan such attacks in the safety of America.

[127] Nation, XL (1885), 111.

[128] Saturday Review, LIX (1885), 130.

[129] Hunt, Crime of the Century, 66.

had introduced rumors of a Home Rule Bill, Parnell had returned from
his two years of seclusion and the parliamentary forces once again
began to take charge of Irish nationalism.  At the same time Sullivan
saw that his grip on the Clan was gradually diminishing, discovered that
funds were no longer available, and realized that the American people
were tired of being accused of harboring dynamiters.  The conservative
forces of the Irish-Americans violently condemned the continuation of
the program and even Patrick Ford had to change the name and nature of
his "Emergency Fund."  Cleveland had entered office and some talk of the
new extradition treaty had appeared.  All these things indicated that
the campaign was over.  England, although shaken, remained firm and
failed to be terrorized into submission.

Chapter VI

The Extradition Treaty

In the spring of 1885 many persons in both England and America
realized the need for a new extradition treaty, but this awareness was
not limited to merely the English and the Americans. It was world-wide,
the result of the increase in international crime, the increase in rapid
means of escape for the criminal,[1] and the growing belief that all nations possess some responsibility for the protection of each other and
humanity in general against the international criminal.[2] As most of the
nations in the world increased both the number and the terms of their
various extradition treaties during the second half of the nineteenth
century, the United States followed the trend and signed no less than
seventeen conventions or supplements to previous treaties from 1868 to
1890, twelve in the decade of the 1880's.[3]

While the American and English interest in an extradition treaty in
1885 can be seen as part of a general world movement, citizens of both
countries participated in the related world-wide discussion of the political offender and his use of dynamite. During the second half of the
nineteenth century anarchists attempted to destroy all civil authority

---

[1] Allen & Rice (ed.), "Extradition of Dynamite Criminals," North
American Review, CXLI (1885), 47.

[2] Burnette, "Senate Foreign Relations Committee," 238.

[3] Walter W. Fifield, "A History of Extradition Treaties of the
United States." Unpublished Doctoral Dissertation. University of
Southern California (1936). Complete copies of all these treaties
can be found in the appendix.

by force. At first they practiced the art of assassination, but after
the perfection of the dynamite bomb, they turned to its use so much
that the anarchist became synonomous with the terrorist and dynamiter.
As this form of political agitation spread during the 1870's and 1880's
a great debate centered around the question, should these acts be considered political in nature and, therefore, not subject to the extradition laws, or were they really beyond the sphere of typical political
agitation and liable for extradition for crimes against humanity. As
time passed more and more people accepted the latter definition of the
anarchist who used dynamite to terrorize authority, since in reality
they attacked the very bases of society.[4] Others considered the mere
terrorist a political offender, yet the exact nature of the crime was
dependent upon the means used, the desired result, and the property destroyed. In effect they argued that the political offender could be
extradited, if he committed a crime against humanity.

While this question absorbed a great deal of discussion in other
countries, Americans who had never heard of the concept of punishing
political criminals accepted the view that the dynamiter and the assassin
were outside the protection afforded the political offender. At least
from 1870 to 1885 the United States, participating in the world-wide interest in extradition, negotiated a number of treaties which stipulated
so. In 1870 the treaty signed with Peru included in the list of extraditable crimes murder or assassination and "severe injuries

[4] Robert G. Newman, "Extradition and the Political Offender." Unpublished Doctoral Dissertation. University of Illinois (1934), 230.

intentionally caused on railroads and telegraph lines or to persons by means of explosions of mine or steam-boilers."[5] In the 1874 treaty with Belgium and the 1880 treaty with the Netherlands no such clause appeared. However, in 1882 a new treaty was signed with Belgium and a railroad clause, similar to that found in Peru's treaty, was included. This treaty was signed on June 13, 1882, delivered to the Senate on August 8, and proclaimed as ratified on November 20, 1882—all within six months.[6] The treaty with Spain, signed in that same year for some reason did not have this clause, but in 1883 a new treaty was signed with Luxembourg which did include it. This took six months to clear the Senate.[7] In 1884 Italy and the United States signed a supplement to their old 1868 Extradition Treaty, one which according to one author included many crimes, formally considered to be of a political nature.[8] By 1885 the United States obviously had moved in the direction of narrowing the definition of the political offender and excluding the terrorist who used dynamite.

In early December 1885 American negotiators in Japan took another step in further narrowing this definition of political crime. In that month negotiations opened in Tokyo for a new extradition treaty. A few months before Calvin Pratt, an American citizen, had fled to Japan

---

[5] Fifield, "Extradition Treaties," 549.

[6] Ibid., 346. The speed could have been caused by the knowledge that a group of extremists had met in Brussels in the previous year.

[7] Burnette, "Senate Foreign Relations Committee," p. 237.

[8] Ibid., 238.

after embezzling funds in the United States. Japanese authorities extradited Pratt when the United States requested his custody, but there was no guarantee that they would do so in future cases, since no extradition treaty relations existed between the two countries.[9] Consequently, the United States sought a treaty that would clarify this procedure and after four months of hard negotiating one was signed on April 29, 1886. It was ratified by the Senate on June 21, and proclaimed by the President on July 13. Of the crimes enumerated the most interesting was

> Malicious destruction of, or attempt to destroy, railroads, trains, vessels, bridges, dwellings, public edifices or other buildings when the act endangers human life.[10]

Richard B. Hubbard, American Minister in Japan, explained that this article "gives sufficient protection against the outrages of that increasing class of scoundrels who pervert the discoveries of science into instruments of savage crime."[11] Thus, the United States officially accepted the belief that dynamite crimes which endangered life were not political, but terroristic in nature and punishable.

Once accepted, the same clause appeared in three other treaties, one with the Netherlands, one with Russia and one with Colombia. In 1887 the United States signed the Netherlands Treaty which included as extraditable the crime of "willful and unlawful destruction or obstruction

---

[9] U.S.F.R., 1886, 564. Hubbard to Bayard, October 11, 1885.

[10] Fifield, "Extradition Treaties," 428. It also made embezzlement an extraditable crime.

[11] U.S.F.R., 1886, 564. Hubbard to Bayard, October 11, 1885.

of railroads which endangers human life."[12]  It was signed on June 2,
1887, but not ratified by the Senate until March 26, 1889, shortly after
Harrison had entered the White House.  Meanwhile, the Russians and Americans concluded their negotiations on March 28, 1887.  Ever since the
assassination of Alexander II in 1881 the Russians had desired to establish as general practice among nations the extradition of all murderers or
attempted murderers.  In 1886 Baron Rosen, the Russian Minister to the
United States, tried to negotiate a treaty which would have included as
extraditable, murder or attempted murder of a monarch or any member of
his family.[13]  Bayard indicated that he was particularly concerned
with safeguarding political offenders, but these differences were quickly ironed out.  The Senate received the treaty, but did not ratify it
until February 6, 1893, just one month before Cleveland returned to the
White House.[14]  They could have delayed it because some may have felt
that the clauses on assassination and malicious destruction of railroads, buildings, etc., could have been used to gain hold of political
offenders.  Yet Bayard seemed convinced that the political offender was
safeguarded.  Finally in 1888 the Cleveland administration negotiated a
treaty with Colombia that contained a malicious destruction clause.[15]
Although signed on May 7, 1888 the Republican controlled Senate once

---

[12] Fifield, "Extradition Treaties," 319.

[13] Rosen, Forty Years, I, 73.

[14] Fifield, "Extradition Treaties," 644.

[15] Ibid., 536.

again refused to accept it until after Cleveland left office, and then
only with certain amendments. These, however, did not change the
malicious destruction clause.

These facts indicate that in the 1880's Americans accepted the
world-wide movement to enlarge extradition arrangements and in particular to exclude the typical terrorist crimes from protection as political offenses. It was in this atmosphere that both Americans and Englishmen began to see the need for a new Anglo-American treaty, but this does
not mean that this particular atmosphere served as the only cause for
this awareness.

A number of factors peculiar to their situation prompted their
desires. Prior to 1886 Anglo-American extradition practice was governed
by the old Webster-Ashburton Treaty of 1842. This fulfilled their mutual
needs for a number of years and few disputes of note developed from it.
Then in 1870 the British Parliament passed an Extradition Act which declared that "no prisoners shall be surrendered unless the country to
which they are to be surrendered shall have provided by law or by arrangement, that he shall be tried only for the offense for which he is
surrendered."[16] Hamilton Fish refused to accept the fact that this purely domestic law could apply to the Webster-Ashburton treaty on the
ground that Parliament could not unilaterally change the binding terms
of English treaties.[17] The dispute came to a head when Ezra D. Winslow

---

[16] A. G. Sedquick, "Extradition," North American Review, CXXXVI
(1683), 497.

[17] Nevins, Hamilton Fish, 870.

fled to England after escaping from jail where he was confined on forgery charges. When the United States asked for Winslow's return, Great Britain demanded assurances that the United States would comply with the terms of the Extradition Act.[18] Grant of course refused to give such assurances, since the old treaty did not state that they were necessary. The British inquired if it would be possible to sign a new treaty which would provide for this point. Grant wanted this, especially since it would provide an opportunity to extend the list of extraditable crimes, but for some reason the matter was dropped until Cleveland entered office in 1885.[19]

The general movement to rewrite such treaties and this peculiar problem of Anglo-American relations caused a number of Americans to ask for a new treaty during the first half of the 1880's. In June 1881 the *American* called for a new treaty to clarify the points raised by the British law of 1870.[20] Later in that year Thompson returned to the same theme, but for a different reason. It seems that at that time the country had "been affected with a succession of defalcations and embezzlements in banking institutions" and he called for a treaty which would put a stop fo this.[21] The *Nation* reported a bank embezzlement incident on March 16, 1882.[22] While these reasons were advanced for a new treaty,

---

[18] FiField, "Extradition Treaties," 25.

[19] Ibid., 28.

[20] American, II (1881), 131.

[21] Ibid., 184.

[22] Nation, XXXIV (1882), 218.

a few Americans declared that it was necessary to stop the dynamite conspirators who troubled England.[23] Finally, in a relatively long article A. G. Sedquick reviewed the history of Anglo-American extradition practice and concluded that the time was ripe for a new comprehensive treaty.[24]

British interest in such an undertaking increased during 1883 and 1884 when the Irish hatched their dynamite plots and when it became evident that under existing laws the United States did not have to extradite Sheridan, Tynan, or any of the other Irish-Americans who had committed crimes in England and who had reached the safety of America. For the British the use of American soil as a base for dynamite attacks was unacceptable, but the only way they could avoid this would be by including such crimes in an extradition treaty. The dynamite attack on the House of Commons and the Tower of London in January 1885 was the straw that broke the camel's back for the British. They wanted a new treaty.[25]

Meanwhile, Americans faced their own extradition difficulty. In various papers and magazines notices of embezzlements appeared more and more as the decade passed. Literally a rash of banks discovered to their dismay that prominent officials had disappeared with large sums only to reappear in the safety of some foreign country with which the United States did not have an extradition treaty that included

---

[23] Gibson, The New York Irish, 402.

[24] Sedquick, "Extradition," 497.

[25] Gibson, The New York Irish, 401.

embezzlement. One such refuge was Canada which, as part of the British Empire, came under the terms of the old Webster-Ashburton treaty. In effect, both the United States and Great Britain wanted a new treaty, but for different reasons; England, to close America to Irish dynamiters; the United States, to close Canada to American embezzlers.

These two ideas and desires dramatically converged in 1885. That year opened with the triple dynamite attack in London which generated in America a great deal of discussion, ranging from the nature of terrorist acts to the extradition of political criminals. James B. Angell, President of the University of Michigan, felt that the public as well as government officials favored the extradition of criminals in general primarily because of the increased speed of communications, but he did not feel that men should be surrendered for political offenses. Although the Irish dynamiter claimed the protection of this clause, Angell argued that they should be considered in the assassination class and, therefore, extraditable. He felt that the United States could not otherwise consider "these other acts by Irishmen," since the government recognized the right to extradite assassins in the Belgium Extradition Treaty of 1882.[26] George T. Curtis felt that those who committed the dynamite crimes and later fled to the United States should be extradited, but those who planned such attacks in the safety of America could not be shipped back. Others argued that the United States would have to give up the Irish dynamiter, if they wanted another country to extend this

---

[26] James B. Angell, "The Extradition of Dynamite Criminals," North American Review, CXLI (1885), 47.

favor to the United States.[27]  Meanwhile, Cleveland took office only
to be greeted by a bankers magazine with a proposed treaty draft that
would "fully meet the requirements for the handing over of criminals
between Canada and the United States."[28]

By the middle of the summer the bankers increased their activities
when rumors appeared that the United States and England would reopen the
negotiations on the extradition treaty as proposed during Grant's administration.  Some bankers felt that this text would not help Americans
against "officials who default in the United States and take refuge in
Canada."[29]  On September 23 they met at the national convention of the
American Bankers Association in Chicago only to hear a rather discouraging report on extradition treaties.  As a result of the large number of
defaulters and embezzlement cases the officers reviewed the thirty-one
existing treaties, found them wanting on this particular point, and
sought the cooperation of the American Bar Association in a campaign to
speed extradition reform.[30]  At the meeting one member proposed that a
special committee formulate treaty provisions that would provide for
the extradition of embezzlement and criminal misuse of funds of any bank,
trust fund or saving institution and present these provisions to the

[27] Ibid., 55.

[28] Bankers Magazine and Statistical Report, XXXIX (1885), 789.

[29] The Bankers Magazine and Statistical Register, XLIX (1885), 70.

[30] Proceedings of the Convention of the American Bankers Association
(1885), 152.

President and the State Department.[31]  After the delegates accepted this

resolution, Washington B. Williams declared that of the thirty treaties

he studied "the most narrow and ineffectual . . . is with England,"

which he felt should be modified to cover the embezzlement of private

and public funds.[32]  At the same convention Albert S. Bolles of the

University of Pennsylvania's Wharton School read a paper entitled, "On

the Protection of Banks and Other Moneyed Institutions from Losses

Through Defaulting Officers."  Of all the causes for the sudden increase

in the number of such cases, he felt the inability to severely punish

the crimes was the most important.  The failure to punish developed

directly from the fact that the individual criminal could escape so

easily, especially to Canada, where he was safe from prosecution because

of the defectiveness of the treaty with England.  Some defaulters actual-

ly lived almost within sight of the scene of their crimes, secure against

arrest.  He concluded that

> the safety of the banks and other institutions of both
> countries imperatively requires that this awfull dis-
> regard of justice should cease.  The business and social
> relations of the two countries are so close, their
> mutual protection so desirable, that neither country
> ought any longer to be an asylum for the criminals of
> the other.[33]

After hearing this address the delegates unanimously approved a resolu-

tion empowering the Executive Council to "procure such amendments to

---

[31] Ibid., 157.

[32] Ibid., 155.

[33] Albert S. Bolles, Practical Banking, 7th ed. (1890).  The complete address appears in the appendix.

existing extradition treaties as will secure the return of fugitives
from justice that at present are at large on account of what are considered defects in the existing treaties."[34]

The pressure for a new treaty had mounted and Cleveland's administration finally took steps to fulfill the need. On August 4, 1885
Bayard ordered the new American Minister to England, Edward Phelps, to
reopen the extradition negotiations.[35]  After discussing the problem
with the British and studying the proposed draft, as it then existed,
Phelps offered a number of recommendations to Washington. The old treaty,
he felt, had adequately served the purpose for forty years "but it is
now found imperative that it should include the crime of larceny and
embezzlement, and as the British government may claim, dynamite offenses."[36]  For nine years the British had demanded a long and elab-
orate new treaty; but Phelps felt this was the wrong approach, because
it would mean, if accepted by both countries, the enactment of new laws
which "our Irish friends . . . will not let" pass without attempting to
arouse opposition in Congress.[37]  Phelps felt that, since the old treaty
had worked so well and since the demand for a treaty was so urgent, the
best approach would be to extend the old treaty to include the new crimes

---

[34] Proceedings of the Convention of American Bankers Association
(1885), 163.

[35] House Executive Documents, 50th Congress, 2nd Session, I, part
2, number 1, p. 1731. Bayard to Phelps, August 4, 1885.

[36] Tansill, Foreign Policy of Bayard, xxxii. Phelps to Bayard,
November 21, 1885.

[37] Ibid., xxiv.

along with one article which would meet the requirement of the
British Extradition Act of 1870.[38]

While Phelps worked on the extradition question, Congress reconvened and Cleveland asked for a commission to solve the fishery dispute.
As was stated earlier, the Senate refused to endorse the idea and Senator
Edmunds, who according to his biographer "shared with many other American politicians of his day, an inordinate passion for proposing anti-
English legislation,"[39] led the fight to reject the idea. Yet in the
midst of this battle Senator George F. Hoar who was no friend of the
administration offered a resolution which requested the President to
enlarge the existing extradition arrangements with England to cover
financial crimes such as embezzlement and breach of trust.[40]

In early February William Gladstone formed his Third Ministry and
appointed Lord Rosebery as his Foreign Minister. Shortly afterwards
Rosebery spoke to Phelps about the extradition treaty and suggested that
there was no need to include a clause specifically excluding political
offenders, since it would merely supplement an already existing treaty
which contained that clause. When Phelps informed Bayard of this conversation, the Secretary merely reminded the Minister that the Irish
question was a very explosive one and that the Senate seemed "adverse

---

[38] Fifield, "Extradition Treaties," 30.

[39] Adler, Edmunds, 318.

[40] Congressional Record, 49th Congress, 2nd Session, XVIII,
part 1, 403.

to going against" it.[41]  He expected opposition to the treaty, since
"Blaine's party controls the dynamite vote" and, therefore, every pre-
caution should be taken to avoid issues that Blaine and his friends
could use.  He felt the political offenders clause had to appear in the
new treaty, if only to avoid this possibility, and specifically told
Phelps to inform the British "that in all arrangements between the United
States and Great Britain the element of Irish hostility to the latter,"
must never be omitted from consideration.[42]  He then went on to imply
that he wanted a treaty signed with the Gladstone government, probably to
take advantage of the good will generated among Irish-Americans by his
Home Rule proposal.  Phelps had already spoken to Lord Rosebery about the
Irish element and he agreed to eliminate anything that would generate opposition.[43]

Bayard's concern for the Republican attempt to gain the Irish vote
did not end with the extradition treaty.  In fact, he saw the Republicans
in the Senate as a group of men who used their office for partisan
reasons only, who would take advantage of every possible issue to gain
the Irish, who refused to accept Cleveland's request for a commission
to solve the fishery troubles for that reason.  To him,

> The Irish vote in the United States, being very potential,
> is being sought most vigorously and unscrupulously by the
> Republican leaders, chief of whom is Mr. Blaine, and . . .
> every issue will be raised by them by which they can se-

---

[41] Tansill, Foreign Policy of Bayard, xxxv.  Bayard to Phelps,
March 7, 1886.

[42] Ibid.

[43] Ibid., 210.  Phelps to Bayard, March 27, 1886.

cure the alliance with the Irish vote, and every British question gives a chance for this.[44]

The Republicans received an opportunity to prove Bayard correct in May 1886, when the Canadians seized the American vessel, David J. Adams, "for violation of Canadian waters." When Phelps heard the news, he immediately wrote to Rosebery and informed him of his regret that such action would come "at this junction when it will be immediately availed of by the party desirous of making trouble with England for the sake of the Irish vote."[45] Whether this was true or not, made little difference to the flow of complaints which arrived in the Senate from New England fishermen. Responding to these calls for aid, Edmunds, the boss of the Senate,[46] on June 3 demanded that American naval forces patrol the fishery areas to defend American rights.[47] The reaction in the Senate prompted Bayard to inform Phelps.

> You will observe how justly I measured the use to which the anti-British sentiment would be put by Blaine and Company. The Irish heart (the Irish vote) is to be fixed to increase the difficulty of settlement of the fishery question. It is expected that in addition to his enlightenment of the public mind on the Irish Home Rule measure, Mr. Blaine is soon to address a public meeting at Portland, Maine on the fishing question. Whether

[44] Ibid., 208. Bayard to Phelps, March 7, 1886.

[45] Ibid., 212. Phelps to Bayard, May 8, 1886. Bayard informed Phelps, "I did not wish him to make public in any way your intimation that we had a party here desirous of provoking collision with England. It is perfectly true that the Irish dynamite element is courted and caressed by Blaine and his fellows and this of course requires expression by them of animosity to everything British on every possible occasion." Bayard to Phelps, May 21, 1886, 219.

[46] Adler, Edmunds, 228.

[47] Congressional Record, 49th Congress, 2nd Session, XVIII, part 5, 5182.

Messrs. Evarts, Edmunds and Sherman will accept his
guidance I do not know, but up to this time I have been
able to discover no higher or better rule of action
with the Senate Committee on Foreign Relations, to
which they belong, and which they control than to ob-
struct and oppose anything proposed or approved by
the Executive.[48]

This and other statements by Bayard concerning the Senate cannot

be taken at face value, but there were some signs that the Republicans

were interested in using diplomatic disputes for purely political

reasons. The Republicans on the committee at this time included

Sherman of Ohio; Edmunds of Vermont; Frye of Maine; Evarts, the ex-

Secretary of State, and Benjamin Harrison, the future President.

Edmunds had cause to dislike the Cleveland administration, since the

President had defeated him on the tenure of office battle and the

question of appointments.[49] In addition he was known for his anti-

English bias. Frye was considered by many to be the Senate mouthpiece

of Blaine, and Evarts had indicated a degree of anti-English sentiment

also.[50] The only Democrat on the committee with any real voice was

John T. Morgan of Alabama who served as the spokesman for the admin-

istration, but he often opposed Bayard's plans and leaned to the Repub-

licans. Consequently, although Bayard's concept of the Committee's

position on many issues was somewhat exaggerated, as will be shown, it

was not completely without foundation.

---

[48] Tansill, Foreign Policy of Bayard, 229. Bayard to Phelps, June 9, 1886. Bayard, referred to Blaine's Home Rule speech which he delivered at Portland, Maine, on June 6 and in which he stated that Ireland's condition resulted from the fact that absentee landlords ruined the country.

[49] Burnette, "Senate Foreign Relations Committee," 276-78.

[50] Ibid., 389.

At any rate within this bitter atmosphere created by the seizure of the "David Adams" and other vessels, an atmosphere enflamed by Republican orators, Phelps signed an extradition treaty with Lord Rosebery on June 25, 1886.[51] He had done so without first getting Bayard's approval of the final text on the pretext that, if he delayed, the Senate would not have been able to approve the treaty before recessing.[52] Moreover, on June 8 the Home Rule Bill had failed to pass its second reading and Gladstone had dissolved Parliament. In all probability Phelps wanted to have the treaty signed by the Gladstone government and, since there was the possibility the Conservatives would win the election, he rushed the treaty as fast as possible to Washington. He might even have hoped for Senate approval before the results of the elections decided the Home Rule issue.

The treaty itself merely enlarged the list of extraditable crimes to include embezzlement, fraud and breach of trust. One clause attempted to include under the terms of extradition the crime of

> malicious injuries to property, whereby the life of any person shall be endangered if such injuries constitute a crime according to the laws of both high contracting parties.[53]

Phelps had originally proposed a clause which followed that found in the Japanese Treaty,

---

[51] Bailey, Diplomatic History, 426.

[52] New York Tribune, July 20, 1886.

[53] Ibid.

> malicious destruction of, or the attempt to destroy,
> railways or trains, bridges, public edifices or dwell-
> ings, where the act endangers human life.[54]

Although the final draft did not follow the exact wording of the Japanese

Treaty which the Senate had accepted, it did not radically depart from

that idea. In fact as was shown earlier thr trend of American extradi-

tion policy was in this direction and the Phelps-Rosebery Treaty was

merely part of that movement.

When the text arrived in Washington, Cleveland immediately sent

it to the Senate on July 8. In his accompanying message he asked for

their immediate approval "on the grounds of the long series of negotia-

tions" and "its great importance owing to the contiguity of Her Majesty's

territories with those of the United States."[55] In executive session

the Senate Committee on Foreign Affairs considered the bill and Sherman

reported it on July 17, 1886 with a unanimous recommendation for approval,

only nine days after it was received.[56] During the committee discussions

Edmunds offered an amendment to the embezzlement clause to the effect

that it would not apply to those under 16, a move which Bayard interpreted

as another example of Edmunds' anti-administration position.[57] This was

not correct, however, for in the course of the fight for ratification

---

[54] House Executive Documents, 50th Congress, Second Session, I,
part II, 1731.

[55] Messages, 4175.

[56] Senate Executive Journal: Proceedings of the United States
Senate in Executive Session (1901), Vol. XXV, 552.

[57] Tansill, Foreign Policy of Bayard, 35. Bayard to Phelps, July
17, 1886.

Edmunds became one of the treaty's best friends. Only one other amendment was offered during the committee hearing—one which would add rape to the list of extraditable crimes.[58] It failed to win approval, but it reappeared in later debates.

While the Senators discussed the treaty, its existence caused a great deal of discussion in both the United States and England as to its probable contents. The British showed "intense gratification for the prospect of a really effective extradition treaty."[59] Some American papers published the rumor that the British would receive the right to demand the dynamiters who would flee to the United States, while the United States "under such a treaty would be interested in the American colony of bank embezzlers now so rapidly growing up in the Dominion."[60] One English paper recognized the possible Irish reaction, however, but most hoped that the Senate would ratify the treaty owing to the desire of Americans to get hold of the absconding swindlers who find a refuge in Canada.[61]

Before the publication of the treaty text Americans seemed divided on the whole question. The New York Sun, a Democratic paper, agreed that dynamiters should be extraditable, but not political offenders. Some papers emphasized the need to include both dynamiters and embezzlers,

---

[58] Burnette, "Senate Foreign Relations Committee," 357.

[59] New York Catholic Telegraph, July 22, 1886. Quoted from a London dispatch dated July 15, 1886.

[60] Public Opinion, I (1886), 288. One paper, the Washington Post, published a story of a bank embezzlement of $100,000 by the bank president.

[61] Ibid., 288. Chicago Tribune, July 17, 1886.

while others emphasized the embezzler clause which would give great security to bank depositors and stockholders. Little disagreement existed on the gains for Americans, but some papers disagreed on the dynamite issue. One dispatch stated that, although most Americans sympathized with the Irish in their desire for freedom, few accepted the work of the dynamiters. This most probably was true, especially after the dynamite scare that followed the Haymarket Riot of May, 1886, but the Ohio State Journal still cautioned Americans about the dynamite clause, since "such a treaty might be made an infernal instrument of oppression."[62]

While such speculation filled the papers the New York Tribune scooped the country on July 20, 1886, by publishing the text of the treaty and the message Phelps sent with it.[63] Why this planned leak was permitted is hard to say, since on July 17, 1886 both Democrats and Republicans on the Committee approved the treaty. The reactions to the rumors of the treaty could have caused its supporters to release the text so as to eliminate any doubt that political offenders would be surrendered. It could also have been released as a trial balloon just to gauge reaction, while the opponents could have released it in an effect to generate enough unfavorable sentiment to

---

[62] Ibid., 289.

[63] Tansill, Foreign Policy of Bayard, xxxv. Tansill states that the London Times published the full text on July 21, 1886, indicating that it was their scoop, but the Tribune got it first. The leak possibly went from Frye to Blaine to Whitelaw Reid, editor of the Tribune, or really from anyone in the Senate. The Tribune had very accurate sources at this time, as will be shown later. As was the case when debating a treaty the Senate would try to keep the terms secret until after its approval so as not to embarrass the Executive branch. However, one could expect a leak if the treaty generated lively debate or attracted public interest.

kill it. At any rate Bayard was not surprised that the Senate failed
to honor the secrecy of executive session.[64]

The Tribune also published a long article which emphasized, first,
that, since the treaty had no retroactive clause, those Irishmen who had
participated in the earlier dynamite campaign were safe; secondly, that
political offenders were protected by a separate clause; and thirdly,
that Americans needed the dynamite clause as much as the English especially after the Haymarket incident.[65] On the next day the same Republican paper reported that the business community had received the
news with great rejoicing. Yet the question of the dynamite clause
had obviously generated some disagreement on the value of the treaty,
since the author of this news article attempted to allay British fears
that the treaty would be destroyed because of it.

On the day following the Tribune scoop the London Times published
the text and British reactions appeared immediately. The Times complained that it failed to suppress the Irish-American societies that
had planned the dynamite plots, something that the British had desired
as early as June 1881.[66] Others complained that the American emphasis
upon the political offenders clause might destroy any real hope of
preventing dynamite attacks. In other words the British felt that they
would not gain the custody of the dynamiters, the only reason for their

---

[64] Ibid., xxxv. Bayard to Phelps, July 31, 1886.

[65] New York Tribune, July 20, 1886.

[66] Tansill, Foreign Policy of Bayard, xxxv.

signing, if Americans considered them to be political criminals.[67]

With the text at hand American opinion seemed to accept both aspects of the treaty without any real disagreement. Godkin saw the treaty as providing for the extradition of only the actual dynamiter and not those who planned such attacks, while the true political offender was as secure as ever and the defaulting colony in Canada would at least cease growing.[68] Both Republican and Democratic papers accepted the embezzlement clause without question and the dynamite clause mainly on the basis of the Haymarket incident.[69]

While the British and Americans accepted the treaty the Irish-Americans rallied their forces against it. Ford declared that it was merely a Bayard inspired prop for British despotism which the Senate would destroy.[70] The New York Irish-American, the Democratic opponent of Ford's Irish World, declared the treaty would make the United States an ally of the English in the work of perpetrating a tyrannical rule, and for this reason Irish Americans would oppose it, since it violated American traditions.[71] Patrick Collins publicly opposed the treaty, while O'Reilly said it was a disgrace to the country and to the Democratic Party. The latter felt that it would effectively eliminate the United States as a refuge for political offenders, since the British would claim every purely political act under the terms of the dynamite

---

[67] Saturday Review, LXII (1886), 109.

[68] Nation, LXIII (1886), 65.

[69] Public Opinion, I (1886), 309-310.

[70] New York Irish World, July 22, 1886.

[71] New York Irish-American, July 22, 1886.

clause and not the political offenders clause. The New York Tablet
(a Catholic paper which reflected Irish opinion) held that the British
at first wanted the right to try Americans who plotted the dynamite
attacks on American soil, but settled for the right to demand those
who actually committed the crime. Yet even if the Senate accepted the
treaty, the British would gain few dynamiters since, as this editor
held, Americans would decide the political issue of the case.[72] The
Chicago Citizen saw the whole thing as a British attempt to gain
political prisoners, but it would not succeed "because Senators Logan
and Riddleberger would fight it."[73]

While Americans generally speaking wanted both clauses, they
recognized the formidable opposition of the Irish.[74] The Emmett Club
of Brooklyn (the organization which staged the March 1883 attack) sent
a petition to the Senate opposing the treaty, along with others from
various Irish organizations, both political and social in nature.[75] In
the midst of these Cleveland submitted the papers on the seizure of
American vessels in the previous May and June. As these inflamed the
anti-British sentiment, latent in many Senators, Van Wyck in an obvious attempt to take advantage of this turn of events proposed that

---

[72] New York Tablet, July 31, 1886. This kind of argument must
have worried the English. See page 224.

[73] Chicago Citizen, July 24, 1886.

[74] Public Opinion, I (1886), 309.

[75] Burnette, "Senate Foreign Relations Committee," 357.

the extradition question be debated in open session.[76] This must have been a move to kill the treaty, since no one would have attempted to appear in public at that time as a friend of England and an enemy of the Irish. However, the members of the Foreign Affairs Committee led a successful fight against this motion, only to have the Senate in a later vote postpone the discussion until the next session.[77]

The Republican New York Tribune, usually well informed, blamed the failure on a heavy work load, and this does seem reasonable.[78] Although the Senate Committee on Foreign Affairs cleared the treaty within five working days, the Senate as a whole had the treaty at the most for thirteen working days. This was hardly sufficient time to allow debate and some Senators wanted debate. At the same time the excitement caused by the dynamite clause obviously helped the Senate to decide for postponement, especially since it was an election year. The Tribune accused the Democrats of opposing ratification, while Bayard implied the Republicans opposed it, since he was not sure what treaty the Republicans would find acceptable to meet party requirements.[79] Both versions are incorrect, since both Edmunds and Morgan wanted the treaty ratified. In all reality both parties split on the question and both must have

---

[76] Senate Executive Journal, XXV, 576.

[77] Burnette, "Senate Foreign Relations Committee," 358.

[78] New York Tribune, August 4, 1886.

[79] Tansill, Foreign Policy of Bayard, 236. Bayard to Phelps, July 29, 1886.

been concerned about the possible effect of ratification on the Irish.[80]

Shortly after the postponement the American Bankers Association met at Boston. The delegates listened to a report from the committee entrusted with the question of extradition treaties in general. The report told of meetings and inquiries made at the Senate and the State Department concerning the Phelps-Rosebery Treaty[81] and especially the dynamite clause. Some effort was made to convince the bankers that this particular clause was not out of context with other recent treaties, namely those with Japan and Belgium. Their emphasis on the dynamite question indicates that those who wanted the treaty ratified recognized it as the greatest single obstacle to the fulfillment of their plans.

The adjournment of Congress immediately preceded the Congressional election campaign and Blaine gave the Republican keynote address when he attacked the administration on the tariff and fishery questions.[82] Other Republicans took up the cry and accused the Democrats under Cleveland's leadership of being pro-British. The Irish themselves accepted Blaine's argument as the ex-peasants condemned Bayard for his pro-British bias. Although the more active Irish-nationalists had accused Bayard of being pro-British before he had accepted the job as Secretary of State, the fact that other Americans accused him of the

---

[80] W. Stull Holt, Treaties Defeated by the Senate (1933), 142.

[81] Proceedings of the American Bankers Association's Annual Convention, (1886), 53-63.

[82] Nation, XL (1885), 167.

same crime in 1886[83] only strengthened the animosity these Irish Americans had for the Democratic party at the national level.  Such native
American attacks, coupled to the publication of the treaty text and
general Republican efforts to paint the Administration pro-British
must have made it easier for these anti-Cleveland Irishmen to "spread
the faith" among their fellow countrymen.  On July 31, 1886 Finerty
condemned both Cleveland and Bayard for being pro-British, while two
months later he placed Phelps on the list as a man always trying to be
friendly with England.[84]  This is understandable, since Finerty had
switched sides to become a "Blaine Irishman" in 1884.  However, even
the Boston Pilot, edited by the ever-staunch Democrat, John Boyle
O'Reilly, constantly belittled Bayard and Phelps.  On October 16, 1886
O'Reilly condemned Phelps for a public statement that only Irish-Americans wanted Home Rule in Ireland and the implication that without
their support the question would evaporate.  A week later he published
articles from the Atlanta Constitution and the New York Sun, both nom-
inally Democratic, that ridiculed Phelps' usefulness.  The Sun also
stated that the only way to get rid of Bayard was to vote Republican
in 1888.  In issue after issue O'Reilly hammered away at Bayard,
Phelps and William C. Endicott, the Secretary of War.[85]  Yet even while
condemning Bayard "as a most unfit and undemocratic Secretary of State,"

[83] Arthur Richmond, "Letters to Prominent Persons; Number One to
the Secretary of State," North American Review, XLII (1886), 90.

[84] Chicago Citizen, July 19, 1886; September 18, 1886.

[85] Boston Pilot, October 30, November 13, November 27, December 4,
December 18, 1886.

proclaimed his loyalty to the Democratic party. No matter how pro-
itish some Democrats were, he would never support the Republicans,
ace, as he argued, they showed the Irish attention only since the
?eat of 1884. His loyalty to the party did not prevent his Irishism
om rising to the surface in condemnation of the pro-English elements
the party.[86] Other Catholic papers found fault with Bayard on both
e extradition and fishery points while some found fault with Phelps'
astant efforts to show his friendship for the English.[87]

It is interesting to note at this point that the Republicans did
o use the Extradition Treaty in their campaign to paint the adminis-
ation in a pro-British light. If they instituted such a campaign for
expressed purpose of capturing the Irish vote it would seem only log-
l that they would use this treaty which was so fresh in Irish minds
for them so characteristic of a pro-British administration. That
y did not implies that they could not, either because of some other
ssures or because to do so would have led to the treaty's defeat.
s they wanted to avoid because the treaty had some real value for
United States. In other words, it is quite possible to believe
t the Republicans were using issues in the election campaigns that
not in reality possess any great significance for Anglo-American

---

[86] O'Reilly's dislike for Endicott could have been the result of
gaining the New England Cabinet seat that Collins wanted. He was
m Massachusetts.

[87] New York _Tablet_, September 18, October 23; November 20, 27,
6; New York _Freeman's Journal_, December 11, 1886.

relations. Non-essential disputes could be used as fodder for the masses, but those which counted were saved from the blinding light of the election campaigns.

With the election over Anglo-American disputes returned to the center of the political stage as the Canadians approved a law which permitted the seizure of American vessels entering Canadian waters for any purpose not permitted by treaty and the United States Revenue Service antagonized the Canadians on the fur-seal dispute. In the midst of all this Anglophobia Congress reconvened and the Senate called up the Extradition Treaty. The American need for the treaty did not lessen in the course of the autumn months. In September, for instance, a number of officials of the Charter Oak Insurance Company embezzled over one million dollars and at least one of them arrived in Canada to enjoy the loot.[88] Yet shortly after the session opened opposition to the treaty must have appeared for on December 14, 1886 Senator Edmunds asked that it be referred back to the committee.[89] Obviously, this was an attempt to get it where its friends could produce a text acceptable to the majority. In the following month Senator Morgan, also a supporter of the treaty, reported it with an amendment to the dynamite clause which merely made allowances for the various laws of the

---

[88] Public Opinion, I (1886), 481.

[89] Senate Executive Journal, XXV, 624.

olitical sub-divisions of both countries.[90]  This was most probably
uggested by the Judiciary Committee after some senators criticized
his point and the Committee on Foreign Relations complied with these
uggestions.  At any rate the treaty with amendments was considered by
ie Senate on January 21, 1887.

In the debate that followed a bitter struggle developed between
enator Riddleberger, one of the most violent of the anti-British pol-
icians, and members of the Committee on Foreign Relations.  Riddleberger
d the fight against the treaty which he disliked in toto but particu-
rly because of the dynamite clause.  At one point Edmunds declared
at no decent Irishman would use dynamite, to which Riddleberger re-
ied that the crimes of England against Ireland justified any kind of
taliation.[91]  Evarts said that the treaty should be accepted because
would enable the United States to capture the "boodle alderman," but
ddleberger replied that "the recovery of one hundred boodles from
nada would not offset the surrender of a single Irish patriot."[92]
ye, Sherman and Morgan entered the debate on the side of the treaty

---

[90] Ibid., 710.  The amendment read "insert after the words 'high
itracting parties,' in the last line of the first paragraph of the
ause numbered 4, in Article I, the following words:  or according to
e laws of that political division of either country in which the of-
ise shall have been committed, and of that political division of
:her country in which the offender shall be arrested."

[91] Chicago Citizen, January 29, 1887; New York Times, January 22,
37; New York Tribune, January 22, 1887.

[92] New York Times, January 22, 1887; New York Tribune, January 22,
37.

and the New York <u>Times</u>, a Democratic paper, accused Riddleberger of merely defending Irish radicals.[93]  In effect, he was fighting against a bipartisan alliance.

During these debates Congress turned to the question of the fishery dispute.  The Canadian actions of late November led to the introduction by Senator Edmunds of the Retaliation Bill.  When this passed on January 24, 1887, 46 to 1, the President received the right to reduce Canadian trade with the United States as a club to gain concessions on the fishery question.[94]  Riddleberger oddly enough voted against the measure, because it was in a sense dealing with England and this he would not do in any form.[95]  The Irish were concerned with this dispute because some felt that the government might use the extradition problem to gain concessions on the fisheries.[96]  In this way what was basic to the Irish in America became somewhat entangled with the whole problem of Anglo-American relations.

This entanglement presents a particularly difficult problem for the historian.  Anglo-American problems rested rather heavily upon Bayard during this particular session of Congress, but he felt he received little sympathy there.  Whatever he tried in the way of a solu-

---

[93] Ibid.

[94] Burnette, "Senate Foreign Relations Committee," 335.

[95] Ibid., 358.  This is indicative of Riddleberger's violent anti-English bias and Burnette feels that this is explained to some extent by the fact that England held most of Virginia's bonds when he was a Readjuster during the 1870's and 1880's.

[96] Chicago <u>Citizen</u>, January 29, 1887.

tion to these problems, the Republicans in the Senate refused to accept. To Bayard, they wanted to use such disputes for mere political gain, the Irish vote. Thus, when discussing these issues in open session, Riddleberger was not the only anti-English Senator. Edmunds, Frye, Morgan and Ingalls of Kansas were especially well-known for this feeling.[97] Throughout these months violent speeches rocked the halls of Congress as one after another Republican, and some Democrats as well, tried to exhibit an anti-British feeling. At one point Ingalls called for war over the fishery question.[98] Bayard felt the weight of this abuse and constantly returned to the inhospitable atmosphere of the Senate in general and of the Committee on Foreign Relations in particular. Even Cecil Spring-Rice, the young, but brilliant, Secretary of the English Legation, noticed the hatred some senators possessed for Bayard personally and the Administration in general.[99] Allan Nevins stated that the Republicans were willing to use almost any means available to gain the Irish vote, and Charles Tansill agreed.[100]

All this fails to take into consideration the Extradition Treaty. The very senators who in open session fought to gain the attention of the anti-British element, fought in closed session for the Extradition Treaty. The Republicans like Evarts, Edmunds and Frye, who appeared to

[97] Tansill, Foreign Policy of Bayard, 229, 260.

[98] Congressional Record, 49th Congress, 2nd Session, XVIII, part I, 929.

[99] Gwynn, Letters and Friendship of Spring-Rice, 57. To Ferguson March 18, 1887.

[100] Nevins, Cleveland, 428; Tansill, Foreign Policy of Bayard, 320-323. Tansill constantly refers to this.

Bayard as being interested only in the Irish vote, refused to make concessions to that vote on the Extradition Treaty.  To infer from this that
they were really not interested in the Irish vote would not be correct,
for they were, as the letters of Bayard would indicate.  The explanation
of their stand can possibly be found in two facts; first one large segment of Americans, especially the powerful bankers, wanted the treaty,
and secondly in order to use the treaty in the scramble for Irish vote,
the Republican would have had to campaign publicly for the removal of
the dynamite clause.  But this in turn would have implied that they
were not against the use of dynamite by political offenders, a position which would have cost them dearly.  By keeping it locked up behind
the closed doors of executive session, they could avoid such pitfalls and
at the same time increase its changes for passage, since the effective-
ness of Irish opposition would be reduced to a minimum.  At any rate on
March 2 Riddleberger asked for an immediate vote on a motion to postpone the treaty debates indefinitely.[101]  Curiously enough, he did not
ask for outright rejection, probably because he realized that this
would not have met with success, although this would have been the
effect of his motion.  Senator Hoar then offered a motion to table the
discussion, which in effect postponed the debate but without a vote.
This news caused Thompson to lament, "If the clauses which enlarge the
number of offenses against business honesty, for which criminals are
to be surrendered, could be taken by themselves, there would be no

---

[101] Senate Executive Journal, XXV, 586.

hesitancy about ratifying them."[102]  When the news reached England,

some Englishmen saw the postponement as the work of wild Irish-Americans,

but the Chicago Citizen declared that the Senate objected to the treaty

because it was unamerican in that it permitted the extradition of polit-

ical offenders.[103]  By March 25 Spring-Rice reported that it "seems  to

have busted."[104]

If those who postponed the discussions did so in the hope that when

they would return to the treaty, they would find a different atmosphere

they must have been greatly disappointed for in the interim things did

not change.  The diplomatic picture remained much the same with Bayard

and the administration trying to solve problems and the Senate Re-

Publicans trying to keep them alive.  Spring-Rice constantly repeated

his earlier observation that Irish political stock continued to rise

seemingly without limit.[105]  Meanwhile, Phelps feared the effect Re-

publican efforts to stir up anti-British feeling would have upon general

Anglo-American relations. By 1887 the British began to react to the

constant talk in America concerning Anglo-Irish relations and the habit

of the American press and politicians to condemn the British failure to

---

[102] American, XIII (1887), 293.  Thompson must have stood in the middle on this point since Barker, the publisher, in all probability took the side of the bankers.

[103] Chicago Citizen, March 13, 1887.

[104] Gwynn, Letters and Friendship of Spring-Rice, I, 59.  To Stephens, March 25, 1887.

[105] Ibid., 56-96.  He constantly makes reference to this.

confer Home Rule on Ireland.[106] Bayard had just the opposite, that

is, the effect this constant talk would have upon the American side,

since in his mind

> it was this underlying and smouldering sentiment that
> even more than the narrow selfishness of the Clouster
> fishermen and their attorneys in and out of Congress,
> that created difficulties in the way of my obtaining
> a just and amicable settlement.[107]

But the Republicans did not let up. When the Irish in New York called

for a mass meeting to protest Balfour's coercion bill, then before Par-

liament, Senators Evarts, Hawley, and Heacock sent telegrams congratu-

lating the Irish National League for carrying on the fight.[108] At the

same time Blaine was traveling through England and Spring-Rice re-

minded the Foreign Office that "it would do no harm to conciliate him

who attempts to recapture the Irish vote which was only partially won

at the last election."[109]

The Irish seemed in a formidable position in the spring of 1887.

Just as American Anglophobia seemed on the rise, the Republicans under

Blaine's leadership sought the Irish vote and worked to increase the

Anglophobia already present. At the same time the Irish at home

needed assistance to destroy Balfour's new coercion act. This com-

bination of events permitted the Irish at least to prevent ratifica-

tion of a treaty which had won the support of the bankers and business-

---

106 Tansill, Foreign Policy of Bayard, 262.

107 Ibid., 262. Bayard to Phelps, April 23, 1887.

108 New York Irish World, March 27, 1887.

109 Gwynn, Letters and Friendship of Spring-Rice, 67, to Stephen,
April 15, 1887.

men of the country. However, it was evident that the Republicans although seeking the Irish vote, did not and could not bring this treaty
into the mainstream of that struggle. They faced an odd dilemma, how
to gain both the support of the moneyed class who wanted the treaty
and the Irish who did not. Spring-Rice recognized this when he stated,
"Blaine, if he accepts the invitation of the rich, offends the Irish;
if he refuses, he offends the capitalists."[110] This more than any
other reason explains why even the Republicans wanted to avoid a showdown on the dynamite clause. By tabling the treaty and postponing a
decision they could avoid offending the Irish, since it was not accepted, and the bankers, since it was not rejected.

---

[110] Ibid., 68. To Stephen, June 30, 1887.

Chapter VII

The Final Rejection

During the late spring and summer of 1887 Bayard devoted much of
his time to the search for a solution to Anglo-American problems.
By early September he had agreed to submit the fishery question to a
special commission of high officials from both countries.

Bayard's hopes for a settlement suffered a setback when the British appointed Joseph Chamberlain as their representative. Chamberlain,
well known to Irish-Americans as the man who wrecked Gladstone's first
Home Rule bill, increased their dislike for him when in late October,
just before sailing for the United States, he delivered a violent attack upon the Irish in America for their support of revolution in
Ireland.[1] His close political friend, Charles Dilke, felt that this
speech was foolish, since it widened differences and exasperated "pas-
sions prior to engaging upon business that required a serene atmosphere."[2] Many of his political friends told Chamberlain to refuse the
appointment, since the work of the negotiations was doomed to failure
from the start. Even after he accepted Dilke cautioned him to be care-
ful of his words, since "the Irish vote was a large object of regard in
the United States."[3] This interest in Chamberlain's presence and its

---

[1] Gwynn, Dilke, II, 270.

[2] Garvin, Chamberlain, II, 320.

[3] Ibid., 325.

effect upon the results of the negotiations was not limited to the British. Cleveland was fully aware of the unfavorable influence he would have among the Irish,[4] while Bayard felt that "the animosities growing out of British domestic questions (Home Rule in Ireland) are sufficient to interfere"[5] with his honest attempt to solve an Anglo-American problem. Phelps felt that no matter what the commission produced, it would encounter the opposition of the Irish party.[6]

While important figures in both countries indicated a fear of Irish power, the fur-seals dispute arose again to further complicate matters. For the second time in as many years Revenue Service cutters had seized Canadian vessels on the high seas for the indiscriminate killing of seals. In an obvious effort to create a feeling of good will just prior to the opening of the Fishery Commission, Bayard not only returned these vessels to the Canadians, but apologized for their seizure. This was only correct, since the United States had no right to seize them in the first place, but Irish-Americans would not accept the concept of an apology and O'Reilly used the incident to condemn Bayard for showing such friendliness to the English government.[7]

Into this atmosphere of Irish opposition and hostility arrived Chamberlain on November 7. Bayard had hired Pinkerton guards to pro-

---

[4] Tansill, Foreign Policy of Bayard, 278. Phelps to Bayard, October 29, 1887.

[5] Ibid., 274. Bayard to G. B. Roberts, November 21, 1887.

[6] Ibid., 279. Cleveland to Bayard, November 7, 1887.

[7] Boston Pilot, October 29, 1887.

tect the distinguished Englishman against the threats of the Clan-Na-
Gael.[8] Reilly felt that this was an insult to the Irish, but said
that it would not matter for in the final analysis the Irish would oppose the Commission's work no matter what resulted simply because Bayard
had called the Commission in the interest of England.[9] It seems that
Bayard could never please the loyal Democrat from Boston.

Two weeks after the Commission opened Congress reconvened with
the extradition question obviously on its agenda. Phelps had indicated
in October that he felt that it would pass and "even the Irish, if the
question is fairly stated, would accept the treaty. I think, if some
judicious and competent person is employed quietly to confer with
Senators, the confirmation can be easily carried."[10] By December, however, opposition had grown to include others besides the Irish. Some
felt that the treaty did not include as many crimes as it should and
that some forms of fraud were still possible as it was then written.[11]
A few Senators did not feel that concessions on extradition should be
made until the British agreed to a settlement on the fishery problem.
In other words, they wanted to use the treaty as a club to force concessions from the British. Irish opposition continued, since in their
estimation the treaty would give the British the right to demand political

---

[8] Garvin, Chamberlain, II, 327.

[9] Boston Pilot, November 21, 1887.

[10] Tansill, Foreign Policy of Bayard, xxxvi. Phelps to Bayard,
October 25, 1887.

[11] Chicago Citizen, December 3, 1887.

offenders. The whole discussion received a shot in the arm only two weeks before Congress met when two Irish-Americans, Thomas Callan and Michael Harkins, were arrested by British authorities for possession of dynamite.[12]

In the face of growing criticism the Senate reopened discussion of the treaty but almost immediately it was sent to the Committee on Foreign Relations.[13] While this Committee under the Chairmanship of John Sherman of Ohio attempted to remove causes for criticism, a deadlock developed in the deliberations of the Fisheries Commission. To bypass the deadlock Bayard invited Chamberlain to his home for a private conversation. In the course of their talk Chamberlain offered a treaty text, but Bayard replied that he was not in a position to accept it. He wanted to avoid antagonizing the "force of Irish feeling." Chamberlain replied that he could understand Bayard's fears especially after "John Sherman had told him the Irish influence had prevented the ratification of the Phelps-Rosebery Extradition treaty."[14] The Chairman of the Committee on Foreign Relations, who was obviously in a position to know, saw the Senate's failure to ratify the treaty as the work of the Irish, that is, if Chamberlain is to be trusted and there is no good cause to doubt him on this point. At least Sherman's interpretation would seem to fit well with the facts that the Irish alone violently opposed the

---

[12] Ryan, *Fenian Memories*, 135. They were later tried, convicted on February 3, 1888, and sentenced to a fifteen year prison term. See the *Annual Register*, 1888, part II, 7.

[13] *Senate Executive Journal*, XXVI, 17.

[14] Tansill, *Foreign Policy of Bayard*, 286. Bayard memo. December 10, 1887.

treaty, that most observers saw the dynamite clause as the main obstacle, and that Riddleberger led the opposition precisely for this reason.

After the Christmas recess it was obvious that another move for ratification would be made and the Irish attempted direct pressure. On January 5 Senator Henry L. Dawes, of Massachusetts, presented a petition from the Father Matthew Total Abstinence Society of Lawrence, Massachusetts, which asked that the Senate reject the treaty.[15]  Meanwhile, the Republicans continued to cater to the Irish vote. In early December Senator Ingalls, the presiding officer of the Senate, met with two visiting members of Parnell's Party and used the opportunity to remind them that the British once sacked Washington.[16]

On January 12, 1888 Senator Morgan reported the treaty from Committee with an amendment and the debate opened on January 30. Riddleberger almost at once offered a motion to consider the treaty in open session, but this was rejected, 11 to 38.[17]  It is interesting to note that every member of the Committee voted against opening the discussion, since in all probability this would have killed it. Riddleberger did not give up, however, and on the next day, while still in open session, he attempted to have his motion reconsidered.[18]  Edmunds rose to challenge the legality of raising executive business in open session and Senator

[15] Senate Executive Journal, XXVI, 106.

[16] Gwynn, Letters and Friendship of Spring-Rice, 89. To Stephen, December 15, 1887.

[17] Senate Executive Journal, XXVI, 161.

[18] Congressional Record, 50 Congress, 1 Session, XVIX, part 1, 829. Riddleberger had voted against his own motion of January 30 in order to be in a position to ask for a reconsideration in open session.

ngalls, president pro tempore, put it over to the next day. On Febru-
ry 1 the Senate united against Riddleberger and prevented the hearing
f his motion for reconsideration by filibustering on other questions and
ngalls refused to recognize him. All this was an obvious attempt to
void having to vote in public against Riddleberger's motion to open the
reaty discussion.[19] When the Senate went behind closed doors the tables
ere reversed, since after the treaty was read for the second time, Rid-
leberger held the floor and refused to yield to permit a vote.[20] Con-
equently, on the next day in open session after Riddleberger again
ried to gain recognition to present his motion of reconsideration
enator Plumb accused him of using obstructionist tactics in his fight
gainst Phelps' handiwork, to which Riddleberger replied that he wanted
o open the discussions because "in executive session no man is re-
ponsible."[21]

Shortly after this encounter Ingalls ordered the visitors removed
nd the doors closed. The treaty, having been read for the second time,
as in the Committee of the Whole and the Senators considered the amend-

---

[19] Ibid., 868; New York Tribune, February 2, 1880. It is interest-
ng to note that on January 30, 1888, Ingalls voted to open the discus-
ions, but on February 1 he refused to give Riddleberger an opportunity
o present his reconsideration motion.

[20] Senate Executive Journal, XXVI, 169; New York Tribune, February
, 1888.

[21] Congressional Record, 50th Congress, 1 Session, XVIX, part 1,
99. The New York Tribune, February 3, 1888, stated that "the treaty
ill be ratified if the vote is behind closed doors, and rejected in
he open." New York Times, February 3, 1888, stated that "Senators
dmunds, Ingalls and Plumb talked so Riddleberger wouldn't get a chance
o talk about his motion."

ment as proposed by the Foreign Relations Committee. The original dynamite clause merely declared that "malicious injuries to property whereby the life of any person shall be endangered, if such injuries constitute a crime according to the laws of both the high contracting parties."[22] It was rather general in its coverage, since any attempt to destroy property where human life was merely endangered, not necessarily taken, was subject to extradition, and as such was substantially different from the clause found in Phelps' proposed draft, which Bayard had received on November 23, 1885. His clause stated that "malicious destruction of, or the attempt to destroy, railroads or trains, bridges, public edifices or dwellings, where the act endangers human life," was extraditable.[23] Here is a much more specific statement which enumerates only certain kinds of property, all of which, oddly enough, had come under the attack of the Irish dynamiter. Phelps must have been guided by this consideration. In addition, his clause was a virtual verbatim reproduction of the one found in the Japanese Treaty which passed the Senate in June, 1886. Why he rejected it and agreed to the more general statement can only be surmised. It would seem that the British would have been interested in a more general clause in order to gain as many offenders as possible. This particular point could have been the one to which Phelps referred when he told Bayard that he was having some difficulty just before the

---

[22] New York _Tribune_, July 20, 1886.

[23] _House Executive Document_, 50th Congress, 2nd Session, I, part II, 1739.

treaty was signed.[24] Yet the change did occur and the final version had the general statement.

All this, of course, was unknown to the general public and they did not learn that two clauses had entered the discussion until February, 1888, and, then, they received the impression that the more specific clause originated in the Committee on Foreign Relations. The amendment to the treaty which Morgan reported on January 12, and the Senate considered on February 2, returned to some extent to Phelps' original proposal. By adding certain words the clause read "malicious injuries to persons or property by explosives, or malicious injuries or obstructions to railroads, whereby the life of any person shall be endangered."[25] In the course of the many discussions on the treaty in open session Riddleberger implied that this amendment "would bring in the Irish dynamiters," which, if true, would "intensify the opposition to the treaty from the Irish element."[26] The New York Tribune said that such rumors caused the Irish in America to fear that they would be "deprived of the right of asylum," that the amendment would "prevent [the collection of] funds for Ireland," and that "political agitators" would be given over to the British.[27] For these reasons the Tribune and the Times wanted the treaty discussed in open session, so that it will be shown

---

[24] Tansill, Foreign Policy of Bayard, xxxvi. Phelps to Bayard, March 27, 1886.

[25] Senate Executive Journal, XXVI, 170.

[26] New York Times, February 3, 1888.

[27] New York Tribune, February 4, 1888.

that "Americans will not surrender political agitators or conspirators or deprive anyone of political asylum."[28] This belief that the amendment changed the original clause was not limited to contemporaries of the debates, since two scholars who have studied the question have agreed that this was the effect of the change.[29]

In the light of certain considerations, this does not seem to be completely true. In the first place, when the New York *Tribune* published the original clause in 1886, American and Irish-American opinion felt that the treaty included dynamiters. Furthermore, the amendment of 1888 originated in the Committee on Foreign Relations whose members wanted ratification. One would imagine they would avoid creating any additional opposition, and at the same time work to reduce the opposition that already existed. It seems inconceivable that they would introduce a measure that would tend to excite the Irish. Any attempt to change the dynamite clause then must be seen as an effort to decrease, not increase Irish opposition. The additional words made the clause somewhat more specific and, therefore, would tend to reduce the possibility that the British would demand and gain political offenders. Instead of bringing anyone who maliciously destroyed any kind of property under the terms of the treaty, the amendment in effect would have limited extradition to those persons who used dynamite in their act of destruction

---

[28] Ibid., New York *Times*, February 5, 1888.

[29] Burnette, "Senate Foreign Relations Committee," 460; Fifield, "Extradition Treaties," 34. Burnette stated that the amendment "expanded" the list of extraditable offenses "to include the Irish dynamiters."

and who destroyed railroads. It still was not as specific as that found in the Japanese treaty, but it was a step in that direction. That this is the correct interpretation seems to be implied in a statement by Sherman to the effect that he felt the original clause was too broad and general and that the amendment would restrict the treaty only to those who used dynamite.[30] Unfortunately, they did not want to state their case publicly and Riddleberger was able to play upon the fear of the unknown. The Irish in America did not know the exact terms and in their ignorance they took the worst possible picture of the new amendment. Although it did specify dynamite, it did not introduce the dynamite issue for the first time as the papers indicated. The change actually helped the Irish, but they did not know this.

After the weekend recess Congress returned to Capitol Hill on February 6 and Riddleberger returned to his previous tactics of discussing the whole question in open session and trying to force the Senate into a public vote on his motion to open the discussions. Riddleberger asked Sherman to explain the contents of the amendment but the Senator from Ohio refused on the ground that it was a matter for secret session only. Riddleberger then declared "I do not believe there is one single member of the Committee on Foreign Relations who would rise today in open session and advocate the amendment which comes from that committee."[31]

---

[30] Burnette, "Senate Foreign Relations Committee," 462. They could have hoped to gain the support of those Americans, and Irish-Americans who abhorred the use of dynamite. By specifying dynamite they could also exclude most political offenders, but not the anarchist types which America had already accepted as crimes against humanity.

[31] Congressional Record, 50 Congress, 1 Session, XIX, part I, 967. This was the same clause as found in the Japanese treaty. See page 206.

He then disclosed that the Russian Extradition treaty had a clause similar to that advocated by the Committee in the form of the amendment and he asked that this be printed in the Record. In this way he was able to give the Irish at least some idea of what changes had appeared.

Shortly after this debate the Senate entered closed session and almost at once signs of opposition to the treaty appeared. Some Senators felt the treaty should be accepted or rejected in toto and, therefore, opposed amendments of any kind. Others felt that it could be used as a club to gain concessions in other disputes.[32] A few saw a British trick in the whole thing, while others feared the political overtones of any attempt to get laws passed to implement the terms of the treaty.[33] Riddleberger continued his fight as he reiterated the belief that the Senate would not dare to ratify it in open session. This argument forced Edmunds to make another attempt to placate the opposition. On February 7 he offered an amendment to the amendment which, by adding the words "whereby the life of any person shall be endangered" after explosives, further limited the clause.[34] But this did not satisfy the opposition which argued that the clause still did not clearly define

---

[32] New York Times, February 3, 1888. Some of these wanted a general treaty with England to solve all problems.

[33] New York Tribune, February 7, 1888. This particular period shows very clearly the inside information which the Tribune always published. The Times published only the discussions of the open session, but the Tribune article did not stop its reporting with the closing of the doors.

[34] Senate Executive Journal, XXVI, 174.

the crime. Senator Eustis further stated that, since the crime of dynamiting was unknown to Americans, each state and territory would have to define it for themselves if the treaty was ratified as it stood.[35] Riddleberger again demanded that his resolution to open the discussion be heard, but no one wanted this and Ingalls refused to recognize him.[36]

After a week and a half of argument the matter came to a head on February 8. In the latter part of the afternoon Senator Isham G. Harris made a motion to enter secret session and Riddleberger used the opportunity to again offer his resolution of reconsideration, but the Senate voted to close the doors.[37] There Eustis argued against the treaty because of potential legal difficulties while Edmunds and Morgan asked for ratification. Riddleberger again prepared to delay the vote when Senator Stewart offered a resolution to postpone further discussion until the next session.[38] This was carried 23 to 21, and on the next day Riddleberger finally withdrew his well-worn resolution "since the Lion's tail had been twisted by a vote of 23 to 21."[39]

Once the postponement became public the papers started to speculate

---

[35] New York *Tribune*, February 8, 1888.

[36] New York *Times*, February 9, 1888.

[37] *Congressional Record*, 50 Congress, 1 Session, XIX, part II, 1056.

[38] *Senate Executive Journal*, XXVI, 175.

[39] *Congressional Record*, 50 Congress, 1 Session, XIX, part II, 1075. It is interesting to note that the *Tribune* published the vote on February 9, the day after it was taken, but the *Times* did not publish it until February 10, the day after Riddleberger's statement in open session.

concerning the reasons behind the final outcome. Almost all, including
the Irish-American papers, felt that the main credit for postponement
went to Riddleberger. The _Tribune_ tried to show that the Democrats,
Cleveland, Bayard, and Phelps, had been tricked by the British and, consequently, the Republicans opposed the treaty. It also stated that the
Republicans wanted to redefine the dynamite clause in order to avoid
the vagueness of the original clause, since a strong pro-British official
could use that vagueness to turn over political offenders.[40] The New
York _Times_ felt that neither party could claim any clear cut party
position, since the vote had split party lines. It saw this as a sign
that neither party wanted to offend the Irish vote.[41] This seems to
be closer to the truth especially when the actual vote indicated that
ten Republicans and twelve Democrats, plus Riddleberger, voted for
postponement, while eight Republicans and thirteen Democrats opposed
it.[42] The _Times_ further stated that the treaty would never pass with
the dynamite clause unchanged and that the Senate failed to discuss the
treaty in open session or "pass it in dark" because they "feared Irish
power."[43] The Chicago _Daily News_ stated that the Senate "lacked the
courage to grapple with the treaty pending a presidential election
lest their party should lose the votes of a certain element whose

---

[40] New York _Tribune_, February 9, 1888. This was an obvious reference to Bayard.

[41] New York _Times_, February 10.

[42] _Senate Executive Journal_, XXVI, 175.

[43] New York _Times_, February 10, 1888.

members might sometimes stand in terror of its provisions."[44] Phelps
had almost given up hope when he told Bayard that it might be ratified
next year "if the Irish faction does not acquire complete control of
the country."[45]

Whether the Irish had this much influence or not is almost impossible to tell. That they had some influence on the postponement is
obvious but by February 8 reasons other than the dynamite clause must
have motivated some Senators to vote as they did. As has already been
indicated, a number of Senators wanted to avoid settling this question
before the fisheries problem appeared solved, while others were actually
concerned about the problem of the new laws which the treaty would
necessitate. These and others, coupled to the Irish question, caused
the postponement.

The postponement became a political football almost immediately
after it was announced. As has already been indicated the New York
Tribune attempted to paint the Republicans in the most favorable light
and blame the whole thing on the British-loving Democrats in Washington. The Philadelphia Press tried to do the same thing when it declared
"the fear that it might be used to serve the political purposes of
England in the prosecution of Irish Home Rulers has made the Republican

---

[44] Public Opinion, IV (1888), 456.

[45] Tansill, Foreign Policy of Bayard, xxvi. Phelps to Bayard,
February 11, 1888.

members of the United States Senate unwilling to approve it."[46]  At

the same time the Democratic Catholic paper, New York _Freeman's Journal_

_and Catholic Register_, tried to offset the Republican distortion of the

facts with the statement,

> President Cleveland is said to be totally opposed to the
> clause in the proposed Anglo-American treaty providing
> for surrender of political offenders.  Mr. Cleveland has
> declared that no proposition of this description will
> meet with his approval.[47]

The Irish, needless to say, applauded the postponement, but O'Reilly

cautioned the administration by reminding them that it was no credit to

them that the Republican Senate stood "in the way of a measure which

would surrender American principles and material interests to a foreign

government."[48]  He still felt Bayard and Phelps wanted to sell American

interests to England.  If the Irish were happy, most Americans lamented

the postponement, but some still hoped for ratification because of the

embezzlement clause.

While this question disappeared from the main stream of American

politics, it occasionally reappeared during the three months following

the vote of February 8.  On the day after the vote Senator Eustis sub-

mitted a resolution to remove the injunction of secrecy from the vote

---

[46] _Public Opinion_, IV (1888), 456.  The _Annual Register_ was so
taken by this propaganda it stated that 23 Republicans voted for the
resolution of postponement, while 21 Democrats voted against it.  See
_Annual Register_, 1888, part II, 403.

[47] February 25, 1888.

[48] Boston _Pilot_, February 11, 1888.

on the postponement motion.[49] Eustis had opposed the treaty and he wanted everyone to know this. A few weeks later Senator William E. Chandler proposed that the treaty also be published,[50] while the bankers of Boston sent a petition demanding its ratification. The question of publishing the text was forgotten, however, until on April 2 Senator Henry B. Payne asked that the treaty and the vote be published in order to "show how Cleveland was in the pay of the British."[51] The Senate voted to publish this information on April 5 and the question openly entered the political campaign for the first time.[52]

By the middle of April, however, attention had shifted to the Bayard-Chamberlain treaty, the result of the work of the special commission. The treaty was signed in the middle of February and Cleveland, asking for immediate ratification, sent it to the Senate on February 15. No one close to the scene really expected ratification and as the Senate's Committee on Foreign Relations continued to discuss the question from February until early May, what little hope did exist, slowly disappeared. Spring-Rice felt that the Senate would reject it "not because the Senate disapproves of it but because they disapprove of the present government."[53] As the discussion continued, he saw the

---

[49] Senate Executive Journal, XXVI, 177.

[50] Ibid., 191.

[51] Burnette, "Senate Foreign Relations Committee," 462.

[52] Holt, Treaties Defeated, 142.

[53] Gwynn, Letters and Friendships of Spring-Rice, 85. To Stephen, February 10, 1888.

only hope in postponement.[54]  Bayard and Phelps both felt that the

Senate would not give the treaty a fair hearing and many others felt

that "Anglophobia" and the "wild Irish" would destroy the treaty.[55]

Carl Schurz stated that "the 'small politician' does, indeed, abound

in these days" but in spite of this, the treaty would pass.[56]  However,

by May Bayard had lost all hope since

> the bitter hatred of many Irish-Americans for everything
> British was an important factor. . . . American welfare
> would be sacrificed by domestic issues between Great
> Britain and one of the dependencies with which we have
> properly nothing whatever to do.[57]

The Republicans in the Senate had decided to make use of the

Bayard-Chamberlain Treaty in the 1888 campaign as an additional device

by which they could point to Cleveland, his Administration, and the

whole Democratic Party as being pro-British.  The tariff would serve

as the principal tool, but the treaty would help.  For this reason the

Foreign Affairs Committee debated the issue from February 15 until

May 7, when in a strict party vote the Republican majority recommended

rejection of Bayard's work and accused the Administration of being whol-

ly subservient to the English crown.[58]  As if this was not enough, the

Republicans next voted to hold discussions on the treaty in open session,

---

[54] Ibid., 87.  To Ferguson, March 6, 1888.

[55] Tansill, Foreign Policy of Bayard, 303.

[56] Bancroft, Speeches of Carl Schurz, IV, 504.  Schurz to Bayard, March 7, 1888.

[57] Tansill, Foreign Policy of Bayard, 307.  Bayard to Judge J.B. Stallo, May 7, 1888.

[58] Ibid., 313.  Edmunds who fought for the Extradition Treaty was one of the leaders of this.

something they did not do in the case of the Phelps-Rosebery Treaty.
As a result from May to August visitors to the Upper House witnessed a
steady stream of violent anti-English speeches. Finally, on August 21,
1888 again by a strict party vote the Senate rejected the treaty. For
six months the Republican managers had milked the issue dry.

In the course of the long summer Bayard made numerous statements
to the effect that the Republicans opposed the treaty only to gain the
Irish vote. Senator Morgan accused Sherman of refusing to compromise
in any way just to advance his own political interests. At one point
Riddleberger, again a leading factor in the development of Anglophobia,
admitted that as far as he was concerned the decision to open the discussions was aimed at getting the "foreign vote."[59]  Bayard felt that
they would even use "the threat of war with Great Britain, under a
policy of retaliation with Canada, . . . in the coming canvass to
catch the 'Hibernian Vote.'"[60]

This Republican tactic forced Cleveland to fight fire with fire.
Shortly after the Senate rejection of the Bayard-Chamberlain treaty,
the President sent a message to Congress, in which he asked for retaliation powers against Canada. Democratic Irishmen throughout the
country praised this "master political stroke," for it forced the Republicans into showing their true position.[61]  Within a matter of days

---

[59] Burnette, "Senate Foreign Relations Committee," 437.

[60] Tansill, Foreign Policy of Bayard, 315. Bayard to Bevani,
June 16, 1888. He felt the same way in July. See page 317, Bayard
to Phelps, July 26, 1888.

[61] Nevins, Cleveland, 412, 428-431. Nevins gives the story in
some detail.

the Democratic House passed the measure 174 to 4, but the Republicans
in the Senate refused to accept it.  Edmunds declared that Cleveland
already had the power to retaliate, if he really wanted to show his
anti-British position.

By then the campaign was well under way and the Republicans intensified their efforts to prove that the Democratic party was the
party of England.  They learned early in September that the British-
Minister Sackville-West had fallen for a Republican trick to get his
advice on how pro-English Americans should vote.  His letter to Mur-
chison urging support for Cleveland was released in late October and
a shower of complaints filled Cleveland's office.  From the date of
the release, October 21, 1888, until the election the front pages of
newspapers across the country carried the story as all other issues
became insignificant overnight.  On the day after the publication
Bayard had a conversation with West and noted that

> he was aware of how the question of Irish relations to
> Great Britain were regarded in this country, and how
> obvious it was that they played an important part in
> our politics, how the party led by Mr. Blaine was in-
> dustriously engaged in fomenting the ill will of the
> Irish element in the United States against Great Britain.[62]

but this had little effect, since the letter had already been written.
Bayard did not ask for West's recall, but O'Reilly informed Cleveland
that, if this did not occur soon, he would lose the Irish vote.  Democratic fears that the Irish would leave the party prompted Bayard to

---

[62] Tansill, _Foreign Policy of Bayard_, 332.

request the recall and, when the British did not reply quickly enough, he gave West his papers and ordered him out of the country. This strong action did not spell success, however; Cleveland lost New York by 14,000 votes and the presidency with it.[63]

In the midst of the campaign a great debate occupied the attention of the various Irish leaders on the question of the Extradition Treaty. John Devoy reminded his Irish friends that, if that treaty should pass the Senate, "there is not an act of resistance to tyranny classed as a crime by an infamous coercion act that cannot be brought under its provisions, and England's heavy hand can be laid on the Irish exile in this country."[64] In other words Devoy felt that "coercion would be brought to the very door of the Irish citizens of the United States,"[65] and the Irish in America would help to bring this about if they voted Democratic. Other Irishmen including Michael Kerwin, William Carroll and Robert Thompson argued along similar lines against the hated English lover, Grover Cleveland. At the same time Patrick Ford tried to place the blame for the amendment to the treaty on the shoulders of the Democrats.[66] The Democratic Irish papers replied that the Republican majority on the Committee changed the amendment so that the "dynamite clause would permit England to gain access to Irish polit-

---

[63] Nevins, Cleveland, 431.

[64] John Devoy, "Irish Comment on an English Text," North American Review, LI (1888), 282.

[65] Ibid., 283.

[66] New York Irish World, October 21, 1888.

ical refugees."[67]  The Chicago Citizen entered the debate by reminding

O'Reilly that he had earlier praised the Republican majority for saving

the Irish from the terms of a treaty negotiated by the pro-British

American Minister in London and supported by a pro-British Secretary

of State.[68]  Finerty accused O'Reilly of circulating the story in

order to offset the effect of the Sackville-West case, but this can

not be true, since Ford started the debate.  As the arguments flowed

back and forth, their purpose was obvious, but the lies were not.

Neither party could claim any merit for the postponement of the dis-

cussion nor the particular merits or demerits of the amendments,

since party lines split over both the amendments and the vote of post-

ponement.

When the news of the Republican victory reached Chicago, Finerty

saw it as an event that saved America from submission to England,

because the Irish did not vote for the Democratic party.[69]  Whether

this was true or not failed to concern the Republicans who reacted as

if they at least owed the Irish a debt.  On November 19, 1888 Patrick

Ford presided at a victory celebration at Cooper's Hall in New York.

Both Blaine and Harrison sent telegrams to congratulate those Irish-

Americans who had fought for the Republican victory.[70]

---

[67] Boston Pilot, October 27, 1888.

[68] Chicago Citizen, November 3, 1888.

[69] Ibid., November 10, 1888.

[70] New York Times, November 24, 1888.

In the midst of such celebrations the lawmakers of America returned to Washington in early December for the reopening of Congress.
Two days later the Senate resumed the debate on the dynamite issue,
but John Sherman introduced additional amendments, which caused a
further delay until they were printed.

In the course of the delay both interested parties tried to influence the outcome by sending petitions to the Senate. On January 21
Senator Matthew Quay presented three petitions from Irish societies
which called for the rejection of the treaty. On the same day H.D.
Lyman, the Vice-President of the American Surety Company of New York,
sent a petition which listed forty-seven embezzlers who had fled to
Canada. For forty-seven reasons he wanted the treaty approved.[71]

Sherman's amendments, finally printed, were distributed and on
January 30 the debate resumed. The crime of rape and some minor sub-
stitutions in the larceny clause formed the major portion of the changes
and after they were read the question reverted to Edmunds' motion to add
the words "whereby the life of any person shall be endangered" after the
word "explosives" in the Committee's amendment to the original clause.
Once the Senate accepted this change, they were faced with the problem
of accepting or rejecting the entire amendment. In the middle of this
debate Edmunds asked that the whole treaty be returned to the Committee.[72] The New York *Times* took this as a move to kill the treaty,

---

[71] Senate Executive Journal, XXVI, 435.

[72] Ibid., 437.

but this seems highly unlikely in view of the fact that Edmunds from the beginning supported it.[73] In all probability he wanted to get it back in the Committee where friendly hands could eliminate elements that had generated criticism. At least this would seem plausible, since both the Republican and Democratic members of the Committee voted for Edmund's motion along with most Democrats, while the majority of Republicans and Riddleberger said no. The motion suffered defeat 23 to 20.[74]

When this occurred the question again returned to the amendment as it came from Committee. It was defeated 34 to 9. Some of the greatest anti-English Senators, along with Morgan, voted to keep this attempt to better define the dynamite crime, but it was of no avail as fifteen Republicans and eighteen Democrats rejected it. Irish opposition surely helped to gain some of these negative votes, but it just as surely did not gain all of them. A few Senators must have agreed with Senator Eustis who was concerned with the legal problem of definition. Once the magnitude of the opposition was realized, Senator George Gray of Delaware, a close personal friend of Bayard's and the man who took his senate seat when he became Secretary of State, offered a motion to eliminate the dynamite clause completely. His friendship with the administration indicates a last minute effort to save the treaty. Nineteen Democrats and twelve Republicans voted to accept this

---

[73] New York *Times*, February 1, 1889.

[74] *Senate Executive Journal*, XXVI, 442.

proposal, while only one Democrat, Morgan, and ten Republicans rejected it. It is interesting to note that some of the most anti-English Senators such as Frye, Hawley, Hoar, Ingalls, Sawyer, and Sherman, all of whom had voted for Edmunds' attempt to get the treaty back to Committee, now supported this effect to kill the dynamite clause and save the treaty. Morgan and Edmunds continued to vote for inclusion of this controversial clause probably because they feared England would never accept a treaty without it. Yet in spite of their arguments the Senate removed the one most obnoxious clause as far as the Irish were concerned. The Irish in America had gained their victory after two and a half years of opposition.

Shortly after this important decision was made and after the Senate rejected an attempt to include manslaughter in the list of extraditable crimes, the lawmakers turned to the final question of either accepting or rejecting the treaty. The final vote occurred on January 31, 1889 when the Senate voted 38 to 15 to reject the treaty even though it did not contain a dynamite clause. Of those who voted to keep it eleven, five Democrats and six Republicans, had voted to eliminate the dynamite clause and, therefore, it may be assumed that they wanted to save the treaty for its embezzlement clause. Of those who voted against the treaty nine Republicans did so most probably because the final version did not contain a dynamite clause since they had voted to keep that clause in the treaty. Yet seven Republicans who had helped to remove the dynamite clause rejected the final treaty. Obviously they found fault in reasons other than the dynamite question.

Thus, sixteen Republicans voted for reasons other than fear of the Irish vote. In like manner one can show that at least ten Democrats rejected the final treaty without thought of Irish power. In other words twenty-six of the thirty-eight negative votes can not be attributed to Irish pressure.[75] American issues, not Irish-American issues killed it. In all probability, Riddleberger's constant harassment of the Senate and his ability to delay the final vote gave individual Senators the opportunity to develop what they considered were legitimate complaints. As a result the treaty in its final form suffered defeat, not because of Irish pressure, but because of basically American complaints.

Within two weeks of the vote the important proceedings and votes were published, but the papers had already learned that the treaty was rejected. The Irish papers received the news with great joy and immediately claimed the honor of forcing the Senate into rejecting it.[76] The American sources tended to analyze the situation with a more objective mind, recognizing the general inadequacy of some aspects of the treaty.[77] Most lamented the fact that it failed and indicated the hope that something could be done to close Canada.[78]

Five weeks after the rejection Benjamin Harrison became President and Blaine became Secretary of State. Shortly afterwards the new Sec-

---

[75] Ibid., 435-445. The various votes are listed in these pages.

[76] Chicago Citizen, February 9, 1889, February 16, 1889; Boston Pilot, February 18, 1889; New York Catholic Review, February 16, 1889.

[77] New York Times, February 2, 1886; American, XVIII (1889), 70.

[78] Gibson, New York Irish, 428.

retary opened negotiations on the extradition question with the recently appointed British Minister, Sir Julian Pauncefote, who has served as a career diplomat for some time.[79] Within less than four months of taking office the new Secretary signed a new treaty, but Harrison had to wait for the return of Congress to submit it for ratification.[80] Then the debate did not begin in earnest until the middle of February 1890.

In the twelve months between the rejection of the Phelps-Rosebery Treaty and the discussion of its replacement a number of things occurred that revolutionized the whole atmosphere of Irish-American hopes and Anglo-American relations. In the first place the return of the Republicans removed from the political arena the necessity of the "outs" calling the "ins" British-lovers. The Democrats could not suddenly begin to accuse the Republicans of favoring the British as the Republicans had cried for four years. That the Republicans had been able to follow such a line had much to do with the intensification of Anglophobia in America, which in turn had helped the Irish cause. Now that they were in office there was no longer any need for this and, consequently, Irish power tended to decline. Secondly, the British indicated their desire to reduce Anglo-American tensions as an aftermath of the Sackville-West incident, when the Conservative government sent England's most able diplomat to Washington.[81] Thirdly, Irish-American nationalism

---

[79] R. B. Mowat, *Life of Lord Pauncefote* (1929), 117. He was the Permanent Undersecretary in the Foreign Office.

[80] *Senate Executive Journal*, XXVII, 195.

[81] Mowat, *Pauncefote*, 118.

suffered a severe blow in May 1889 from which it did not recover for
at least a decade.  On May 4 members of the Sullivanite faction of the
Clan murdered Dr. Philip H. Cronin, one of Sullivan's most persistent
enemies.[82]  Cronin's fight against Sullivan's leadership of the Clan
began 1884, when Sullivan failed to satisfactorily account for the
financing of the dynamite campaign.  This led to Cronin's expulsion
from the Clan in 1885, the creation of a rival organization, and, finally, in 1888 an attempt to bring the two groups together.  Cronin's charges
of serious misappropriation of funds against Sullivan led to the formation of a special committee which cleared Sullivan and the "Triangle."[83]
Cronin did not destroy his private notes of the hearings, however, and
even wrote a minority report which he read to his own organization.
His disclosure of secret information supposedly led to his murder.[84]
When the investigators gathered the information, Sullivan himself was
indicated but the charge was later dropped.  The others involved were
convicted.  The murder itself and the disclosures at the trial completely
discredited secret and violent forms of Irish-nationalism,[85] so much so
that the Clan was forced to issue a statement that attempted to prove
that its members were nothing more than peace-loving Irish patriots.[86]

---

[82] Hunt, _Crime of the Century_, 67.

[83] Anderson, _Sidelights on Home Rule_, 133.

[84] Hunt, _Crime of the Century_, 84.

[85] Anderson, _Sidelights on Home Rule_, 134.

[86] O'Brien, _Post Bag_, II, 314.

But Americans in general failed to believe this description as they violently condemned what amounted to political murder.[87] Finally, on December 24, 1889 Captain William O'Shea filed for a divorce and accused Parnell of living with his wife from 1880-1886.[88] For the first time in ten years Parnell was the center of a struggle which did not directly involve Irish nationalism. That this happened indicated to a degree that Irish agitation was at last subsiding. The factors that had helped to create the atmosphere in which the Irish-Americans worked during the decade were rapidly disappearing.

In this changing atmosphere the Republican Senate opened the debate on Blaine's Extradition Treaty. This version had some substantial differences from the earlier one, differences which reflected the nature of the debates against Phelps' work. In the first place, it did not contain a dynamite clause, since the Senate had already indicated that it would not approve such a clause. Pauncefote very possibly accepted this because, as a result of the disclosures at the hearings of the Parnell Commission in the winter of 1888-1889 and the reaction against the Cronin murder, he felt that the threat of Irish dynamiters no longer really existed. The fact that he desired to reduce tensions must have entered his mind also, and he did not insist upon a dynamite clause because this would only have created a potential trouble spot. The text also increased the number of crimes, included an embezzlement

---

[87] Public Opinion, VII (1889), 24.

[88] O'Brien, Parnell and His Party, 279.

clause which did not place limits on the amount that had to be stolen, and added a separate clause which stipulated fraud, "by a bailee, banker, agent, factor, trustee, or director, member or officer of any company" as an extraditable crime.[89] Each of these changes obviously attempted to eliminate the earlier criticism. Blaine had learned from Phelps' attempt.

While the treaty did not become public property until late January, rumors of its existence had caused a number of papers to comment about its possible contents. The American felt for sure that it contained a dynamite clause and on this basis predicted Irish opposition. Then, the New York Times, when it published the text on January 27, 1890, accused Blaine of specifically omitting the dynamite clause in order to "take care of his Irish friends who voted with him in 1884 and 1888."[90] However, the Times did agree with Blaine that the main objective of the treaty was the prevention of defaulters from fleeing to Canada. A number of papers agreed that it should be ratified for this reason,[91] while the American stated that, since the treaty did not raise the dynamite aspect, expressly excluded political offense, and recognized the right of final judgment by the country in which the crime was committed, it avoided the objections which led to the rejection "of the earlier

---

[89] William M. Malloy, Treaties, Conventions, International Acts, Protocols, and Agreements Between the United States of America and other Powers. 2 Vols. (1910), I, 740. The original text was published in the New York Times, January 27, 1890.

[90] New York Times, January 27, 1890.

[91] Public Opinion, VIII, 402.

treaty."[92]  The almost universal support for Blaine's work did not in-

clude Godkin's Nation which decried one major complaint, the clauses

were too vague and would only generate future disagreements.[93]

With such major backing the Senate discussed the treaty on February

13, 1890. Almost at once Senator Gray offered an amendment which was

eventually defeated by an almost strict party vote.[94]  The Democrats

made another attempt to modify the treaty when Senator Faulkner pro-

posed that manslaughter be removed from the list of extraditable crimes

since each country had its own definition of the crime. Again the Re-

publicans defeated this Democratic attempt to change Blaine's handwork.

Next Sherman offered a resolution to accept or reject the treaty as

written, but this time the Democrats defeated it. Sherman knew that

he could not get the necessary two-thirds vote and he voted against the

treaty to be in a position to reconsider. He went to Gray, the Dem-

ocratic leader, and learned what he would have to give to get the neces-

sary Democratic support.[95]  He then moved to reconsider the treaty with

the changes demanded by Gray included and the treaty passes unanimous-

ly.[96]  Six days later Harrison officially ratified the treaty and pro-

---

[92] American, XIX (1890), 309.

[93] Nation, I (1890), 85. Godkin never really found any good in anything Blaine did.

[94] Senate Executive Journal, XXVII, 463.

[95] New York Times, February 12, 1890.

[96] Senate Executive Journal, XXVII, 470.

claimed it on March 25, 1890, just one year after entering office.[97]

The Irish-Americans indicated their pleasure that the dynamite question had not appeared in the treaty and, therefore, they played little role in these discussions.[98]  The role they played in the Phelps Treaty, however, had just one additional sidelight.  Although the United States signed numerous treaties in the 1890's which contained clauses referring to the malicious destruction of railroads and even one which followed the lines of the malicious destruction clause found in the Japanese treaty of 1886 and the Phelps-Rosebery treaty, England and the United States did not sign a railroad clause until 1900[99] and a malicious destruction clause until 1931.[100]  It took the two countries forty-five years to gain what Phelps and Rosebery had accepted in 1886.

---

[97] Malloy, Treaties, Conventions, International Acts, I, 474.

[98] New York, Irish World, February 9, 1890.

[99] Fifield, "Extradition Treaties," 236.

[100] Ibid., 246.

Chapter VIII

Conclusion

This study began as an attempt to analyze the years from 1880
to 1888 in order to discover what role the Irish in America played
in Anglo-American relations. This necessitated the establishment of
the atmosphere in which the Irish worked; that is, first of all,
the relationship of Irish power in America to American politics, secondly, the relationship of that power to the Anglo-Irish struggle and,
thirdly, the state of Anglo-American relations. In effect it was
necessary to discover if the same general conditions that existed in
the years immediately following the American Civil War existed in the
decade of the 1880's.

During the last half of the 1860's the Irish question became en-
meshed in American politics and Anglo-American diplomacy. The Irish
in Ireland organized a revolution in 1866-67 and its preparation, execution, and suppression aroused the Irish-American's hatred of England and his desire to help in the struggle to gain Ireland's freedom.
These aroused hatreds and desires prompted the Irish in America to
openly support the plans for revolution in Ireland and organize their
own invasions of Canada. The American politician, because of specific
political problems characteristic to this period of American history,
used these aroused emotions in an effort to intensify his appeal to
the Irish voter. At the same time responsible American diplomats used

269

Irish-American preparations to invade Canada and to support the revolution in Ireland as a club to gain concessions from the English on basic
Anglo-American questions which had arisen out of the war. In other
words the American politician and the American diplomat found the Irish
agitation a convenient tool which they could use to gain their own ends.

Before describing the general atmosphere that existed during the
1860's and answering the question did conditions remain the same as in
the 1860's, an attempt was made to discover just how ready conditions
were on the eve of the decade. This meant an evaluation of how ready
the Irish in Ireland were to launch an attack against the English, how
ready the Irish in America were to influence the outcome of such a battle, and finally in what direction were American politics and Anglo-
American relations moving.

Irish power to disrupt English life had suffered a severe setback
with the events of the 1840's, but in 1872 a revival of that power began with the creation of the Home Rule League. When Butt converted his
League into the Home Rule party, Irish capacity received another lift,
but the real boost came when Charles Stewart Parnell won his first seat
in the House of Commons in 1875. While he slowly emerged as the leader
of the left-wing of the Home Rule party, Davitt devised a plan that he
hoped would unite all factions of Irish and Irish-American nationalism
behind a concerted attack upon the Irish land system. Eventually, he
tied Parnell to the majority of the more revolutionary elements under
the banner of the "New Departure." This, coupled to the disastrous
economic situation in the winter of 1879-1880, laid the foundation for

the most significant decade in Anglo-Irish relation between the Great
Famine and World War I. Ireland was indeed ready.

While events in Ireland readied her people for the leadership of
Parnell, events in America prepared the Irish population there for
their significant role in the battle Parnell was to wage. The revolutionary failure in 1848 drove Irish politicians to America where they
found hundreds of thousands of their fellow countrymen, victims of the
famine. Both the leaders and the led arrived with bitter memories of
the hated land system, English oppression, and absentee landlords of the
Anglo-Irish Ascendency. These, kept alive by experience in America
where the Irish suffered abuse for their poverty, drunkenness, religion
and crime-infested "Irish towns," nourished and produced Irish-American
nationalism with its sole purpose of the freeing of Ireland, which
would automatically help Irish-Americans enter the mainstream of American life. The failures of the late 1860's caused a basic division to
appear in Irish-American ranks and, although it continued throughout the
remaining years of the struggle, Davitt temporarily healed the wound
with his scheme of war for the land. In late 1878 both Devoy and O'Reilly
had accepted the "New Departure." By the same time the Irish in America
had risen to relatively respectable positions in American society,
especially in the political world. Irish-American nationalism, kept
alive by the Irish struggle, experiences in America, and the numerous
social, beneficial and athletic associations, had helped to cement the
natural clanish instincts of the Irish spirit into a potent political
force which both major parties had recognized on a national level as early

as 1866. By 1870 many Irish-Americans had risen to political fame on the local level and during the decade this number grew. At the same time the Irish rose in national prominence with an active member of the Clan serving as a Republican in the Senate of the United States. By the end of the decade Irish-Americans had risen to important positions in the Democratic party, and even the Republicans were willing to pass out political plums to men like Edward Condon. In this question of rising Irish political power the career of Patrick Collins is most instructive. This Boston politician, active in Irish-American politics as well as American, had risen to a power position in Massachusetts politics by 1880 and continued to rise during the following decade. As the Irish in America stood united behind the aim of freeing Ireland, supporting Davitt's land war and Parnell's leadership, they possessed political and material power in abundance. If the Irish in Ireland were prepared by December 1879, the Irish in America were just as ready.

In these very years of Irish preparation American politics and Anglo-American relations seemed headed in the proper direction. In 1876 American political life entered the twenty year "Era of No Decision" during which few issues were placed before the public and even these split party ranks down the middle, thereby reducing the hope for a clear victory in a campaign fought over them. The basic numerical and territorial balance of political power hardly shifted and elections turned on mere handfuls of voters, which increased the importance of the large and pivotal states in national races. In many of these, especially New York, the most important state in the Union, the Irish held considerable

political power which rested firmly on their numbers and sentiment.
At the same time a number of minor clashes with England tended to arouse
the latent flame of Anglophobia to the surface of American life. The
Halifax Award, the Fortune Bay incident, the War of the Pacific, and
other questions indicated that Anglo-American relations would suffer a
bumpy future. In other words, just when the politician discovered a
need for votes in certain key states, the diplomatic situation created
an atmosphere in which he could use an anti-English line which would attract the attention of the Irish who could deliver the necessary votes,
especially in New York.

It seems on first glance that all these factors converged at a most
opportune time to produce a climate in which the Irish American could use
his political power as a lever to force American politicians to intervene in the Anglo-Irish struggle on the side of Ireland. As favorable as
things looked on February 2, 1880 when Parnell addressed the House of
Representatives of the United States, in the final analysis the conditions of the 1860's did not completely reappear in the 1880's. It
can not be doubted that both political parties made active and sustained
bids for the Irish vote throughout the period under question, starting
late in the election of 1880 and carrying through the election of 1888.
Nor can there be any doubt that the Irish in America made significant,
if not indispensable contributions, to Parnell's cause and that his
struggle greatly influenced the whole range of Irish-American activities.
Yet it cannot be stated that American diplomats used these Irish activities to inflame Anglo-American relations or to gain concessions from the

English in purely Anglo-American disputes. Each responsible American
diplomat worked to avoid open clashes with England and this includes
Evarts and Blaine, as well as Frelinghuysen, Bayard, Lowell and Phelps.
Evarts and Blaine seemed more prone to inflame these relations than the
others, yet Evarts tried to compromise on the Fortune Bay incident and
Blaine offered the British flag a twenty-one gun salute at the Yorktown
Centennial Celebration in November 1881. The latter four were especially interested in reducing tensions and refused to utilize the Irish question to enhance their diplomacy. What clamouring for this that did exist came from those out of office, Blaine, his Republican allies, and
the Democrats, when Frelinghuysen ran the State Department; Blaine and
the Republicans, when Bayard held that position. The non-responsible
politician would use the Irish question to gain office, but once there
he would not use it as a club to gain concessions from the British.
Blaine himself followed this pattern, even though he had earned the
reputation of loving the dynamite Irish. Thus, of the three pillars
which supported the influence of Irish Americans upon Anglo-American
relations during the late 1860's, the all important one was missing in
the 1880's. Nevertheless working under this handicap the Irish in America did play a rather interesting, though negative, role in the formation of America's relations with England.

During 1881 and 1882 the most important question in relationship
to this Irish influence upon Anglo-American relations centered around
the question of the arrest of American citizens in Ireland. In the
spring of 1881 the Boynton case was debated in the Senate, while Blaine

sought his release on terms of international comity. When Lowell discovered that he really never acquired American citizenship and withdrew from the case, an action endorsed by Blaine, the Secretary of State
indicated things would have been different if he had acquired American
citizenship. Thus, when the case of Walsh arose Blaine asked Lowell to
intervene. Some authors would have us believe that this American intervention eventually led to his release, but, as has already been shown,
other factors must have influenced the British decision. When Frelinghuysen became Secretary, the question greeted him and by late January
it had entered the House of Representatives where it consumed long
hours of debate. These debates forced Frelinghuysen to send a rash
of telegrams to Lowell in an effort to end the dispute and these in
turn caused the British to extend their offer to release all the suspects on the one condition that they leave the country. This can be the
only explanation, since the idea of such an offer had appeared as early
as March 30 and the official offer was extended on April 6. At that time
Ireland was in a state of chaos, so much so that Gladstone **had decided**
to negotiate with Parnell, but even these unofficial negotiations did
not begin until April 10, four days after the British made their offer.
In other words conditions in Ireland and England did not prompt this,
American pressure must have. Yet even here both sides were looking
for a settlement and neither side wanted to embarrass the other. Thus,
the "Irish Suspects" did not increase Anglo-American tensions. However, when the British mistreated Henry George in September 1882,
the United States sent a very stiff note and the British immediately

apologized. This was a different case and it hints to the fact that maybe Irish-Americans were not completely accepted at this time, an observation made by many authorities. At any rate the British finally released the "Irish Suspects" without condition in August and September 1882, but only after they received assurance that Parnell would reduce land agitation. The final outcome again rested upon conditions in Ireland and not necessarily upon conditions in America.

While this question occupied the energies of many diplomats the Irish revolutionaries in America tended to arouse British fears and forced them to seek aid from the United States in the suppression of revolutionary and terroristic activities of these radicals. Here one finds a degree of success for the Irish in their efforts to inflame Anglo-American relations because, first of all, government suppression of Irish activities would immediately attract the full weight of Irish political power and, secondly, such activities had a tendency to enrage English public opinion against the failure of the United States to prevent such expeditions. When the British complained about the newspaper attacks to Blaine and Frelinghuysen, both had to reply that they could do nothing to stop such articles, since the Constitution guaranteed freedom of the press. This was a legitimate reason to a degree but at least Frelinghuysen realized that, if such attacks continued, Anglo-American relations would deteriorate. When the British continued to raise the question of the dynamite bombs, Blaine merely indicated that he would have to have proof of the Irish intensions, but he did not offer to help the British discover this proof. This action, plus his failure to

intervene in the case of the Fenian Ram, where the proof of the Clan's
activity was public information and their purpose most obvious, would
indicate that the politician in Blaine told him not to interfere for
fear of the Irish vote. Even Frelinghuysen, who entered the Department
with the expressed desire to reverse Blaine's policy and reduce Anglo-
American tensions, succumbed to the political pressure of the Irish
in America, when he accepted Patrick O'Donnell as an American citizen
in spite of the fact that the available information at least left grave
doubt as to the validity of his claim. His position in the Sheridan and
Tynan cases also indicated a desire to avoid any affront to the Irish in
America even though in private conversation he intimated that he did not
appreciate his inability to act.

The most sensational attempt to create friction between England
and the United States centered around Sullivan's dynamite campaign of
1883-1885. The British lived in a state of constant fear and their
anxiety produced an Explosives Law within twenty-four hours. The proof
that the attacks were organized, financed, and executed by Irish-Americans
caused the British to accuse the United States of failing to live up to
her obligations as a neutral and friendly state. Such complaints
prompted the vast majority of the Senate to condemn the last of these
attacks in an official resolution. They also caused a number of state
governments to officially condemn these acts and even President Arthur
was forced to issue an executive order demanding all government officials
to enforce the law that prohibited the shipment of dynamite by boat.
The continued attacks caused a number of Americans to lose their sympathy

for the Irish cause and some stated that the United States could not
afford the luxury of having a large segment of the population abuse
their rights of citizenship. A few asked for the extradition of all
dynamiters as enemies against humanity. By the summer of 1884, however,
both parties were gearing for the fall election and the Republicans with
Blaine as their candidate made a decided effort to appear attractive to
the Irish voter by enlisting the aid of the radical wing of Irish-
American nationalism. Sullivan, Finerty, Ford and other less radical
men all supported Blaine's candidacy, so much so that he was often accused of befriending the "dynamite Irish" throughout the remainder of
his political career. In other words the political power of the Irish
permitted them to engineer terrorist attacks upon England which in
turn inflamed the British public against the United States because official Washington failed to prevent such attacks. However, nothing came
of this, simply because responsible American diplomats were not willing
to use this agitation in their negotiations with England.

The discussions concerning these dynamite attacks greatly influenced
the whole question of extradition treaties. During this time a world wide
movement increased the number and scope of such treaties, especially in
respect to what had formerly been considered political crimes. These
trends greatly influenced treaty making in the United States so that,
when the Irish activities of the early 1880's commenced it seemed only
natural that the British and the Americans would sign a new extradition
treaty. The British obviously wanted one that would include under its
terms the crime of dynamiting, while Americans wanted one that would

close Canada to bank embezzlers and similar crooks. Interestingly enough, the United States was not especially against the inclusion of the dynamite clause in extradition treaties as evidenced by the Japanese Treaty of June 1886.

Negotiations on the question opened shortly after Phelps arrived in London. By November he had offered a shorter draft which fulfilled the American desires and which, of course, included a dynamite clause. His draft of the latter clause was identical to that found in the Japanese treaty which received Senate approval in June 1886. However, the treaty he signed on June 25, 1886 contained a much broader clause which must have been what the British wanted. The vague terminology later caused some of the opposition that developed in the Senate.

His handiwork arrived in Washington in the middle of the fishery struggle and the Republican attempt to paint the Democratic administration as being pro-British. Oddly enough, however, both the Republicans and the Democrats on the Senate Committee on Foreign Affairs approved the treaty, including that outspoken anti-British New Englander, Senator Edmunds. Then the text conveniently leaked to the front page of the New York Tribune. This caused the Irish in America to attack the dynamite clause and the resulting outcry in all probability caused the politicians to postpone the question until after the fall congressional election. In that campaign the Republicans continued their efforts to paint Cleveland and the Democrats as pro-British, but they did not use the Extradition Treaty. It would seem only natural for them to use every possible opportunity to prove their point which would have included the work of Phelps and Rosebery. However, they did not and, when Congress returned in December to take up the question of the Extradition Treaty in the following month the great anti-English voices that resounded in the Senate during open session did not oppose the treaty. Edmunds, Sherman, Hawley, Ingalls and others fought for it against the arguments of Senator Riddleberger, but behind closed doors. At the same time Edmunds fought for his Retaliation Bill, an anti-British measure and Ingalls called for war over the fishery dispute. Their failure to take advantage of the possibilities that the Extradition Treaty offered in the way of proving the pro-British bent of the administration raises some doubt as to the sincerity of their anti-British outbursts in the Senate. Maybe they acted because the moneyed interests of America wanted the Extradition Treaty and the Senate, which had a wide reputation as being the most exclusive millionaires club in America, was not interested in losing this opportunity to close Canada to America's embezzlers. Riddleberger's public statements generated a degree of opposition and, when he asked for a vote of acceptance or rejection, Senator Hoar saved the day by offering a motion to table the discussion. Hoar was not necessarily known as a friend of the Irish and his action killed their hopes of defeating the treaty outright.

When the question reappeared in late January and early February 1888, Riddleberger again led the opposition. At the same time Edmunds and other Republicans fought this attempt to dump the treaty, while in open session continued to accuse Bayard, Cleveland and the Democrats of selling American interests to the British by agreeing to a special

commission to solve the fishery question. In February opposition had
developed on points other than the dynamite clause to a point where
the Irish combined with this new irritation to postpone the debate for
the third time. The Irish must share the credit for this postponement
with native-Americans, however.

From February until November the Republican managers worked with
a great deal of energy and numerous issues to prove to the voters of
America that the administration had remained pro-British. However,
once again the Republicans did not utilize the question of the Extradition Treaty, although the Irish themselves did attempt to place the burden of responsibility for the dynamite clause upon their political enemies. This led to an interesting battle at the end of the campaign,
when both Democratic and Republican Irishmen tried to show that the
other party wanted to extradite Irish patriots. Even the Democratic
party in its official campaign handbook tried to show that the Republicans were responsible for the harsh wording of the treaty. Yet
the Republicans did not counter this move with any official literature.
Again it would seem that they were caught in the dilemma so aptly described by Spring-Rice, when he said that Blaine could not avoid offending either the rich or the Irish.

When Congress returned again to discuss the treaty for the fourth
time a personal friend of Bayard's offered a resolution to reject the
dynamite clause. When the Senate accepted this, the Irish in America
with Riddleberger's aid had earned their point. However, in spite of the
removal of this clause which had caused so much criticism the treaty was

still rejected. Other factors besides the opposition to that clause caused the rejection. In fact some of those negative votes were inspired by the very elimination of that clause. Thus, though the Irish had won their point, they did not cause the rejection.

Riddleberger's role in the whole struggle is hard to surmise. He was bitterly anti-English, so much so, that he even refused to vote for Edmunds' Retaliation Bill of January 1887 because it implied a possible settlement with England. This bitterness prompted him to defend the Irish dynamiters in January 1885 and to fight against their possible extradition to England. These actions can only be explained by his extreme hatred of things British and, although some have tried to explain this, it would seem impossible really to adequately define why his hatred was so strong. It may have been the bond issue question, but the actual cause is unknown.

When the confusion of the 1888 election settled Blaine entered the State Department for the second time and almost immediately opened negotiations to close a new treaty with the British. The resulting handiwork eliminated the majority of complaints, aired against the work of Phelps, including the dynamite clause. He must have realized that many Senators had questioned the vagueness of the law and the problem of definition. This coupled to the fact that the Senate had just rejected the old clause, plus the fact that he did have some obligations to reward his Irish friends, led to his opposing its inclusion in the new treaty. The fact that the immediate threat of such attacks had subsided possibly motivated the British into accepting its elimination. At any rate, it cannot be clearly stated that Blaine did this merely to keep his Irish friends happy. By this time he was again a responsible diplomat and to a degree he was forced to act like one. Although he did use his influence to reward his Irish political friends with patronage positions in foreign posts, which was completely in keeping with the practice of the day, he cannot be accused of considering the Irish and the Irish alone in the negotiations leading to the new treaty.

From the foregoing it is obvious that the Irish in America did not greatly influence the trend of Anglo-American relations, either in the long run or the short and this was true primarily because America's responsible diplomats refused to use the opportunities the Irish activities afforded to intensify Anglo-American relations. In fact, even the Republican party failed to cause any real concern for the safety of Anglo-American relations because the British recognized the peculiarities of the American system and accepted the wild political talk for what it was. The Republican Senators' response to the Phelps-Rosebery Extradition Treaty indicated the true nature of the many wild anti-English speeches in the Senate. They were made for political capital and the British realized that the sincerity of these statements were open to question. Even though all things seemed headed in the right direction in early 1880 the important pillar that had sustained the earlier agitation failed to materialize. The Irish had little real influence upon Anglo-American relations in the decade of the 1880's.

# THE IRISH-AMERICANS

An Arno Press Collection

Athearn, Robert G. **THOMAS FRANCIS MEAGHER:**
An Irish Revolutionary in America. 1949

Biever, Bruce Francis. **RELIGION, CULTURE AND VALUES:**
A Cross-Cultural Analysis of Motivational Factors in Native
Irish and American Irish Catholicism. 1976

Bolger, Stephen Garrett. **THE IRISH CHARACTER IN
AMERICAN FICTION, 1830-1860.** 1976

Browne, Henry J. **THE CATHOLIC CHURCH AND THE
KNIGHTS OF LABOR.** 1949

Buckley, John Patrick. **THE NEW YORK IRISH:** Their View
of American Foreign Policy, 1914-1921. 1976

Cochran, Alice Lida. **THE SAGA OF AN IRISH IMMIGRANT
FAMILY:** The Descendants of John Mullanphy. 1976

Corbett, James J. **THE ROAR OF THE CROWD.** 1925

Cronin, Harry C. **EUGENE O'NEILL:** Irish and American;
A Study in Cultural Context. 1976

Cuddy, Joseph Edward. **IRISH-AMERICAN AND NATIONAL
ISOLATIONISM, 1914-1920.** 1976

Curley, James Michael. **I'D DO IT AGAIN:** A Record of All My
Uproarious Years. 1957

Deasy, Mary. **THE HOUR OF SPRING.** 1948

Dinneen, Joseph. **WARD EIGHT.** 1936

Doyle, David Noel. **IRISH-AMERICANS, NATIVE RIGHTS
AND NATIONAL EMPIRES:** The Structure, Divisions and
Attitudes of the Catholic Minority in the Decade of Expansion,
1890-1901. 1976

Dunphy, Jack. **JOHN FURY.** 1946

Fanning, Charles, ed. **MR. DOOLEY AND THE CHICAGO
IRISH:** An Anthology. 1976

Farrell, James T. **FATHER AND SON.** 1940

Fleming, Thomas J. **ALL GOOD MEN.** 1961

Funchion, Michael F. **CHICAGO'S IRISH NATIONALISTS,
1881-1890.** 1976

Gudelunas, William A., Jr. and William G. Shade. **BEFORE
THE MOLLY MAGUIRES:** The Emergence of the
Ethno-Religious Factor in the Politics of the Lower Anthracite
Region, 1844-1872. 1976

Henderson, Thomas McLean. **TAMMANY HALL AND THE
NEW IMMIGRANTS:** The Progressive Years. 1976

Hueston, Robert Francis. **THE CATHOLIC PRESS AND
NATIVISM, 1840-1860.** 1976

Joyce, William Leonard. **EDITORS AND ETHNICITY:**
A History of the Irish-American Press, 1848-1883. 1976

Larkin, Emmet. **THE HISTORICAL DIMENSIONS OF IRISH CATHOLICISM.** 1976

Lockhart, Audrey. **SOME ASPECTS OF EMIGRATION FROM IRELAND TO THE NORTH AMERICAN COLONIES BETWEEN 1660-1775.** 1976

Maguire, Edward J., ed. **REVEREND JOHN O'HANLON'S THE IRISH EMIGRANT'S GUIDE FOR THE UNITED STATES:** A Critical Edition with Introduction and Commentary. 1976

McCaffrey, Lawrence J., ed. **IRISH NATIONALISM AND THE AMERICAN CONTRIBUTION.** 1976

McDonald, Grace. **HISTORY OF THE IRISH IN WISCONSIN IN THE NINETEENTH CENTURY.** 1954

McManamin, Francis G. **THE AMERICAN YEARS OF JOHN BOYLE O'REILLY, 1870-1890.** 1976

McSorley, Edward. **OUR OWN KIND.** 1946

Moynihan, James H. **THE LIFE OF ARCHBISHOP JOHN IRELAND.** 1953

Niehaus, Earl F. **THE IRISH IN NEW ORLEANS, 1800-1860.** 1965

O'Grady, Joseph Patrick. **IRISH-AMERICANS AND ANGLO-AMERICAN RELATIONS, 1880-1888.** 1976

Rodechko, James Paul. **PATRICK FORD AND HIS SEARCH FOR AMERICA:** A Case Study of Irish-American Journalism, 1870-1913. 1976

Roney, Frank. **IRISH REBEL AND CALIFORNIA LABOR LEADER:** An Autobiography. Edited by Ira B. Cross. 1931

Roohan, James Edmund. **AMERICAN CATHOLICS AND THE SOCIAL QUESTION, 1865-1900.** 1976

Shannon, James. **CATHOLIC COLONIZATION ON THE WESTERN FRONTIER.** 1957

Shaw, Douglas V. **THE MAKING OF AN IMMIGRANT CITY:** Ethnic and Cultural Conflict in Jersey City, New Jersey, 1850-1877. 1976

Sylvester, Harry. **MOON GAFFNEY.** 1947

Tarpey, Marie Veronica. **THE ROLE OF JOSEPH McGARRITY IN THE STRUGGLE FOR IRISH INDEPENDENCE.** 1976

Vinyard, JoEllen McNergney. **THE IRISH ON THE URBAN FRONTIER:** Nineteenth Century Detroit. 1976

Walsh, James P., ed. **THE IRISH: AMERICA'S POLITICAL CLASS.** 1976

Weisz, Howard Ralph. **IRISH-AMERICAN AND ITALIAN-AMERICAN EDUCATIONAL VIEWS AND ACTIVITIES, 1870-1900:** A Comparison. 1976